UNIVERSITY OF NORTH CAROLINA AT CHAPEL HILL
DEPARTMENT OF ROMANCE LANGUAGES

NORTH CAROLINA STUDIES IN THE ROMANCE LANGUAGES AND LITERATURES

Distributed by:

UNIVERSITY OF NORTH CAROLINA PRESS

CHAPEL HILL
North Carolina 27515-2288
U.S.A.

NORTH CAROLINA STUDIES IN THE ROMANCE LANGUAGES AND LITERATURES
Number 256

THE POETICS OF INCONSTANCY

THE POETICS OF INCONSTANCY

Etienne Durand and the End of Renaissance Verse

BY

HOYT ROGERS

CHAPEL HILL

NORTH CAROLINA STUDIES IN THE ROMANCE LANGUAGES AND LITERATURES

U.N.C. DEPARTMENT OF ROMANCE LANGUAGES

1998

Library of Congress Cataloging-in-Publication Data

Rogers, Hoyt.
The poetics of inconstancy: Etienne Durand and the end of Renaissance verse / by Hoyt Rogers.
p. – cm. – (North Carolina Studies in the Romance Languages & Literatures; no. 256).
Includes bibliographical references.
ISBN 0-8078-9260-2
1. Durand, Etienne, 1586-1618 – Technique. 2. Love poetry, French – History and criticism. 3. French poetry – 17th century – History and criticism. 4. Petrarchism. I. Title. II. Series.

PQ1794.D795Z8 1998 98-4924
841'.4 – DC21 CIP

Cover: The Goddess Inconstancy, from Cesare Ripa, *Iconologia...* (1603).
Cliché courtesy of the Bibliothèque Nationale de France–Paris.

Cover design: Shelley Gruendler

ISBN 0-8078-9260-2

IMPRESO EN ESPAÑA

PRINTED IN SPAIN

DEPÓSITO LEGAL: V. 787 - 1998

ARTES GRÁFICAS SOLER, S. A. - LA OLIVERETA, 28 - 46018 VALENCIA

TABLE OF CONTENTS

For all my parents

Alles prüfe der Mensch, sagen die Himmlischen,
Daß er, kräftig genährt, danken für Alles lern,
Und verstehe die Freiheit,
Aufzubrechen, wohin er will.

HÖLDERLIN, "Lebenslauf"

ACKNOWLEDGEMENTS

The initial version of this book was written in Oxford, Paris and Munich during my tenure of a Marshall Aid Commemoration Scholarship and an Oxford-Sorbonne Exchange Fellowship. I owe a profound debt to the British and French peoples and to my frequent hosts in Germany, Friedhelm Kemp of the Ludwig-Maximilians-Universität, München, and Cornelia Kemp, for their generous assistance in completing the first stage of my project. Marie Wells of Cambridge University, William Davenport of the Northwood Institute, and Roselle Davenport were also instrumental in achieving that goal.

Above all, I wish to express my deep gratitude to Terence Cave of St. Johns College, Oxford University, for his unstinting aid in the conception of this work; it could truly be described as a collaboration, in every aspect but its faults. I would like to thank Yves Bonnefoy of the Collège de France for originally suggesting the subject, and for inspiring my reading and reflection since early youth. Ian McFarlane of Wadham College, Oxford, and Donald Stone of Harvard University encouraged my Renaissance studies at key points in my education.

In recent years Roy Rosenstein of the American University of Paris provided me with long-distance library consultations, Steven Lonsdale of Davidson College and Mark Newville enabled me to carry out additional research at Georgetown University, and Renaud and Nelia Anselin facilitated the finishing touches at the Bibliothèque Nationale. Attendance of the 1995 Aston Magna Academy under the direction of Raymond Erickson and Sally Sanford influenced me to examine the musical aspects of my topic. Carol Sherman, Editor of the NCSRLL at Chapel Hill, patiently eased the book through its final revisions. With the cooperation of the Vice-Rector, Celsa Albert, funds obtained through the Universidad Católica de Santo Domingo helped defray the cost of publication. My students there have often been my teachers.

Many other friends, especially those known as family, have contributed their moral support at one time or another; but "there is always more than should be said." The dedication to all my parents echoes a constancy which – as Hölderlin's words imply – is the origin of freedom, in literature as in life.

Introduction:

THE POET OF INCONSTANCY

Late Petrarchism differs notably from its earlier stages. Its transformation reflects a profound shift in cultural values – a "crisis of the Renaissance"[1] which opens new perspectives in poetic theory and practice. On a broad level, this book will identify a distinctive "poetics of inconstancy" which comes to the fore at the end of the sixteenth century, and which pervades the love verse of the age. At the same time, as a study based on the inductive method, it will take a single poet as its point of departure: Etienne Durand, whose *Poésies complètes* are now widely available for the first time in a modern critical edition, published in the standard series *Textes littéraires français*.[2] Yves Bonnefoy's preface to that volume illustrates the extent to which Durand's literary stature has grown in recent years; he goes so far as to call him "un grand poète: la grande poésie étant ce qui renflamme l'une par l'autre – comme dans l'arc électrique – la sensibilité la plus spontanée et le travail clarifiant de l'intellect."[3] Like Bonnefoy in the rest of his essay,[4] I would maintain that Durand's work is not only valuable in itself: it is also an emblem of his time, a crystallization of its esthetic concerns.

---

[1] Cf. André Chastel, *La Crise de la renaissance, 1520-1600.*

[2] Ed. with introductions by H. Rogers and R. Rosenstein and with a preface by Yves Bonnefoy, published in Geneva by Librairie Droz in 1990. It has been an impediment for Durand scholars that they had no access to a reliable edition of his verse. F. Lachèvre's "réimpression" of the poet's *Méditations* was printed in 1906 in only 300 copies, and is marred by numerous errata, arbitrary changes, etc.; it does not include the poems scattered throughout his pastoral novel and ballets which were added to the recent edition.

[3] Ibid., p. XIII; all further page references refer to the same text.

[4] Reprinted under the title "Etienne Durand" in Bonnefoy's *Dessin, couleur et lumière*.

The short life-span of Etienne Durand, 1585-1618, coincided with the middle phase of one of the most chaotic periods in French history, 1570-1630. Throughout the latter part of the sixteenth century, France was torn by the Religious Wars; but even after the Peace of Vervins and the Edict of Nantes (1598), the country remained unstable for several decades. It was not until the rise of Richelieu and the suppression of the Fronde that central authority won definitive control.[5] This social disequilibrium is mirrored in the poetry of the age; exuberant in its profusion, it displays no dominant pattern. After 1570, the influence of Desportes comes to the fore; but that of Ronsard continues almost unabated. As G. Mathieu-Castellani has pointed out, alongside the suavity and blandness of the "néo-pétrarquistes blancs," the bitterness and violence of the "néo-pétrarquistes noirs"[6] also asserts itself. Even after Malherbe's rise to eminence – which did not really come about until the 1620s – adherents of Ronsard, Desportes, and Du Bartas still persist.[7] Because of his frequently anthologized "Stances à l'Inconstance,"[8] Durand has often been identified as "the poet of inconstancy." But in fact the theme of universal change is a hallmark of his contemporaries as well. Far more than just another *topos*, it signals a fundamental alteration in technique, a "poetics of inconstancy" which appreciably informs their verse, both sacred and profane.

The poetry written between 1570 and 1630 has been variously described as "late Renaissance," "pre-Classical," "*précieux*," "metaphysical," "Baroque," and "Mannerist"; scholars have made many attempts to prove the validity of one or the other of these terms, delimit the span of time to which they apply, and so forth. In recent years the last two epithets have gained ascendancy; but the attempt

---

[5] Cf. J. Morel, *La Renaissance 1570-1624*, pp. 9-10.

[6] These terms are borrowed from her book *Les Thèmes amoureux dans la poésie française (1570-1600)*.

[7] Cf. H. Lafay, *La Poésie française du premier* XVIIe *siècle (1598-1630)*, pp. 65-70. On p. 446 Lafay points out that Malherbe's influence over his contemporaries has been grossly exaggerated: "Malherbe est un poète parmi les autres."

[8] Ed. Rogers and Rosenstein, pp. 186-7. All further page numbers given for Durand's poetry refer to this edition. Sonnets will be designated by their sequence number rather than by page. For anthologies in which the "Stances à l'Inconstance" appear, see the relevant listings in the bibilographies of the edition and the present work.

to use them as all-encompassing period names is still inconclusive.[9] When they are invoked in the present book, I will normally be applying them to individual stylistic traits, not to blocks of history. In my view none of the above-mentioned labels has any absolute priority over the others; but this does not mean that they are useless. Each of them alludes to an important aspect of a highly eclectic phase in French verse. The "Baroque" element seems typified by the powerful rhetoric of Jodelle, d'Aubigné, or the late Ronsard, while the "Mannerism" of an emphasis on smooth technique may be observed in Desportes and his followers. The term *précieux* might be applied to the dainty exercises of Lingendes or Porchères, with their effervescent turns of phrase; the "metaphysical" wit of certain poems by Sponde or Durand (particularly the "Stances à l'inconstance") springs from a deeper source: in them as in Donne, it contributes to a *raisonnement passionné.*[10] When referring to the period as a whole, I will follow the excellent example of Mathieu-Castellani and H. Lafay (and more recently of David Lee Rubin's anthology *La Poésie française du premier 17e siècle)*, by speaking simply of the late sixteenth and early seventeenth centuries wherever possible – or when this seems cumbersome, I will use the phrase "late Renaissance" as a form of shorthand.

The terminological debate, necessary and fruitful though it has been, has often tended to channel critical attention away from individual authors. Vast generalizations about "Mannerism" or "Baroque" highlight significant aspects of late Renaissance verse, but they can also distort one's view of the single poet, the single poem. Many years have now elapsed since Gisèle Mathieu-Castellani and Henri Lafay published their comprehensive *thèses d'état* on the history of

[9] Cf. the extensive bibliographies in Morel, Mathieu-Castellani, and Lafay. For a succinct *mise au point* see M. Raymond, "Aux frontières du maniérisme et du baroque"; the distinction between these two trends is also examined by J. V. Mirollo in his *Mannerism and Renaissance Poetry*. The most thorough and up-to-date survey of the terminolology debate is J. M. Steadman's *Redefining a Period Style: "Renaissance," "Mannerism," and "Baroque" in Literature* (1990). As he remarks (p. 162): "Whatever the value of these abstract categories for the cultural historian and the philosopher of civilization..., in practical criticism [they] frequently seem superfluous." "Frequently" but not always, I would add, as long as they are applied with caution.

[10] A. M. Boase makes repeated use of this phrase in his "Étude sur les poésies de Jean de Sponde" (in Sponde, *Poésies*, ed. Boase and Ruchon).

French poetry in this period.[11] The time has come for scholars to devote full monographs to individual poets – and more importantly, to re-edit their works. That kind of focus has already been given to devotional poets such as La Ceppède and Chassignet;[12] they are now appreciated in their own right, rather than as mere representatives of a style. Much less has been done to resurrect their contemporaries who excelled in love verse: though Durand is being rediscovered, I would cite Expilly, Deimier, Du Mas and Bouchet d'Ambillou[13] as but a few of the unjustly neglected. The objection that these poets are less interesting than La Ceppède or Chassignet cannot be proved or disproved until their works have been thoroughly examined; readers who take the trouble to do so will be rewarded for their efforts.

While it was necessary to gain a general perspective on this little-known epoch of French verse, a more empirical approach may now produce unexpected results, and the perception of new norms to replace some of the less accurate old ones. This is where Durand provides a signal opportunity. His work is unique but also representative: more clearly and more adamantly than the other poets of his age, he embodies their attachment to a literary tradition as well their rebellion against it. The thematic and stylistic features of his verse mark the culmination of a poetics of inconstancy in late Renaissance France – a poetics of which his own life, for many observers, forms a strangely suggestive metaphor.

The meteoric success of Durand as "maître de ballet" at the unstable court of Marie de Médicis, his foolhardy role in the conspiracy against Luynes, and his dramatic death by execution at the age of thirty-three – these biographical elements have traditionally led both admirers and detractors[14] to view Durand's destiny as a sym-

---

[11] Though very different in approach, these two works constitute between them a vast fresco of French poetry 1570-1630. Since Mathieu-Castellani concentrates on love verse, Terence Cave's *Devotional Poetry in France c. 1570-1613* remains indispensable to an understanding of the period. Cf. also M. Clément's *Une poétique de crise: poètes baroques et mystiques (1570-1660).*

[12] Cf. P. A. Chilton, *The Poetry of Jean de La Ceppède*; and R. Ortali, *Un Poète de la mort: Jean-Baptiste Chassignet.*

[13] See my bibliography; for further information on these and other poets who will be mentioned in the course of my book, the reader should consult the comprehensive studies mentioned in the previous footnote. Cf. also the standard bibliographies of sixteenth and seventeenth century French literature.

[14] Among the former class of "mythmakers" cf. Jean Tardieu and Amelia Bruzzi; among the latter class, cf. Pierre de Boitel and Théophile de Viau – all discussed below.

bolic whole, a living metaphor of inconstancy, the poet's most powerful theme. Durand's career as a master illusionist and the drastic reversal of fortune which befell him correspond to two traits often identified with "l'âge baroque": theatricality and sudden metamorphosis. No one can affirm that the poet himself was aware of these parallels, much less that he "foresaw" his gruesome end. But where life, work, and period so closely correlate, many readers have chosen to perceive a representative unity; for them, Durand's myth resembles that of Giordano Bruno or Théophile de Viau. For sceptics such as myself, this web of cross-references presents an intriguing coincidence, nothing more: its interest lies in a series of ironies, not in the inevitability of an emblematic fate.

Durand's disgrace suddenly eclipsed the brightest literary star of an era: apart from the warm reminiscences of Guillaume Colletet (which remained unpublished until the nineteenth century) [15] and an obscure historical novel by the Romantic writer "Bazin," [16] the very name of Durand virtually vanished for almost three hundred years; it was only in 1906, when the bibliographer Frédéric Lachèvre published his edition of the *Méditations* with a lengthy introduction, that the poet was rediscovered. The fact that Durand was officially engaged as *poète ordinaire* to Marie de Médicis testifies to the esteem in which he was held at Court. The success of his elaborate ballets of 1615 and 1617, [17] which were hailed enthusiastically, [18] confirms the impression. In his brief memoir of Durand, [19]

---

[15] First printed in E. Tricotel's "Note sur un poëte peu connu..." (1859). As a would-be political figure, Durand had also been mentioned in Deageant's *Memoires* (see below).

[16] Pseudonym for Anaïs de Raucou, who made Durand a principal character in his historical novel *La Cour de Marie de Médicis, mémoires d'un cadet de Gascogne, 1615-1618*, published in 1830. Though "Bazin" was interested chiefly in the foolhardy and sensational sides of Durand's career, he also expatiates on his supposed stance vis-à-vis the literary currents of the time. In a key scene, where a group of poets meet in a tavern, Durand is reckoned decidedly to the *libertins*, who are depicted as reckless opponents of the social order; he meets his doom, like "son meilleur ami" Théophile de Viau (p. 189), as a rebel without a cause. These conjectures are belied by Durand's attachment to the Court, and by Théophile's cruel sonnet on his death (see below).

[17] See bibliography for the "descriptions" of these ballets published at the time of their production.

[18] On the favorable reception of both ballets, cf. the full chapters devoted to each of them in M. M. McGowan's *L'Art du ballet de cour en France, 1581-1643.*

[19] For the full text of Colletet's reminiscences see intro. to the *Méditations*, ed. Lachèvre, pp. X-XVII; all subsequent page references are to that edition.

Colletet (1598-1659) clearly states that by 1618 he was widely considered the most eminent poet of his time. "Je me souviens en ma jeunesse," he relates, "que l'estant un jour allé visité en son logis sur la grande réputation qu'il s'estoit acquise à la Cour de faire des vers aussi bien que pas un de son siècle, je le trouvay sur son disner à table..." Colletet had no difficulty in accepting the notion that, at the time of their interview, Durand was twenty-eight rather than thirty-three.[20] This impression of youthfulness is in accord with his description of the poet's character and appearance: "Comme il estoit homme de petite taille, mais de belle apparence, il avoit beaucoup de belles qualités intérieures. Il dansoit, chantoit et touchoit le luth à merveille. Son entretien étoit fort agréable et fort divertissant."

For Colletet, Durand's literary gifts seem to have been a felicitous extension of his personal qualities: "Ses vers estoient esgallement ingénieux, doux et forts, sa prose étoit pleine d'esprit et fort pathétique..." In addition to his descriptions of the Court ballets, Durand had published a pastoral novel, *Les Espines d'Amour*, in 1604 (re-published 1608). Around 1611[21] he had also printed a poetry collection, *Méditations de E. D.* Colletet's copy of the last-named work, a gift from the poet, is the only one to have come down to us. It is divided into three parts: the *Méditations* proper, a self-contained cycle of Petrarchist verse; two narrative poems, "Joconde" (drawn from Ariosto) and the "Adventure de Sylvandre" (modeled on Desportes's "Eurylas"); and a *Meslange* which includes the "Stances à l'Inconstance." Of the first section Colletet remarks: "Il y a des sonnets, des stances, des chansons, des odes et des élégies si passionnées et si pleines de nobles sentiments que son siècle n'a peut-être rien produit de plus fort ny de plus relevé."

But all was not cloudless in Durand's character; as though reminded of this darker side by the word "pathétique," Colletet continues on a different note: "Mais, plût à Dieu qu'avec un esprit si propre à la Cour il eût joint un peu plus de conduite et de juge-

[20] Lachèvre fixes the date of Durand's birth as the year 1585, based on bibliographical considerations (cf. p. VIII; also p. 240, note 3). The year 1586 has also been proposed, though most scholars favor 1585; cf. Puleio's monograph, note 14, pp. 19-21. It all depends on what months one assigns to the birth and the publication, and this is only guesswork.

[21] The work was printed without a date and without a "privilège du Roy"; but Colletet states that it appeared seven years before his meeting with Durand.

ment, il ne seroit pas tombé dans le funeste précipice où nous l'avons vu perdre." Brilliant, charming, impetuous – such is the portrait that emerges from our only direct testimony.

"Un esprit si propre à la Cour..." Natural inclination is enough to explain why Durand was drawn to the Court. Certainly it was not material need which impelled him to take up the duties of "maître de ballet" and "poète ordinaire" to Marie de Médicis and Louis XIII. According to Colletet, Durand was born in Paris "d'une famille de condition assez relevée et fort riche en biens." Independently of his Court activities, he occupied a position as "controlleur provincial des guerres." He is referred to by this title in the *Description du Ballet de Madame* (1615),[22] and the title is corroborated by Colletet. As with most bureaucratic posts, it is hard to determine exactly what this office entailed; in his introduction, Lachèvre notes that "les commissaires des guerres faisaient les revues, les contrôleurs tenaient les contrôles de ces revues" (p. X). The province which Durand supervised was apparently the Ile de France; since he did not have to stray too far from Paris, he was able to pursue his artistic vocation at Court.

The combination of such disparate offices as "poète ordinaire" and "contrôleur provincial des guerres" may seem odd, but it was normal in the seventeenth century for one person to accumulate several posts. As Lachèvre has demonstrated through his painstaking archival research, Durand probably owed the position of "contrôleur" to the patronage of his relatives. Though there is little cause to question Lachèvre's findings with regard to Durand's family ties and "état civil," some of his other speculations arouse serious doubt: above all, his analysis of Durand's pastoral novel as a *roman à clef*. As Lachèvre would have it, the novel "proves" that the "Uranie" to whom the poet dedicated the *Méditations* is none other than his cousin Marie de Fourcy, the dedicatee of the *Espines d'Amour* – now, in 1611, a high-ranking married woman, the Marquise d'Effiat.[23] According to him, this would explain the "secrecy" surrounding the printing of the poems.

---

[22] See p. 4; the *Description*, which gives an account of one of Durand's ballets, was probably written by himself.

[23] Through a strange twist of fate, the Marquise was the mother of Cinq-Mars, the ill-starred favorite of Louis XIII. Like Durand, he was a handsome and headstrong young man whose meteoric career ended in execution for *lèse-majesté*. Lachèvre even goes so far as to speculate that he may have been the illegitimate son of the poet. This would indeed have been a miracle, since Durand died in 1618 and Cinq-Mars was born in 1620.

While many pastoral novels did depict real persons under fanciful names,[24] mining them for actual events will usually lead the reader astray; at best one can only recognize famous figures like Henri IV about whom a good many factual details are already known. But Lachèvre's suppositions do underline a serious conundrum: *were* the poems published clandestinely? and if so, why? Lachèvre rightly asserts that without "privilège du Roy," the edition must necessarily have been limited to a few copies; equally enigmatic is the absence of the author's full name and the date and place of publication. Other aspects, not cited by Lachèvre, add to the anomaly. For example, one can surmise from Colletet's account that he did not know of the *Méditations* before his visit to Durand; had he known of the book, given the respect in which he held the author because of his eminence as Court poet (the reason he gives for having sought out Durand in the first place), he would probably have acquired the volume for himself. Were the *Méditations* intended after all as a private message of some kind? The anthologies of the period further reinforce this notion: only in two of them did any of the poems from Durand's book appear. Given his influential position at Court, and the high reputation attributed to him by Colletet, this seems unusual; the prominence of other literary courtiers of the time, such as Jacques Davy du Perron, is amply reflected by their ubiquity in the anthologies. There may be many explanations for the lacuna, but in my opinion the most plausible one is that Durand himself prevented his poems from being printed in any widely distributed publication. The three poems anthologized in 1615 all appeared anonymously in the same collection, the *Satyres Bastardes* – presumably the handiwork of a notorious plagiarizer;[25] the same three poems were published, again anonymously, in the *Cabinet*

[24] When the *Espines d'Amour* was written, the popularity of Antoine de Nervèze was at its height; the loves and mishaps of well-known Court figures often provided the thinly veiled plots of his pastoral tales. On the biographical and autobiographical elements in the novels published 1594-1610, see Reynier, *Le Roman sentimental*, pp. 273-7.

[25] The *Satyres Bastardes* were published under the name of "Cadet Angoulevent," the pseudonym of Nicolas Joubert; but according to Lachèvre *(Biblio. des recueils collectifs de poésies libres et satyriques*, pp. 31-2), the true compiler was Antoine Estoc. Estoc tried to pass this anthology off as the work of a single author, but in fact it consists of *folâtries* by various poets, particularly of the sixteenth century.

Satyrique of 1618 – probably another incidence of pirating.[26] In any case, they are not among the poems which address themselves directly to "Uranie," since they all derive from the *Meslange* rather than from the *Méditations* proper: as the titles of the anthologies imply, they belong to the genre of satirical verse, not that of love poetry. Even if Durand did release them himself, this would not have jeopardized the secrecy surrounding the *Méditations* as a whole.

Not only the circumstances cited by Lachévre, but other evidence as well seems to point to a deliberate campaign of concealment, particularly with regard to the love poems. Whether "Uranie" and the Marquise d'Effiat are one and the same does not affect the usefulness of Lachèvre's primary suggestion: that the dedicatee was in some way a dangerous figure (or perhaps an endangered one), and that Durand could expect awkward consequences if his offering were openly made. But two further questions – which apparently did not occur to Lachévre – must also be asked. If the edition were to be kept secret, why did Durand have the *Méditations* printed at all? Why do the *vers liminaires* hail him as the "Interprete d'Amour/Qui paroist aux yeux de la Cour" (p. 38) if his poems were meant to be hidden from the public? The four introductory panegyrics, and the very fact of printing, seem to explode Lachèvre's thesis. Despite the unusually urgent and personal tone of the dedicatory letter "D. à son Uranie," it resolves into the usual set of *topoi*. By a form of self-abnegation, the death in life of Petrarchist love, the poet is translated into words: "amour.../Faisant mourir [s]on coeur, faict vivre [s]es complaintes" (p. 124). In Durand's time real events were converted as a matter of course into literary themes – in the pastoral novel, the topical theatre,[27] or official panegyrics, for example; understandably, though misguidedly, Lachèvre tried to trace the *topoi* back to the events.

With the abruptness of those coups de théâtre which he himself had designed for the stage, Durand's fame and prosperity vanished virtually overnight in 1618, shortly after Colletet's visit. Among the papers which led to the poet's arrest were found "des lettres qui

---

[26] This anthology was also published by Estoc; as in the case of the previous volume, the fact that the author's name is omitted may indicate that Durand's poems were again borrowed without asking – a common practice at the time.

[27] See below, note 37.

l'assuroient de la Charge de Secretaire des commandemens de la Reine Mere, laquelle étoit haut levée par ces lettres."[28] A contemporary asserts that Durand was possessed by "une rage alteree d'argent, pour assouvir son extreme avarice"[29] – but this may be a partisan judgment. A few months before the end, Durand indiscreetly told the young Colletet that "sa table n'estoit alors que celle d'un simple philosophe, mais qu'il espéroit que dans peu de temps elle seroit la table d'un grand seigneur."[30] Expecting high rewards for his services to the Queen, Durand had sold himself on that "marché commun" of the Court evoked by his fellow poet, La Roque, "où sans toucher finance,/Chacun perd sa jeunesse et vend sa liberté."[31]

Lachèvre has described the circumstances which led to Durand's arrest and execution in great detail,[32] and there is no need to repeat all his findings here. Briefly stated, the conspiracy was but one of the many attempts to topple the adolescent Louis XIII and his favorite the Duc de Luynes which followed on their coup d'état of 1617; these attempts, if they did not always have the direct approval of the former Regent Marie de Medicis, at least issued from her entourage. In their various plots, the Queen's party could count on support from certain foreign powers, particularly Tuscany: this explains the central role played by two Florentines, the Siti or Sizi brothers, in the affair which cost Durand his life. One of them, Francesco, had been the secretary of the Archbishop of Tours, the brother of the Queen's executed favorite, Galigai. In 1618 the Siti brothers were living in the Paris residence of Bartolini, envoy of the Grand Duke of Tuscany. Because of a dispute between the French and Florentine governments over the ownership of the Italian properties which had belonged to Concini and his wife Galigai, Bartolini had fled to the court of Lorraine, leaving the Sitis in charge of his house and belongings. In retaliation, the brothers undertook the composition of a libel against Luynes and Louis XIII, in which

[28] Deageant, *Memoires*, p. 127. Deageant (a pseudonym?) was the "chief intelligence agent" employed by Louis XIII's favorite, the Duc de Luynes; his memoirs were published by his grandson in 1668.

[29] Pierre Boitel de Gaubertin, *Le Théâtre du malheur* (1621-2), p. 105.

[30] Lachèvre edn. of the *Méditations*, p. XI.

[31] *Les Oeuvres* (1609), p. 766.

[32] See his edn. of the *Méditations*, pp. XLV-LVI, with special attention to the extensive footnotes. In his *Biblio. des recueils collectifs de poésies libres*, pp. 190-2, Lachèvre lists all the official documents concerning Durand's trial and execution (cf. also the supplementary volume, *Additions et corrections*, pp. 35-6).

the latter was compared to Nero; they called on Durand to correct and amplify the document. Prompted by the extravagant promises mentioned earlier, Durand unwisely agreed to help. Copies of the libel, which the authors had sent to Bartolini in Lorraine and the Queen in Blois for approval, were intercepted by agents of the King. Durand and the Sitis were arrested, summarily tried, and condemned to death for lese majesty. Their execution took place in the Place de Grève on July 19, 1618.

An important source of information about these events, one which neither Lachèvre nor subsequent biographers draw upon, may be found in the memoirs of Deageant, the "chief of intelligence" employed by Luynes. His account[33] of the discovery of the conspiracy illustrates once more the curious correspondence between the life and the "myth" of Durand. Deageant admits that he was able to gather evidence against the conspirators only through a "rencontre fortuit." A messenger who was carrying a "gros paquet" of incriminating documents, "pensant bien mettre à couvert son paquet..., l'enfonça si avant dans un buisson qu'il coula dans la riviere." An acquaintance of Deageant's happened to be riding near the same spot just then; "voyant flotter ce paquet sur l'eau," he retrieved it. "La subscription étant moüillée" and illegible, he returned the parcel to Deageant under the assumption that the latter had sent it out in the first place – when in fact it contained the very evidence which he had been trying unsuccessfully to obtain.

This is a remarkable series of coincidences, worthy of a "théâtre de mutations." The plays of Durand's age are rife with similar tricks of fortune, reversals of identity, and "Baroque" developments in plot. The river which carries the papers away, effacing the names of those to whom they were addressed, is a typical metaphor of inconstancy; in the poetry of the period, comparable images often recur: in the flowing stream the poet "vo[it] couler ensemble, et les eaux, et [s]es jours."[34]

At the moment of his death, Durand himself became a symbol to his contemporaries. The metamorphosis took place on several

[33] Op. cit., pp. 116-19.

[34] Jacques Davy du Perron, *Recueil de toute la poésie* (part II of *Les Diverses Oeuvres* [1622]), p. 74; reprinted in Rousset's *Anthologie*, vol. I, p. 201. Cf. the other poems on the theme of "l'eau en mouvement," pp. 197-227; cf. also the chapter on this theme in Rousset's *La Littérature de l'âge baroque*, pp. 142-57.

levels. In the first place, his execution was used by the regime for symbolic ends: the highly placed participants in the plot against Luynes suffered no harm; only the authors of the libel were singled out for punishment, as a warning to the populace. Sedition will be crushed – this is the lesson drawn by Boitel de Gaubertin in his account "Du Poëte Durand qui fut rompu sur la rouë dans la ville de Paris," published in 1621.[35] In a drastic sonnet addressed to Louis XIII, "Sur la mort de Durand et des deux Siti, frères,"[36] Théophile de Viau also applauds the vengeful spectacle offeredby the monarch to his subjects, both present and future:

> C'est un supplice doux et que le ciel avouë,
> On oyra toujours dire à la posterité
> Que c'est le chastiment qu'un traistre a merité,
> Et la fin miserable où luy mesme se vouë.
>
> Heureux qui vous cherit, bien-heureux qui vous louë,
> Le Sort doit travailler à sa prosperité,
> Mais ces lasches ingrats qui vous ont irrité
> Doivent ainsi perir, et seicher sur la rouë.
>
> J'ai veu ces criminels en leur supréme sort,
> J'ai veu les fers, les feux, les bourreaux, et la Mort,
> Mon Ame en les voyant benist vostre bon Ange.
>
> Le peuple à cét object a prié Dieu pour vous,
> Mesme les patiens ont trouvé bien estrange
> D'avoir eu la faveur d'un traictement si doux.

Significantly, Boitel and Théophile both stress that they were actually on hand to see Durand's sentence carried out: like a play, the

---

[35] In *Le Théâtre du malheur*, pp. 105-6.

[36] *Oeuvres poétiques*, ed. Streicher, vol. II, pp. 203-4; this sonnet was first published in 1620 (cf. p. 203, note 1). Discussing the poem in *Théophile de Viau et la libre pensée francaise en 1621* (p. 92), A. Adam comments: "Il ne saurait être question d'excuser Théophile de cette insigne lâcheté. Mais il faut l'expliquer. Comment a-t-il pu se laisser entraîner à la commettre? Quels liens l'attachaient donc à Luynes? Ce que nous avons vu de la situation des hommes de lettres à cette époque fournit l'explication désirée. Le poète est un écrivain à gages. Ses maîtres, Rohan et Candale sont du 'party de la faveur.' Il devra donc, pour eux, sous leurs ordres, célébrer les pires méfaits de la dictature. Théophile, domestique de Candale, fut un publiciste docile et complaisant."

current event should move the "audience" to pity and fear. Boitel's account appears in a book entitled *Le Théâtre tragique*, or the *Théâtre du malheur sur qui la fortune présente les divers accidents tragiques des hommes Illustres*; and real-life tragedies such as that of the execution of Galigai[37] were re-enacted forthwith on the stage. In his comments on the execution of Durand (p. 493), Boitel elevates it to a sign of the times – a "time out of joint":

> ...Durand Poëte & pensionnaire de sa Majesté fut executé publiquement à la Greve avec deux freres Florentine, de la maison des Patrices, tous trois attaints & convaincus de crime de leze Majesté.
>
> Exemple qui apprendra desormais à ces brouilleurs de papier, à ces triparagraphes philoxenes, & capricieux esprits a dompter leur fougue pour ne donner trop de license, à l'excez de leurs conceptions. Mal-heur du siecle, & misere du temps qui par sa vagabonde course a renversé les Pons & les escluses d'ignorance. C'est pourquoy aujourd'huy ces fleuves de Parnasse, sont desbordez, & les flots desbridez de la doctrine bouleversent, & le monde & les hommes que nous voyons confusement comme ceux qui regardent dans la pierre angulaire.

In condemning Durand as the representative of a "Parnasse" in revolt, Boitel seems almost to rejoin the Romantic conceptions of "Bazin." His attitude also partially confirms Jean Tardieu's image of Durand as a "poète maudit avant la lettre"; the "silence universel fait autour de son nom" after his death – to borrow Lachèvre's phrase – further reinforces the notion. The life-history of some poets does suggest – not an ineluctable unity – but a complementary relationship between fate and work; arbitrary and coincidental though they are, such poetic legends belong to the tradition of literature.

Lachèvre approached Durand from a biographical point of view, showing scant interest in his poetry per se. After the publication of the 1906 edition – except for a brief allusion here or there – Durand once again dropped out of the picture for almost fifty years. But this time his return proved more lasting and more signif-

[37] She is the subject of the play *La Magicienne estrangère, tragédie* (1617), attributed to Pierre Matthieu.

icant. In a seminal article "Étienne Durand, poète supplicié," which appeared in 1952, Jean Tardieu called attention to the literary interest of Durand's work, hailing him flamboyantly as a "lointain précurseur du Romantisme" (p. 194). He also stressed the capital importance of the "Stances à l'Inconstance": in the first burst of attention sparked by Tardieu, scholars tended to portray him as the poet of a single poem. This is the role accorded him by Jean Rousset, for example, in his influential book *La Littérature de l'âge baroque en France*, published in 1953 (see pp. 45-7); Rousset's standard anthology of French verse 1570-1700 also gives prominence to the "Stances à l'Inconstance,"[38] while rejecting Durand's other poems. The most extreme example of this approach was S. A. Varga's article of 1955,[39] which focused on Durand's "Stances" while disdainfully dismissing the rest of his work. Though with nuances, Luca Normanno and Bernd Rathmann followed a similar line in their brief articles of 1963 and 1981, respectively.[40] All the same, by 1981 Rathmann is an exception; and when he speaks in passing of the "rapport mutuel entre le motif littéraire et sa réalisation rhétorique" he adumbrates a different concept of Durand as "the poet of inconstancy" – one to which I will return at the close of this introduction.

In the long run, most appraisals of Durand have become more balanced; he remains the "poet of the 'Stances,'" but other facets of his oeuvre also receive their due. The sensitive essay "Sulla poesia di Étienne Durand" by Arnaldo Pizzorusso, which appeared in 1956, touches on Durand's novel and ballets, as well as analyzing a number of sonnets from the *Méditations*. In the same year, A. J. Steele included three poems by Durand in his *Three Centuries of French Verse, 1511-1819*. This publication marked an important turning point for two reasons: first, because it demonstrated that poems by Durand other than the "Stances à l'Inconstance" were worthy of being anthologized; and second, because it implied that his work could appeal not only to devotees of the Baroque, but also to a

[38] *Anthologie de la poésie baroque française*, vol. I, pp. 74-5; cf. also the remarks in Rousset's intro., p. 8.

[39] "Un poète oublié du XVIIe siècle. Étienne Durand et les Stances à l'Inconstance."

[40] Cf. also Alvin Eustis, who dismisses the rest of Durand's work in the *apparatus criticus* of his edition of the "Stances" (in D. L. Rubin, ed., *La Poésie française...*, pp. 201-4).

more general readership. Frank Warnke also included several other poems by Durand besides the "Stances à l'Inconstance" in his anthology *European Metaphysical Poetry* (1961); in his introduction (pp. 34-5), Warnke relies on a number of different references from Durand's work to link his "conversational style" with that of Sponde and the English poets. A broader view of Durand's verse was published by Amelia Bruzzi in 1962; the second of her *Studi sul barocco francese* purports to examine "metafore e poesia" in the *Méditations*, though it actually concentrates on several prevalent themes (nature, instability, etc.). Margaret McGowan's definitive work on *L'Art du ballet de cour en France, 1581-1643*, which appeared in 1963, contains full chapters on each of Durand's best-known exercises in that genre. Both Gisèle Mathieu-Castellani and Henri Lafay, in the vast *théses d'état* mentioned earlier, draw on a variety of poems by Durand, not just the "Stances à l'Inconstance." In the early 1980s Maria Teresa Puleio published two articles on poems other than the "Stances," and also addressed herself to the Ariostan element in Durand's work.[41] In 1990 Roy Rosenstein contributed an analysis[42] of the fire motif in Durand's sonnets, without referring to the inconstancy theme at all.

Despite all the critical attention Durand has received, this is the first full-length monograph on his verse. Here "verse" is the operative word. Puleio's brief study *Estienne Durand tra manierismo e barocco* (1983) provides a succinct overview of the author's total production – including the pastoral novel, the narrative poems, the satyrical pieces, and the ballets – but devotes less than fifty pages to the lyric work as such.[43] Even then, as her title denotes, she is mainly concerned with placing Durand in the framework of the period styles.[44] This seems regrettable, since he has emerged in his own right as one of the most rewarding and characteristic poets of his time. On the other hand, Puleio's systematic treatment of the other

---

[41] See entries under her name in the bibliography.

[42] "Etienne Durand et les flammes de l'amour," in Rogers and Rosenstein, ed. cit., pp. 1-12.

[43] I exclude from this tabulation the pages (39-51) which retrace Lachèvre's biographical theories.

[44] It is worth noting that we both came to the same conclusion about how Durand's poetry fits into the Mannerism-Baroque parameters (with the "Stances à l'Inconstance" assigned to the Baroque), even though neither of us had read the other's work.

aspects of his oeuvre possesses the signal merit of comprehensiveness, freeing me to concentrate almost exclusively on the love lyric here. I do so not only because – in purely esthetic terms – Durand's amatory verse is his most memorable achievement; but also because an examination of these poems in their literary context affords many insights into late Renaissance poetics as a whole. In our articles of 1987, 1988, and 1990, Roy Rosenstein and I have attempted to pave the way for a new conception of Durand as "the poet of inconstancy": we would maintain that his verse illuminates the writing of his time, and leads "De l'inconstance thématique à une poétique de l'inconstance."[45]

In quest of these broader perceptions, my book will stress the *Méditations* proper, the Petrarchist cycle which gives its name to Durand's only surviving volume of poetry. In the light of the inconstancy motif which comes to the fore around 1600, in open contradiction to the original tenets of Petrarchism, how can such a self-declared monument to amorous fidelity be understood? Does the "late Petrarchism" of Durand and his contemporaries differ significantly from the Petrarchism of their predecessors? Are these differences chiefly thematic, or do they permeate the poets' diction and style? Here we open out on a still larger field of inquiry. How do the thematic and rhetorical conventions of poetry influence individual creation? What is the capacity of a tradition to generate new *topoi*? How quickly and how fully can the latter be assimilated into the pre-existing order? Do changes in theme reflect a shift on the plane of language? Are certain new motifs and techniques so disruptive to a tradition that it ends up collapsing from within?

Though I have touched on many features of Durand's social milieu in the preceding pages, my main purpose is to demonstrate the extent to which his poetry both reveals an individual talent and reflects the esthetic preoccupations of his age. In every chapter I have tried to approach the general through the individual, according to the precepts of empirical induction. In the interests of structural clarity, the book has been divided into two sections. The first, "Poetry of Sameness," approaches the question of *topos* and style from a familiar angle; it examines the use of literary conventions by Du-

[45] This is the title of one of our collaborative essays on Durand, published in *Neophilologus* in 1988; for full details regarding this and our other articles on Durand see the bibliography.

rand in particular and late Renaissance love poets in general. Chapter I, "Durand and the Petrarchist Tradition," analyzes the manner in which Durand and his contemporaries reiterate the standard themes of Petrarchism, while subtly transforming them through subversion, deflation, or other means. Crisscrossing echoes link any Petrarchist poem with past, present, and future exercises in the genre; at the same time, even here certain characteristics which distinguish the "poets of 1600" from their predecessors will already become apparent. Chapter II, "The Rhetoric of Repetition," focuses on a different kind of reduplication: like *topoi*, rhetorical tropes preserve a pattern of identity from work to work, age to age, despite the endless variants. By surveying the figures of repetition in the *Méditations* and many other verse collections of the time, I hope to demonstrate how reiteration shapes the basic substance of literary discourse at the turn of the sixteenth century – and for that very reason, leads to ever more daring and complex forms of *conduplicatio* and *annominatio* as the Renaissance draws to a close.

Especially in an effervescent period such as this, "Poetry of Sameness" goes hand in hand with "Poetry of Change." The second section of my book explores the notion of inconstancy, one of the central motifs of late Renaissance thought and the key to its stylistic expression. Chapter III traces the rise of the motif from its origins as an attribute of older themes (the vicissitudes of fortune, antifeminism, etc.) to a fully-fledged *topos*: the invocation to Inconstancy, a thematic genre which finds its most powerful embodiment in Durand's "Stances à l'Inconstance," but which is also the hallmark of the age. Chapter IV links the prevalence of this motif to a change in poetic technique. The unstable boundaries between the devotional and the profane, as well as the restless alternation between the *topoi* of constancy and inconstancy, betray the "thematic inconstancy" of late Renaissance verse. But the predilection for mutability can be observed on a still more fundamental plane: in the *Méditations* as in many other works of the time, a labile rhetoric insistently calls attention to itself, almost to the point of obscuring the putative content.

I am referring here to the degree to which a poet actively calls attention to the mode of expression as opposed to the literal meaning of a poem by multiplying its sudden twists of syntax and trope. At the same time, I recognize the truism that "rhetoric" and "content" are always interdependent, and that how something is said inevitably determines what is being said. Successive schools of literary theory in the twentieth century have convincingly exploded the old assumption of a facile balance between *forme et fond* – though rehearsing all their tenets and taking positions on each of them would take the reader and me far beyond the compass of this book. Deconstructionist critics in particular have forcefully demonstrated that any text is constantly undermining and rebuilding itself from within, "saying and unsaying itself" in a perpetual indeterminacy.[46] My point is simply that some poems bring that process closer to the verbal surface, acting it out as ostentatiously as possible. Relying on close textual analysis, I will suggest that this kind of emphatic enactment is characteristic of late Renaissance verse.

I would like to say a special word about a hypothesis which is central to this book: the notion that Durand and his contemporaries actually possessed a thorough-going poetic technique which functioned by its own inner laws. From the mid-seventeenth century till the rise of Romanticism, critics condemned the final stage of Petrarchism for its obscurity and ornateness; in the nineteenth century they denounced its lassitude, artificiality, and insincerity; and in the twentieth century, they have censured its blandness, frivolity, and stylistic unevenness. I would submit that in all three cases, these judgements flow from the application of an alien esthetic: in the first period, an insistence on clarity and simplicity; in the second, a preoccupation with depth of feeling; and in the third, an admiration for direct force of expression. These trends are pan-European in scope, and an example from outside France will illustrate most tellingly what I mean.

On an international scale, Shakespeare was arguably the greatest poet of Durand's age; the reception of his amatory verse reveals the evolution in attitudes toward late Petrarchism in general. His "sugared sonnets" were highly esteemed at the time of their composition. Their collection and publication in 1609 is a tribute to the favor they had already enjoyed in private circulation for a number of years. But the fashion of "sonneteering" at the close of the Elizabethan era was short-lived: "[a]fter the 1609 edition, the sonnets were pretty well forgotten for over a century and a half."[47]

---

[46] Cf. J. D. Kneale, "Deconstruction," in *The Johns Hopkins Guide to Literary Theory and Criticism*, pp. 185-92.

[47] W. H. Auden, intro. to Shakespeare, *The Sonnets*, p. xxiii; the succeeding

The renewal of interest in them in the eighteenth century was largely negative. The verse form as a whole, and Shakespeare's poems in particular, were taxed with "affectation, pedantry, circumlocution, and nonsense." These strictures against late Renaissance poetry echo those of French Classicism, which served as the model for all of Europe in the age of the Enlightenment. In the nineteenth century the major Romantics were just as harsh toward the sonnets, though from a drastically different point of view. Despite the advent of "Bardolatry" in relation to the plays, they decried Shakepeare's lyric production for its "sameness," "tediousness," and "artifice," its lack of any "genuine sense of nature and passion."

In the twentieth century the focus has shifted somewhat, from strength of feeling to power of expression: but like their Romantic predecessors, modern critics often demand a sustained intensity from poetry which late Renaissance practitioners were at no pains to cultivate in every line or every poem. For example, W. H. Auden deems less than a third of Shakespeare's sonnets to be "excellent throughout"; for him the vast majority of them are "inferior" poems, and many can only be tolerated out of a "sense of duty." He feels particularly uncomfortable with the final couplets, dismissed as "glib and trite": "all too often, even in some of the best, the couplet lines are the weakest and dullest in the sonnet, and, coming where they do at the end, the reader has the sense of a disappointing anticlimax." In similar terms, he complains that "the sequence as we have it concludes with two of the worst of the sonnets, trivial conceits about, apparently, going to Bath to take the waters." According to Auden, this is incontrovertible proof that the order of the series cannot have been planned by Shakespeare himself. "Any writer with an audience in mind knows that a sequence of poems must climax with one of the best."

Other recent critics have made comparable observations,[48] without stopping to ask themselves why a poet of Shakespeare's

---

quotations from Auden and earlier critics are all from the same essay, pp. xxii-xxv. Though mainly concerned with the plays, the texts collected by D. N. Smith in *Shakespeare Criticism: A Selection 1623-1840*, provide valuable insights into the evolution of literary taste.

[48] Cf. Barber and Wheeler's remarks (p. 164) in their book on Shakespeare, published in 1986: "...letdown or overreach or turnabout in the couplet is the most

stature would have persisted in writing so many "weak" lines and "trivial" poems. I would maintain that these "deflationary" features are part of a global strategy, which contrasts lighter with heavier elements – playfulness with gravity, relaxation with tension, lethargy with flashes of ardor – in order to convey both the vagaries of Petrarchist love and the myriad modes of poetry itself.[49] The tactic of ending poems and entire sequences with a "grace note," a leavening to what has gone before, is consonant with a "poetics of inconstancy" which delights in changing stylistic registers and creating countercurrents to the dominant tone. The *chute* – to borrow the term which was common in France in the era – implies a falling-off of energy: a deliberate "anticlimax," but not a "disappointing" one. Like the subsiding cadence frequent in early music, it is an appropriate termination, not a defect. Whether it was Shakespeare himself or his editor who assembled the sonnets of the Quarto text, the order chosen necessarily tells the modern reader something about late Renaissance sensibilities.[50] Since the poems directed to the young man are carefully divided from those addressed to the "dark lady," there was clearly some kind of conscious procedure at work. In any case neither author nor publisher would have placed the two light-hearted sonnets at the end if they thought them likely to displease the reading public. In other words, their position bespeaks the prevailing taste of the epoch, which was not averse to abrupt

---

common defect in the Sonnets; with tactful reading it usually can be kept from being troublesome (but not always)." Similarly, in terms of the series as a whole, W. Kerrigan and G. Braden write dismissively: "If we cut away the two trivial cupid sonnets, Shakespeare's sequence ends with the explosion of its genre" (*The Idea of the Renaissance* [1989], p. 177). On the contrary, I would suggest that the mockery of these two sonnets is instrumental in imploding the genre from within.

[49] On a psychological plane, the abrupt shifts of late Petrarchism have been more readily understood. Cf. Helen Vendler, intro. to Shakespeare, *The Sonnets and Narrative Poems*, p. xxvii: "Shakespeare's chief psychological invention is to make his speaker change his mind... during the course of a sonnet. This is not an entirely new technique; after all, lovers from Petrarch on had expressed remorse after expressing desire. But Shakespeare's speaker does not deal only in such direct antitheses; he frequently alters his position subtly from quatrain to quatrain..." Compare Robert Ellrodt, "Shakespeare the Non-Dramatic Poet," p. 38: "The quick alternation of moods appears at times improbable, but hardly more surprising than in many plays, where such an alternation is supposed to reflect the unpredictibility of life." I would argue that the rapid fluctuations in style enact a parallel instability on the level of discourse, and reflect a "poetics of insconstancy" which comes to the fore at the end of the Renaissance.

[50] R. L. Cole makes the same point in "Criticism and the Analysis of Craft: The Sonnets," in the critical collection *William Shakespeare's Sonnets*, p. 29.

changes in tonality: from high seriousness in one moment to mockery in the next, especially in the form of a parting jest or *pointe*.

In the literary culture of a remote epoch, the nuances of humor are difficult to pin down; but as in Mannerist art, the sardonic manipulation and travesty of preexisting motifs is one of the main pursuits of late Renaissance verse. The problem is in determining exactly where and to what degree that note of sarcasm intervenes: this must be done with tact and flexibility. On points of such delicacy – having to do with mood and inflection – I do not expect other readers to agree with me in every instance, or even on general grounds. In literary studies no critical proposal can be objectively "proven" in the exclusive sense that a logical syllogism or scientific theory can be. In my opinion there is always room for a variety of approaches, and any perspective is worth hazarding if it sheds a ray of light here and there. Though "wit" is an accepted category in discussions of Petrarchist poetry (despite the discrepancies about where it occurs), in the following pages I will expand on the concept and posit other forms of the ironic deflation of discourse. The release of poetic pressure through pallid recitatives, the displacement of strong emotions by farcical mythology, and the wry twists and turns of a pseudo-logic, can all be understood as "puncturing devices" which an overripe tradition skillfully deploys to flaunt and parody itself. This is one way – among many others, equally valid – of grasping the technique of Durand and his age, a technique which is decidedly sui generis. The critical re-evaluation (and revaluation) of Shakespeare's alleged deficiencies is already well underway;[51] in part, I have invoked his name in broaching this topic because he commands a universal respect. Indirectly, he is also the "poet of inconstancy" described in this book. Some specialists in other literatures may be more likely to alter their attitudes toward the poetics of late Petrar-

[51] The exhaustive commentary by Stephen Booth which accompanies his 1977 edition of Shakespeare's sonnets marks a turning point, in that he gives equal weight to all the poems without arbitrarily distinguishing the "good" from the "bad." I will return to this topic in the Conclusion, but here I would like to invoke – on behalf of own my analyses of French verse – his caveat (pp. x-xi): "...when I say 'suggestion' or 'overtone,' and when I talk about ideas and echoes that merely cross a reader's mind, I mean only what I say... Some of the puns, allusions, suggestions, and implications I describe are farfetched; ...but these poems go in generally for farfetched effects. As long as my reader remembers that I am describing *effects*, not trying to substitute ideational static for obvious surface meaning and intent, then the incidentals I describe and justify deserve, and can safely receive, a hearing."

chism where he is concerned, and then extend that reconsideration to his European contemporaries.

The poets of early seventeenth century France have been judged inferior ever since Classicism swiftly eclipsed them; despite their scholarly rehabilitation as a group in the last forty years, their individual works – aside from a few often-anthologized pieces – are still largely unknown. From my own experience of frequenting them, it is clear to me that some aspects which may strike current readers as "dull" or "glib" are not the result of incompetence, but simply correspond to another kind of competence. Repetition or "sameness" may betoken, not careless monotony, but the artful preparation of surprise. Levity or "triviality" may function, not as doggerel, but as a jocose complement to other modes of verse. Relaxation or "weakness" may involve the lowering of poetic tension in order to heighten an adjacent intensity, or languidly abolish it. In perceiving strategies where other critics see inadequacies (or nothing at all), I am giving these poets the benefit of the doubt. While others may choose not to regard the final stage of Petrarchism in this light, I trust they will at least allow for the possibility of an interpretation which differs from their own.

Though I am an interested follower of literary theory, specialists in that domain will detect few innovations in this work. I introduce a certain "deconstructionist" perspective from time to time, but for the most part I try to "construct" an accurate account of Durand and his period through philology, rhetoric, literary history, and *explication de texte*. I hope that some readers will find the sparing use of neologisims refreshing, and that others will accept both my diverse critical approaches and my stress on the "difference" of late Renaissance technique as tributes to a "postmodernist" pluralism.[52] By adopting a wide variety of *optiques*, I have tried to demonstrate my belief in the open-endedness of literature, which confounds any strict adherence to a school of methodology.[53] On the other hand,

[52] Cf. John McGowan's remark about how the "valuing of heterogeneity over unity" is linked to "postmodern theory's... concern with 'difference' " ("Postmodernism," in *The Johns Hopkins Guide...*, op. cit., p. 585). Cf. also his assertion (p. 587): "Postmodernism... is just part of the very complex rereading of history taking place in the current climate of a critical questioning of the Western tradition. Paradoxically, most of the materials for a radical questioning can be found in the tradition itself if we look in different places (noncanonical works) or with new eyes at familiar places."

[53] In *Appropriating Shakespeare: Contemporary Critical Quarrels*, Brian Vickers demonstrates the pitfalls of systematically applying a critical model to literary texts,

that very openness implies that exegetes of all persuasions have genuine contributions to make; accordingly, I will cite a broad spectrum of comments by critics in every period from the sixteenth century to the present. In the first chapter I survey the Petrarchist themes in the *Méditations* as a repertory of inherited conventions, which the poet subtly varies to express both a period style and a personal strain within that style. Chapter II examines Durand and his contemporaries from the angle of normative rhetoric, the foundation of Renaissance verse; again, by reviewing a corpus of tropes I will study how age-old conventions are recapitulated with distinctive nuances, both historical and individual. By contrast, Chapter III explores the capacity of a highly formulaic tradition to generate new *topoi*, even at the expense of inner contradiction. Chapter IV takes this investigation of esthetic instability to its most essential level, where rhetoric and theme run at cross-purposes, or suddenly revert to a deeper unity of vision.

The poetics of inconstancy in the late Renaissance is so heterogeneous and all-embracing that it frequently returns to balance as one of its modes, to continuity as one of its disguises. On a broader level, that tension between tradition and novelty, between fixed formulae and shifting forms, is the driving force of all art. Repetition and change proceed in concert, just as "metaphor" and "reality," "poetry" and "life," cannot be wholly disentangled. In this sense readers are still entitled to think of Durand as the "poet of inconstancy" – no longer as the author of a single poem, but as the exponent of a certain stance toward language and the world. In his preface to the *Poésies complètes* (p. VIII), Bonnefoy writes: "Autant qu'une philosphie, autant qu'une théorie du langage, les *Stances à l'Inconstance* sont évidemment une poétique..." The identification of that underlying poetics, the analysis of how it shapes late Renaissance verse and informs the arts of the era as a whole, are the objects of the pages which follow – though like Petrarchist "objets de désir," always in retreat, they can only be attained *as* desires.

---

without regard to their historical context and primary semantic charge. His attacks are often overstated, and he discounts the valuable contributions which twentieth century theorists have made to the understanding of literature; but his general argument for a less doctrinaire approach – especially to earlier periods such as the Renaissance – is well worth considering.

PART ONE: POETRY OF SAMENESS

CHAPTER I

THE PETRARCHIST TRADITION

Given its date of publication, the love poem cycle of Durand's *Méditations* belongs inevitably to the Petrarchist tradition. Beginning with Scève,[1] all French love poets of the sixteenth and seventeenth centuries draw heavily on the common fund of themes, images, and vaguely Platonic theories inherited from Italy.[2] Any global definition of Petrarchism would have to include the style and motifs used by Petrarch himself, the classicism of the Bembists, the freer variations of Tansillo and others, and the imitations of all these Italian sources in other languages – with the latter inspiring further imitations in their turn.[3] But since the *Méditations* do not –

[1] In the preface to his edn. (p. XXXII), V. L. Saulnier characterizes the *Adolescence Clémentine* of Marot (1532), as an example of "prépétrarquisme francais." By contrast, the *Délie* (1544) is organized as a Petrarchist cycle; in his edition of the work, I. D. Mcfarlane notes that "the homage to Petrarch is unmistakable" (p. 26).

[2] Anti-Petrarchist poems, such as the *Contr'Amours* of Jodelle, are precisely that: conscious revolts against a dominant strain, which define themselves in relation to it alone. Du Bellay's "Contre les Pétrarquistes," to cite another example, can be understood only by contrast with the amorous conventions of the poet's own *Olive*. Anti-Petrarchism represents but another aspect of Petrarchism itself. Characteristic of this underlying unity is the fact that most writers of "anti-Petrarchist" poems had been, or continued to be, "Petrarchists" in their other works. (Cf. R. J. Clements, *Critical Theory and Practice of the Pléiade*, p. 40. Cf. also Arturo Graf's essay "Petrarchismo ed antipetrarchismo" for a discussion of the relations between these two movements in Italy. For a convenient set of anti-Petrarchist poems in various languages, see the *Texte zum Antipetrarkismus*, ed. J. Hösle.) Similarly, less programmatic departures from the norm – the charnelhouse imagery of d'Aubigné, for instance, or the "realism" of the late Ronsard – do not abolish, but rather build upon the inherited themes of the love poem cycle. (Cf. Henri Weber's article on the "Transformation des thèmes pétrarquistes dans le Printemps d'Agrippa d'Aubigné.")

[3] For a comprehensive short evaluation of the topic, see the article on Petrarchism in the *Princeton Encyclopedia of Poetry and Poetics* (pp. 612-13).

as far as I can ascertain – reflect any direct Italian influences,[4] it seems both logical and practical to restrict the discussion here to Petrarchism in France.

For a French poet writing around 1600, the mainstream of Petrarchist tradition consisted of two major currents: one deriving from the Ronsard of the *Continuations*, and the other from Philippe Desportes.[5] Though Durand displays an affinity with the Ronsardian *style bas*, the love poem cycle of the *Méditations* seems closer in theme and technique to *Diane*, *Hippolyte*, and *Cléonice*.[6] The "Adventure de Sylvandre" (pp. 153-60) contains passages which follow Desportes's "Eurylas" almost word for word; other allusions throughout the *Méditations* confirm Durand's close familiarity with the older poet's works.[7] All the same, the eclecticism of the period around 1600[8] excludes attachment to a single master: in his own in-

[4] An examination of the *Fiori delle Rime*, the most famous anthology of Italian Petrarchist verse in this period, reveals no direct influence. Similarities occur only where Desportes had imitated an Italian original. Cf. Durand's sonnets IV, XXXI, and XXXVIII – and compare Desportes (ed. Graham), *Cléonice*, pp. 19-20; *Diane*, p. 285; and *Cléonice*, p. 21. Where Desportes departs from the original, Durand's versions follow Desportes.

[5] Throughout her study of French love poetry 1570-1600, Mathieu-Castellani constantly stresses "la double tradition 'magistrale' (Ronsard et Desportes)" (p. 398) on which that poetry is founded. But she also points out that the imitators of Ronsard in the latter half of the sixteenth century are drawn chiefly to his *style bas* – and this only in its most superficial aspects (cf. p. 204).

[6] The two aspects of the Ronsardian *style bas* which found the greatest favour among his successors were the *mignard* and *folâtre* elements; both of these are a matter not only of theme, but also of diction. On pp. 161-69, 177-9 in the Durand edn. will be found a group of poems which exploit the *gaulois* vein of Ronsard's work; the vivid "Folastrerie" on pp. 164-8 contains innumerable samples of *style mignard*, particularly in the repeated use of diminutives. The fact that the latter are both dainty and highly erotic seems more characteristic of Ronsard than Desportes. The three "Odes" on pp. 88-95 – and particularly "Ode I" – also appear more "Ronsardian" than "Desportian," both in theme and style. But in general, the *Méditations* proper follow the neo-Petrarchist model of Desportes rather than the mixed style (Petrarchist, "Catullan," *folâtre*, *mignard*) of the *Continuations*. Most of Durand's "Ronsardian" poems are confined to the *Meslange* (an exception is formed by the *gaulois* sonnet XLII).

[7] On "Sylvandre" and "Eurylas" see the note in the Durand edn., p. 234. In addition to the examples of imitation already given, cf. sonnet VII, sonnet XXIV, sonnet XLI – and compare Desportes, *Diane*, p. 110, *Hippolyte*, p. 104, *Diane*, p. 196. One could cite other instances. In the proportion of "Desportian" to "Ronsardian" influence, with the former having the edge over the latter, Durand appears to typify the era in which he wrote.

[8] Cf. Lafay, pp. 15-16, 312; and Jean Tortel, "Le Lyrisme au XVIIe siècle," p. 351. Dieter Janik asserts: "Um das Jahr 1620 bietet die französische Lyrik eine bunte Vielfalt, wie Frankreich sie seit der Plejade nicht mehr gekannt hatte" (p. 149).

dividual manner, Durand reflects that general trend. Desportes differs from his predecessors not only by the bland fluidity of his style and the abstraction of his imagery, but also by a renewed emphasis on the "Platonic" vein in Petrarchist verse.[9] Following Italian prototypes more closely than the Pléiade had done,[10] he purged French love poetry of the sensuous detail and sensual frankness which Ronsard had brought to the genre.[11] By its relative openness in declaring the poet's desires,[12] Durand's verse occupies a middle ground between the two sixteenth century models. This hybridization of the main poetic currents is but one example of the way in which – against the backdrop of inherited themes and images – a distinctive sensibility makes itself felt at the end of the Renaissance in France.

By charting Durand's debt to the Petrarchist tradition, one can also assess his thematic originality. The word "originality" should not be understood in the modern sense of "innovation"; late Renaissance readers prized novelty less than readers do nowadays, and the writers of the age claimed a firm allegiance to literary precedent. The originality they admired was the ability to shift familiar themes through subtly altered developments, or to form ingenious combinations from the pre-established elements.[13] In this sense Durand's "exclusions" – the *topoi* he neglects – sometimes reveal even more than his "inclusions" – the themes he develops most fully. All the Petrarchist motifs in Durand's work cannot be treated here in-

---

[9] Cf. Mathieu-Castellani, pp. 228-31, on the "thèmes néo-platoniciens" in Desportes; cf. also R. M. Burgess, *Platonism in Desportes*.

[10] Cf. J.-M. Vianey, *Le Pétrarquisme en France au* XVIe *siècle*, p. 224: "Tout compte fait, Ronsard et ses amis doivent à l'antiquité plus qu'à l'Italie. L'inspiration de Desportes fut, au contraire, presque toute italienne, et l'on sait que son imitation ressembla souvent à un esclavage."

[11] Cf. Mathieu-Castellani: "Le néo-pétrarquisme de Desportes... est précieux et abstrait, sa poésie est moins sentimentale que *psychologique*: on dirait volontiers que l'analyse du sentiment se substitue chez lui au sentiment... Ce qui est donné chez Ronsard dans l'immédiateté de la sensation première, cette unité du sens et du mouvement, passe chez Desportes par l'intermédiaire de la rhétorique et de la casuistique amoureuses" (p. 220).

[12] In addition to the poems already cited, cf. lines 168-72 of the "Discours" (p. 130), or the highly insinuating dedication of the "Joconde" translation ("E.D. à son Uranie," pp. 135-6).

[13] See Terence Cave's chapter on Renaissance principles of imitation in *The Cornucopian Text*, where he compares them (pp. 76-7) with modern concepts of intertextuality.

dividually: the list would run into the hundreds. In the following pages I will focus on those themes or groups of themes which are generally considered to be most characteristic of Petrarchism. In assembling this canon I have relied particularly on Mathieu-Castellani, and on Henri Weber's survey "La Poésie amoureuse de la Pléiade, étude de thèmes" (*La Création poétique au* XVIe *siècle en France*, vol. I, ch. V). I have also drawn on my own experience of reading hundreds of the original sources. Through a systematic analysis of Petrarchist themes in the *Méditations*, certain idiosyncratic threads will become apparent. These may be roughly described as follows: 1) a poetic "elimination" of the beloved, 2) a focus of attention on the lyric *je*, 3) an absence of vernal imagery, 4) a tendency toward abstraction, and 5) an ironic deflation of traditional themes. I will begin by examining the basic "building blocks" of Petrarchism in Durand's verse; then in the second half of the chapter I will address the major *topoi* he chooses to include – or to omit.

1. Basic Elements of Petrarchist Convention

A number of Petrarchist motifs are all-pervasive in Renaissance love verse: the opposition of water and flames, ice and fire, etc.; the comparison of the poet's sufferings with those of mythological figures; the lover's death in life, a death which is perpetually renewed; the stolen heart; the prison of love; the presence-absence dichotomy; and so on. Though one could lengthen the list considerably, for the sake of brevity I will limit myself to the themes just mentioned, examining each in the order I have given. Such motifs usually do not appear as fully-fledged *topoi*, in the sense of "the invocation to Sleep" or "the fading flower"; instead they constitute the building blocks of a Petrarchist rhetoric, based on paradox and antithesis (cf. Mathieu-Castellani, pp. 56-69). While any discussion of the *Méditations* would be incomplete without a rapid survey of such diffuse and ubiquitous elements of the Petrarchist scheme, an exhaustive treatment of each instance where they appear would be gratuitous. In passing I will point to certain cases in Durand's work where they take on a cardinal interest, since their development reveals the immense variety a skillful poet can draw from the most common clichés.

The water-fire opposition probably recurs more often than any other Petrarchist motif.[14] In Durand as elsewhere, it usually symbolizes the tears and the burning passions of the lover; cf. for example sonnet VII: "Mes yeux veulent noyer mon coeur avec des larmes,/ Mon coeur veut desseicher mes yeux avec des feux."[15] These lines, with their chiastic arrangement, illustrate how verbal acrobatics held far more fascination for the poets of Durand's day than newness of imagery. In a longer poem, Durand does enlarge on the water-fire motif to create a more innovative visual effect:

> Plusieurs rochs vont jettant des flammes dans les nuës,
> Et font durant l'esté de leurs testes chenuës
>   Distiler un ruisseau:
> Me voyant souspirer et plorer à l'extreme,
> Tu peux bien asseurer que j'ay dedans moy-mesme
>   Et des feux et de l'eau. (p. 96)

The image of the volcano serves mainly as the pretext for a *pointe*; ultimately, the emphasis remains on verbal wit and cunning. The same is true of sonnet XXV: despite its unusual depiction of a young eagle mounting to the sun and then shedding its plumage in a brook, the whole poem hinges on a clever twist of the water-fire dichotomy. In both cases the image adds a resonance which lingers in the *pointe* itself.

A corollary of the water-fire motif is that of fire and ice, where the latter most often represents the cold indifference of the beloved as contrasted with the passion of the lover: "...tant plus j'ay de feux, et plus elle a de glace" (sonnet XXIV).[16] Though she treats her suitor with coldness, she inspires his flames as well; the fire of passion

---

[14] Though the dichotomy is common, Roy Rosenstein has pointed out in his art. cit. on the "flammes d'amour," that the fire component of the motif recurs more obsessively in Durand than in his contemporaries.

[15] The sonnet in which these lines occurs is a classic example of another Petrarchist theme: the debate between the eyes and the heart of the lover. For other examples, see Filbert Bretin, *Poesies Amoureuses* (1576), fol. 36 vo; and Scalion de Virbluneau, *Les Loyales et Pudicques Amours* (1599), fol. 2 ro, sonnet IIII.

[16] In this sonnet the central simile compares the beloved to a flint which can cause fire, but not catch fire itself. This unusual image has a precedent in Desportes (*Hippolyte*, p. 104); but a later poet seems to have been influenced by Durand's poem: see Ch. de l'Espine, *Le Mariage d'Orphée... Et autres oeuvres Poëtiques* (1623), p. 66.

dwells in her even if she does not feel it. Protesting against Uranie's reproaches, the poet exclaims: "Suis-je pas malheureux d'estre en une mesme heure/ Gellé par vostre bouche, et bruslé par vos yeux?" (p. 85). The mistress is depicted as a living paradox: "Son oeil est plein de feux, son coeur est plein de glace" (p. 86); here the lover is only "projecting" his own confusion onto the beloved. But he cannot exorcise his demons merely by transferring them; his fate is to bear the full weight of inner contradiction, to "Geler dedans les feux, et brusler dans la glace" (sonnet III). This line, with its semantic chiasmus, expresses the typical Petrarchist fusion of passion and torment.

The frequency of the water-fire and fire-ice motifs in Petrarchist verse cannot be attributed to psychological "realism"; above all, such dichotomies allow the poet to display his verbal virtuosity.[17] Durand provides an example of these gymnastics at the end of the "Stances" on pp. 86-7, where he combines both motifs in a small tour de force:

> Belle, si la froideur qu'on voit en vostre face
>   Ne veut changer un peu,
> Ou prenez de mon feu pour fondre vostre glace,
> Ou donnez des glacons pour esteindre mon feu. (p. 87)

The meaning of these lines counts far less than the cleverness of their formulation: in a sense, the poet's pleasure contradicts the lover's pain. This ambiguity inheres in Petrarchism from its origins. Mathieu-Castellani has rightly observed that in Petrarch, the "bonheur de la création poétique est inséparable... du tourment...; c'est la rhétorique pétrarquienne qui permet la stylisation des passions et l'accès à un monde heureux, où les mots ont tout pouvoir" (p. 57).

The figures of Classical mythology fall into two categories: gods and mortals. In searching for parallels with the suffering lover, Durand draws on both; but predictably, he identifies him more readily with men than with gods. The few gods he does evoke in this connection are not members of the Olympic pantheon. The only comparison with divine victims in the *Méditations* places the poet, by implication, in an abject position: that of the Titans after their de-

---

[17] Cf. Odette de Mourgues's comments on the use of antithesis in *précieux* poetry (*Metaphysical, Baroque & Précieux Poetry*, pp. 126-27).

feat and banishment to Tartarus. Their torments form the unifying theme of the "Stances" on pp. 76-7, and reference is made to them again on p. 79. Both poems hyperbolically proclaim the lover's pains to be greater than those of hell; but the inferiority of the Titans is an equally important aspect. Tellingly, Durand ends the "Stances" with a prayer to Uranie:

> Comme plus que les Dieux je vous trouve puissante,
> Retirez de ces maux mon âme languissante:
> Pour damner et sauver il n'appartient qu'à vous. (p. 77)

The lover is the passive victim of his mistress' whims; like the higher gods, she has absolute sway over the fate of underlings. At best, he can only take the role of a lesser deity.

The mortals Durand evokes are far more numerous: Battus (sonnet II); Orestes (sonnet XXI); Dido, Piramus and Thisbe, Alcyone, Leander (p. 92); the victims of Achilles (p. 102); Semele (p. 86); and Daedalus (p. 121). In addition to these legendary figures, the list includes those who actually did exist, but whose history is shrouded in myth: Brutus, Cato, Hannibal, and Socrates (sonnet IV); Mithridates (sonnet VIII and p. 78); the Trojans (sonnet XXXV); the Cumaean Sibyl (sonnet XLVII); and Sappho (p. 92).

Durand does not hesitate to compare his lot with that of women as well as men: in sonnet XLVII, for example, he pictures himself as the Cumean Sibyl in the throes of prophetic inspiration. As she was lashed into a frenzy by Apollo, so he is possessed by a "fol Amour." At the end of a long strophic poem, he addresses this plea to Uranie: "Faictes que ma mort soit une mort de Semelle,/ Qui ne puisse venir que par embrassement" (p. 86). The lines imply a curious parallel between the mistress and Zeus;[18] similarly, the reference to Achilles on p. 102 sets up an equivalence between Uranie and the fiercest of Greek warriors.

More traditional is the comparison of the lover's fate with that of Icarus, a theme featured dramatically by Desportes in the first

---

[18] Though odd, the Sibyl and Semele comparisons were not unheard-of in the late Renaissance: for examples from Durand's contemporaries, cf. Joachim Blanchon, *Les Premières Oeuvres Poétiques* (1583), p. 124, sonnet LIIII (Sibyl); Vital d'Audiguier, *Les Oeuvres Poetiques* (1614), fol. 10 vo (Semele); Flaminio de Birague, *Les Premieres Oeuvres Poetiques* (1585), fol. 89 vo (Semele); S.-G. de La Roque, *Les Oeuvres* (1609), p. 86 (Semele).

sonnet of the *Amours d'Hippolyte*. Durand gives the idea a new twist in the "Elegie VI," when he likens himself to Daedalus instead: as the father had to look on helplessly while his son drowned, so the poet must "voir [s]on Amour traversé,/ Et [s]on espoir mourant en [s]es pleurs renversé" (p. 121). Another conventional theme is the parallel between the beloved and doom-saying Cassandra; Ronsard used this motif to great advantage in his *Amours de Cassandre* (cf. e.g. sonnets XXIV and XXXIII). Unlike Ronsard, Durand emphasizes the inconsistency of the comparison; the Trojan princess was – in contrast to the beloved – as much the victim as the prophetess of woe:

> Le sort est tout pareil des Troyens et de moy:
> Ils sont morts pour n'avoir à Cassandre mis foy,
> Moy pour n'avoir pas creu la belle qui me tue.
> Mais Cassandre et ma belle ont bien du contredict,
> Car Cassandre perit en sa perte preveue,
> Et ma belle triomphe au mal qu'elle a predict. (sonnet XXXV)

In general, Durand shows a tendency to point out such incongruities between the torments of myth and his own dilemma; in this he is at one with the thematic practice of his contemporaries. Like them,[19] he proclaims almost invariably that his afflictions far surpass those of his legendary antecedents. Drawing a parallel in sonnet VIII between himself and Mithridates,[20] the poet ends on a well-turned *pointe*:

> On dict qu'un Roy jadis se paissoit de poison,
> Et que d'autres n'ont peu vivre ailleurs qu'en prison:
> Hé! que je leur ressemble en mauvaise habitude!
> Je n'ayme que mes fers, et ne vis que de pleurs.
> Mais vivant dans l'ennuy comme en la servitude,
> Que ne puis-je comme eux estre aussi sans douleurs?

---

[19] Cf. e.g. La Roque, *Les Oeuvres*, p. 131; Birague, fol. 18 ro; Desportes, *Diane*, p. 182; B. Baddel, *Poëmes d'amours* (1616), fol. A vo; François Berthrand, *Les Premieres Idees d'Amour* (1599), p. 6, sonnet 10.

[20] For another example of this comparison in Durand, see p. 78; cf. also Jean Bertaut, *Les Oeuvres poétiques*, ed. A. Chenevière (1891), p. 324: "Las je me puis bien dire un second Mithridate;/ Je me pais de douleur comme luy de poison."

As I noted above, the "Stances" about Tartarus (pp. 76-7) center on the notion that the poet's sufferings exceed those of any of the denizens of hell, because in him their torments are united in one person. As a variant, Durand complains that his suffering is equal to that of mythical figures, but much less deserved. For example, comparing himself to Orestes pursued by the Furies, he laments:

> Comme Oreste je suis de fureur enflammé:
> Mais las! il enduroit pour sa mere meurtrie,
> Et je n'endure rien que pour avoir aimé. (sonnet XXI)

As opposed to comparisons with the gods, parallels with human victims allow Durand to place himself in a position of far greater inferiority vis-à-vis the beloved: if Uranie could hold sway over the Titans, her domination of a mortal will be infinitely more crushing. In "Ode II" the poet elaborates on the conceit that Amor himself has been dethroned by his mistress:[21]

> Amour, tu n'es plus ce grand Dieu
> Autrefois aux Dieux redoutable:
> Mon infidelle tient ton lieu,
> Car son oeil est inevitable. (p. 92)

But despite the grand assertions made throughout, the tone of the ode, with its jaunty rhythm and teasing frivolity, seems to mock Uranie's "apotheosis" rather than to affirm it. This ambiguity of intention permeates the *Méditations,* and is a typical stylistic trait of Durand's age.[22] Here already a significant shift in thematic practice can be perceived.

The evocation of mythical predecessors in the torments of love belongs to the most powerful conventions in the Petrarchist canon. Comparisons with Piramus or Leander bestow a kind of universality on the lover's woes, heightening their significance. Conversely, the renewal of a well-worn motif through unexpected metrical, syntactical, or rhetorical means can lend an urgency and intensity to the poet's voice which would be far less potent without the contrast

---

[21] For parallel passages see Desportes, *Hippolyte*, p. 145; and Racan, *Oeuvres complètes*, ed. T. de Latour (1857), vol. I, p. 393.

[22] Cf. Odette de Mourgues on the frequent use of wit in the poetry of Durand's age, with or without a serious intent (op. cit., pp. 135-8).

between hackneyed theme and fresh expression. The Acteon sonnet of Sponde[23] is a fine example of this phenomenon. When the poet cries: "Je suis cet Actéon de ces chiens deschiré!" he summons up both the tragic grandeur of the legend and the poignancy of a private agony. He is not only the reincarnation of Acteon, he is *this* Acteon, suffering here and now.[24] The effect produced by Durand and his immediate contemporaries is just the opposite: rather than intensifying the mythical resonance, they deliberately deflate it. For example, Durand comes nearest to a heightened tone in the Cumaean Sibyl sonnet (XLVII), where the terrible gift of prophecy is likened to poetic inspiration; but even here the intrusion of the *pointe finale* tips the scale toward the trivial. On the whole, his evocations of Classical legend are undermined by playful repetition or an undertone of mockery;[25] as I will suggest in the course of this book, such "puncturing devices" contribute to a global ironic strategy.

The theme of "death in life" belongs to the most common of Petrarchist clichés. In the fourth strophe of the poem on Tartarus (p. 76), Durand addresses Tityos with these words:

Toy qui de ton poulmon pais une aigle affamee,
Voy qu'Amour prend en moy sa proye accoustumee,
Et que j'ay plus que toy de renaissantes morts,
Car ton mal eternel tourne en accoustumance,
Mais tantost plein d'espoir, tantost sans esperance,
La tresve de mon mal en accroist les efforts.

The poet remains at the mercy of Amor's cruel whims: his mistress is the "beauté qui [lui] donn[e] ceste mort immortelle" (p. 77). Like the ice-fire or bitter-sweet dichotomies, the death in life motif

[23] *Poésies* (ed. A. Boase and F. Ruchon), p. 177.

[24] Cf. Terence Cave, "The Love-Sonnets of Jean de Sponde: A Reconsideration," pp. 53-4. I follow Cave in preferring the reading "ces chiens" to "ses chiens," the version adopted by Boase and Ruchon in their edition. Cf. also J. P. Porter's remark about the line (p. 46): "This dramatic ellipsis for *I am like* is a significant gain in concision and vividness of expression. It is one of those seemingly small shifts of phraseology which actually contribute to the identification of a new phase of style."

[25] Cf. Mathieu-Castellani's comment that when Durand compares his fate with that of the "grands vaincus" of Tartarus, "l'énumération des supplices a pour principale fonction de préparer leur traduction métaphorique, et l'Enfer, souvent nommé, a perdu sa réalité épouvantable, pour devenir un réservoir d'images et de motifs" (p. 430).

permits the poet to indulge in endlessly clever variations on a seeming paradox. Durand is particularly adept at this type of game: whatever the polarity involved, the tricks for exploiting it remain the same. The main idea is to play at self-contradiction, as when Durand laments: "Vivant je ne vis pas..." (p. 191). The reader's interest is aroused because the sentence appears to fall apart: one meaning cancels out the other. But in fact the statement is completely logical, as the rest of Durand's verse makes clear: "Vivant je ne vis pas, ou je vis en douleur." The conjunction "ou" marks a qualifier: "Living I do not live – or [if I do], I live in pain." The paradox of death in life is only an apparent one, and is recognized as such by the poet and his audience. Contradictions simply belong to the language of amorous verse.[26]

Durand is not content with one false paradox; he can show his skill to better advantage by balancing two or three at once. For example, at the beginning of a set of "Stances" (p. 101) he combines the "morts renaissantes" motif with that of the "coeur volé":

Quel lieu vous tient cachez, nourrissons de ma flamme,
Cependant qu'aveuglé je m'esgare à tous coups?
Si vous estes mon coeur, si vous estes mon ame,
Comment puis-je estre en vie, et separé de vous?

Beaux yeux, mon cher soucy, dont j'adore les charmes,
Si vous me vistes bien en partant de ce lieu,
Vous vistes bien mes yeux se couvrir de leurs larmes,
Pour ne point voir mon coeur qui leur disoit adieu.

Depuis si j'ay vescu, j'ay vescu par miracle;
Ou bien j'eus en naissant plus d'un coeur par le sort:
Non pour pouvoir jamais croire à plus d'un oracle,
Mais pour pouvoir vivant souffrir plus d'une mort.

The first strophe presents the reader with a riddle: what are the "nourrissons"[27] of the poet's passion? The knowledge that Pe-

[26] By the mid-seventeenth century, the antithetical style appears to have fallen out of fashion: perhaps a sign of the transition to "Classical" taste. Colletet, commenting in 1656 upon some *stances* written in his youth, disavows them as follows: "Ces Stances precedentes furent faites par l'Auteur en sa jeunesse, pour plaire à quelques grands Seigneurs de la vieille Cour, qui aimoient encore cette facon d'escrire par Antitheses, et qui estoit à peu pres le style pointu de leur temps..." (*Poésies diverses*, p. 189).

[27] The dictionaries of Cotgrave and Richelet give only the modern definition of

trarchists conceived love to be transmitted by the eyes, the plural *s* of "nourrissons," the word "aveuglé" – these bits and pieces imply that the poet is addressing the "beaux yeux" of his mistress. Certainly, the third line does not help – for now; the references to the lover's "ame" and "coeur" seem merely to prepare the *pointe* of line 4, which rests on the pseudo-paradox of living death. The second strophe takes up anew the theme of sight versus blindness. The apostrophe to the mistress' eyes solves the initial riddle: the "nourrissons" are hidden because the beloved is absent. But why should the lover be "aveuglé"? Once again, an elegant *pointe* ends the stanza, this time as an answer rather than a question. The poet's tears have blinded him, so that he will not have to endure the sight of the beloved's departure. Here is where the *pointe* of strophe one also falls into place: the retreating eyes – source of the mistress' amorous power – take with them the lover's heart, because it has no life apart from them. A chain of equivalence collapses the ostensible contradictions: "nourrissons" = "coeur" = "ame" = "yeux" = "coeur"; "aveuglement" = "larmes"; "nourrissons cachez" = "yeux absents" = "coeur volé" = "mort."[28]

This last correspondence still poses a problem. The equation of the mistress' eyes with the poet's heart has been grasped, but the question in lines three and four ("Si vous estes mon coeur, si vous estes mon ame,/ Comment puis-je estre en vie, et separé de vous?") remains unanswered. The third strophe builds on the anomaly without conclusively resolving it. Alternative solutions are offered: either the death in life the poet has experienced is an inexplicable "miracle," or else he was simply born with a spare heart to lose. He hastens to add that his double heart does not enable him to pledge fidelity to two different mistresses ("oracles"), but only to suffer more than one death. Now the reader sees through the conundrum completely: the "death" occurs on a spiritual plane, not interfering with the continuance of the lover's physical life. By using pseudo-

---

"nourrisson," a "suckling child." But this makes no sense in the context of Durand's poem. In Godefroy one finds that "nourrisson" is an alternate spelling of "norreçon," which can mean "nourriture." This meaning, already archaic in 1611, is surely the one intended here: the mistress' eyes nourish the poet's "flame."

[28] Cf. Helmut Hatzfeld's discussion of this passage in "Mannerism Is Not Baroque," p. 227. His analysis of the phrase "nourrissons de ma flame" seems inconsistent with the Petrarchist doctrine that the "flame of love" originally issues from the eyes of the beloved (and not from those of the lover). As I noted in the previous footnote, the explanation may lie in an archaic use of the word *nourrisson*.

arguments, the poet playfully makes manifest the underlying skeleton of logic on which his false contradictions are draped. In the act of reading, these rationalizations are far from explicit: the author's dexterity presupposes the dexterity of his readers, their familiarity with the inbred "syntax" of late Petrarchist verse.

Within his love – or within his poetics of love – the lover is trapped; in the Petrarchist scheme, his dilemma is expressed by the symbol of a prison.[29] This motif is particularly well developed in the *Méditations*. Durand's variations on the theme illustrate how Renaissance poets achieve a certain freedom within the bounds of convention. By straining at narrow limits, they invest their verse with added force. Just as the Petrarchist lover glories in his chains, the Petrarchist poet thrives within the confines of tradition.

In a set of "Stances" (pp. 77-8) Durand employs the prison image in two diverse but complementary senses:

> Je n'eusse jamais creu que parmy tant de flame
> Un corps attenué peust retenir une ame
> Si long temps en prison:
> Et qu'un attraict charmeur d'une beauté cruelle,
> Ayant causé son mal, la peust rendre rebelle
> Contre sa guarison.
> . . . .
> Les desdains coustumiers de l'oeil qui me possede
> N'estoient que trop puissans pour servir de remede
> Contre leur cruauté,
> Si mon astre fatal qui vers mon mal me pousse
> Ne m'eust faict estimer ceste prison plus douce
> Que n'est la liberté.

Strophe one plays on the age-old Western concept of a dualism between mind and body. Though this notion transcends the domain of Petrarchism as such,[30] the second half of the strophe already shifts perceptibly to a Petrarchist interpretation of the common-

---

[29] Cf. Petrarch, sonnet CXXXIV: "Tal m'à in pregion, che non m'apre né serra,/ né per suo mi riten né scioglie il laccio" (ed. Cudini, p. 195).

[30] The notion of the soul as imprisoned in the body had been popularized by Renaissance Neoplatonism. For example, Ficino maintained that man's "immortal soul is always miserable in the body"; it "sleeps, dreams, raves and ails" in it (cited by Erwin Panofsky, *Studies in Iconology*, p. 138).

place. While the general paradigm depicts the soul as an *unwilling* prisoner of the body, here the soul refuses freedom, "rebelle/ Contre sa guarison": the prison surrounding the poet consists not only of the body, but also of the lovesick soul itself. Cleverly, Durand has converted the prison of dualism into a redoubled symbol of Petrarchist love.

The second strophe presents the theme in a purely conventional manner. The lover has suffered so bitterly from the "desdains coustumiers" of his mistress that he should have learned his lesson by now. But his fatal attraction toward her prevents him from throwing off his shackles: this is a familiar Petrarchist conceit (cf. Mathieu-Castellani, pp. 41-3), based once again on an inner contradiction. The grim prison of passion seems "plus douce/ Que n'est la liberté."

The "Stances" on pp. 181-2 demonstrate how the meaning of a conventional phrase such as the one just quoted "collapses" or "deflates" once it is taken to its ultimate conclusion. The first four strophes of this poem consist of a lengthy and coquettish development of the prison motif. The torture-chamber has become a paradise:

Voir alentour d'un lict mille amours voltiger,
Des attraicts aux desirs les ames s'obliger,
Avoir pour fers des bras, et l'amour pour estude;
Du nombre des baisers à l'envy contester:
Cela ne doit-il pas bien faire rejetter
La liberté des champs pour telle servitude?

Instead of a "vieux Geollier," the lover has as his keeper a beautiful and kindly-disposed mistress. These "Stances" appear in the third section of the *Méditations*, the *Meslange*; they do not belong to the *Méditations* proper, which are modelled on the Petrarchist *canzoniere*. In fact the poem does not correspond to the essence of the prison motif at all, but only to the form; the *topos* has been humorously perverted. The usual Petrarchist lover *suffers* in his prison, abandoning all hope of winning his beloved's favors; by contrast, here the prison stands for the ties binding the two in carnal union, a source of unadulterateded joy.[31] Since the beloved has fulfilled the

---

[31] For another example of the "happy prison" motif, see Desportes, *Diane*, p. 104.

lover's wishes, the "doux-amer" of Petrarchist passion ceases to exist. Even so, the pleasantry would lose its force outside the context of thematic convention: like the lover in his blissful jail, the poet enjoys the "prison" of Petrarchist tradition; by skillfully recasting the set motifs, he exults in the "bonheur de... la rhétorique pétrarquienne."

Of all the Petrarchist antitheses, the most prevalent is the presence-absence dichotomy: from Petrarch to Bertaut by way of Scève and Ronsard, the polarity oscillates through every stage of Renaissance love verse.[32] In an intricate passage from the "Stances de l'Absence" (p. 82), Durand knots a string of contradictions around this fundamental axis:

> Je cherche ma raison qui s'esloigne de moy,
> L'absence d'un bel oeil mon vainqueur et mon Roy,
> Absente aussi mon coeur qu'il a pris pour le suivre;
> Et quand au souvenir mon bien je vay cherchant,
> Ce mesme souvenir se monstre si meschant,
> Qu'il me donne la mort en le faisant revivre.
>
> Mais las! en ceste mort je renais à tous coups,
> Je vis de mes douleurs, et n'ay rien de si doux
> Que l'aigreur que je souffre en mon obeissance;
> Et pensant à mon mal, je m'y plais tellement
> Que je fuy les pensers qui peuvent seulement
> Destourner les douleurs que j'ay de mon absence.

The "Je" at the beginning of the first verse is echoed by the "moy" at the end, with a telling shift to the objective case: the inner distance of the subjectivity from itself is dramatized by the structure of the line. Without wishing to over-interpret, I would suggest that the cunning rhythm and syntax, which balance "cherche" against "s'esloigne" and "raison" against "moy," reinforce the sense of widening disjunction. The two verbs, both verbs of motion, enact an expansive movement: in the search for its vanishing reason, the self is losing ground.

---

[32] Mathieu-Castellani calls the theme of absence a "thème majeur du lyrisme néo-pétrarquiste, chez Bertaut notamment" (p. 231). Around 1600 this motif does seem to assume an even greater importance than previously. Cf. the study of another of Durand's contemporaries: *Siméon [de] La Roque, poète de l'absence*, by J. G. Perkins.

The rest of the passage depicts a progressive disintegration of the lover's faculties. After the loss of reason in line 1, lines 2-3 trace an emotional estrangement: in a variation on the "coeur volé" motif, the suitor's heart follows the beloved into absence, like a courtier accompanying his king. The lover's memory betrays him as well (lines 4-6). Through memory his "bien," the "coeur" of his passsion, is revived; but the resuscitation leads only to a further "mort," the painful awareness of the mistress' absence. Repetitions ("cherche" – "cherchant," "absence" – "absente," "souvenir" – "souvenir")[33] convey the halting, obsessive movements of a divided consciousness. The rhythmic opposition of "mort" and "revivre" in the final verse – like that of "raison" and "moy" in the first – drives home the wedge of inner contradiction.

The relative vividness of the life-in-death motif in these verses derives from the purely imaginative sphere in which it appears. In this case the reader is not confronted with two clearly distinguishable levels of reality, as in the passage examined earlier ("Nourrissons de ma flamme" [p. 101]): the spiritual plane on which death occurs and the physical realm in which the body continues to live. Here both life and death are a function of thought. The combat is wholly interior, evenly matched – a symbol not only of passion, but of poetic antithesis itself.

The second strophe forcefully develops the thematic contraries of the first. Across the confines of the stanzaic form, "la mort" is intensified into "ceste mort." In the Acteon sonnet by Sponde, the indicative pronoun renders myth acutely personal; here it invests an abstraction with sudden immediacy. By comparsion Durand's invocation to Tithyos, quoted above, remains coolly disengaged; when the poet boasts to his infernal twin, "j'ay plus que toy de renaissantes morts" (p. 76), the deaths he mentions seem hoarded up like possessions, rather than experienced in the living flesh. In the strophe under review the conversion of "la mort" into "ceste mort" is enacted by the passage from a passive to an active stance, from "il me donne la mort" to "en ceste mort je renais." As opposed to the impersonal, almost autonomous proliferation of "morts renaissantes" in the other poem, here the suffering subject occupies the center of the stage.

[33] The first two of these pairs are good examples of *derivatio* (see Chapter II).

The rest of the strophe gradually relaxes the tension of its initial verse. "Je vis" takes up the active affirmation of "je renais"; but it is instantly challenged by the phrase "de mes douleurs." Similarly, the enjambment between lines 2 and 3 underscores the contradictory union between sweetness and bitterness – again a classic Petrarchist dichotomy.[34] "Je souffre," in turn, finds its pendant in the subsequent verse: "je m'y plais." In the second strophe, no longer venting his emotions, the poet stands at one remove from himself; even his pain has become an object of thought ("pensant à mon mal"). At a further remove, he flees his own thoughts ("je fuy les pensers"). The last two lines, with their rhythmic monotony, portray a will paralyzed by inner conflict. The verb "Destourner," thrown into relief by enjambment, is doubly pivotal: it resumes in one word the dynamic of the lover's self-estrangement. Turning away the thoughts which might turn away his pain, the poet turns away from himself. Whereas the first strophe still alluded to the beloved's absence, made more poignant by the memory of her presence, the second strophe focuses on the lover. But the final reference is to his own "absence"; at this point, the cadence is rife with ambiguity.

Repetitions, *reprises*, reversals – the second strophe, like the first, is an echo-chamber in which words and concepts reverberate from line to line. These crisscrossings set in motion on a smaller scale what the thematic conventions of Petrarchism generate on a larger: a closed circuit of cross-reference and variation, running from work to work, century to century. Where development of the stock dichotomies runs dry, the repetitions sink to a monotone, the opposites freeze into a colorless immobility. At the end of the "Stances de l'Absence," the exhaustion of the lover is matched by that of the poet:

> Absent comme present mon malheur est egal;
> Absent, pour ne voir point cet oeil qui m'est fatal,
> Et present, pour le voir toujours impitoyable. (p. 82)

But the poetic commonplaces also correspond to the cyclical rhythm of Petrarchist love, its obsessive oscillation between passion

[34] In employing this oxymoronic theme, Petrarch was drawing on an ancient tradition. For a concise history of the *dulce malum* motif, see Hugo Friedrich, *Epochen der italienischen Lyrik*, pp. 217-19.

and listlessness. In a sense, this poem enacts the presence-absence theme at the level of "content": though the supposed love-experience is absent, it provides the verses with their only *raison d'être*.

Then again, perhaps Durand's poetry has shifted here to a different register entirely. In discussing the gods he evokes, I did not stress the principal one: Urania, the Muse of Astronomy and Geometry, associated with abstractions as universal as they are inhuman. His choice of this name for his beloved suggests that the religious overtones of the "Stances à l'Inconstance" are prefigured in the Petrarquist cycle of the *Méditations*. As Yves Bonnefoy remarks of the "Stances de l'Absence" (p. II), "l'Uranie des *Méditations* n'est pas la femme réelle qui manquerait à un désir ordinaire, ce qui ne la rendrait que plus violemment présente dans la parole qui la voudrait, elle emblématise une absence qui semble à la fois moins repérable et plus vaste, celle qui creuserait, déferait toute figure dans l'experience du monde et affecterait donc tout vocable, toute parole." I will return to this point in Chapter III.

The passages examined in this section lead to several conclusions. First, that Durand treats the conventional themes not as prefabricated parts which always mean precisely the same thing, but as focal points around which various meanings can gather. Second, that he profits doubly from the Petrarchist vocabulary, appealing to the accepted sense of the motifs and then playing tricks with them as well. In the space of a few lines, he will often use a *topos* in its normal denotation, then turn it on its head through slight but crucial alterations. This process of thematic subversion resembles that of punning; the result is a *calembour* writ large. The ambiguity is not confined to a few passages: it permeates the *Méditations* throughout. Just as the tone of individual lines or strophes differs markedly within a given poem, so entire poems contrast with others in inflection, casting an ambivalent light on the work as a whole. In Chapter IV I will expand on the ways in which this "poetics of inconstancy" informs the verse of Durand and his contemporaries in the late Renaissance.

2. The Major Themes: Inclusions and Exclusions

The previous section dealt with small-scale motifs which, constantly re-used and transformed, compose the building blocks of an inbred Petrarchist discourse. This section will examine larger constructions, those which recount the supposed love-experience according to a preconceived model. In the schematic narrative of Petrarchism, I distinguish four major "moments," each of which is surrounded by a group of related *topoi*: 1) the fateful first encounter with the beloved; 2) the obsessive contemplation of her beauty; 3) the lover's retreat into the solitude of nature, to which he appeals for sympathy; and 4) the amorous dream, which grants him an illusory fulfillment. Apart from 1), these moments do not occur in a distinct order; instead, they mark recurring states of mind within a chronic disorder. Since the lover often relives the instant of falling in love with the mistress, 1) also recurs on the imaginative plane, the only sphere which concerns the reader (and arguably, the poet himself).[35] The way in which Durand presents these four major groups of themes reveals a consistent stance toward the tenets of Petrarchism: as I noted earlier, his "exclusion" of certain motifs seems as characteristic of that stance as his frequent "inclusion" of others.

In the Petrarchist paradigm, the first encounter implies a precise succession of events, an almost scientific process. The English expression "love at first sight" comes nearer to the Renaissance concept than the French *coup de foudre*, because everything depends on the initial glance. In that instant an allegorical assault takes place: Amor, dwelling in the eyes of the beloved, shoots an arrow through the poet's eyes into his heart; from then on the lover bears a wound which is painfully reopened each time he sees the mistress (cf. Weber, vol. I, pp. 237-8).

This image of the "flèche du regard" occurs repeatedly throughout the *Méditations*. It appears already in the first poem (p. 35), the liminary sonnet by A. P.: "Et sur toy tous les traicts et toute l'amertume/ De ce Tyran des coeurs se plongent d'un instant." It returns on the final page of the book (p. 195): "...un oeil parfaict en beauté/ N'a poinct de blesseure imparfaicte." The fullest expression of the

---

[35] Cf. Gérard Genot's remark that throughout the *Canzoniere*, "qu'il s'agisse de la louange répétée de Laure, de celle du moment où le poète s'est épris d'elle, qu'il s'agisse de l'expression du remords d'avoir perdu tant de temps en l'amour d'une mortelle, le moteur est toujours le même: il s'agit de répéter un moment, ou plutôt un discours sur un moment, de recommencer par la parole le cycle d'une existence circulaire, infiniment changeante, mais qui trouve dans la permanence de son flottement une unité qui se meut en l'*image d'une histoire*" (intro. to his edn., p. 32).

theme can be found in the "Complaincte" on pp. 52-3, where the poet addresses Amor:

> Que te sert d'enfoncer en mon coeur tant de bresches,
> Si la chère beauté qui te fournit de flesches
> Mesprise ainsi les coups qu'elle va provoquant?
> Ou blesse-luy le coeur, ou guaris ma blessure... (p. 53)

This passage underscores another element of the convention: the wound is not mutual, since the beloved remains untouched by the lover's gaze.

The arrow allegory was such a standard *topos* that Durand normally alludes to only part of the process, rather than describing it in its entirety. For example, on p. 99 he brings out the visual aspect in order to execute a clever pointe: "Regardez par vos yeux," he says to Uranie, "les maux qu'ils ont sceu faire." On p. 83 he couples the ocular motif with that of the assault's immediacy:

> Que fais-je en m'esloignant, ayant l'ame offensee
> Du traict qui me blessa dès que je l'apperceu,
> Sinon que commander à ma triste pensee
> D'enfanter les douleurs que mes yeux ont conceu?

Here the conceit rests on the notion that memory continues to generate the same torments in the beloved's absence as those to which the lover's eyes "gave birth" in her presence. Though the initial wound is immediate, the "douleurs" are reproduced eternally, either by the appearance of the mistress or by her remembered image: again, event and imagination merge. Without a previous knowledge of the allegory, such a passage would be incomprehensible to the reader.

Closely connected to the "flèche du regard" motif is that of the "flamme du regard," a theme common to all Petrarchist poets; in fact, Durand uses it more often than most.[36] To cite one example among many: "Peux-tu bien voir la braise/ Qu'ont allumé tes yeux[?]" (p. 61). Typically, the "flames" transmitted by the mistress' gaze burn so powerfully that they threaten to turn the poet's heart to ash. Similarly, at the beginning of "Elegie I" (p. 106) the lover asks:

---

[36] See the essay by R. Rosenstein in our edn.

Mais pourquoy donc [vos yeux] ont-ils employé tant de peine
Pour captiver un coeur, si leur flame inhumaine
Veut le reduire en cendre apres qu'elle l'a pris?

In order to add a touch of realism to the evocation of the first encounter, Petrarchists often attribute a specific time or place to the meeting. Accordingly, Durand claims in his "Discours" that Uranie "appeared to him" at a ball (p. 125).[37] Here as in general, his portrayal of the first encounter corresponds exactly to convention (cf. Mathieu-Castellani, pp. 37-9). The opposite is true when it comes to the group of themes which praise the beloved's beauty.[38] These tend to be conspicuous by their rarity; even when they do appear, they seldom evoke the mistress directly.

A lyrical enumeration of the beloved's traits is found in only two passages of the *Méditations*. Sonnet XXVII conforms to the classic model of a series of exclamations.[39] Grammatically speaking, each verse introduces another subject; and each consists of a noun followed by a chain of modifiers. The predicate does not make its entrance until the tenth line. Durand gives this highly conventional poem a new accent by turning the reader's attention away from the beloved entirely in the final tercet:

Mais admirant toujours ses beautez admirées,
Je suis comme un dragon sur les mines dorées,
Qui n'en peut recevoir plaisir que par les yeux.

In fact, the shift of emphasis toward the lover already begins two lines earlier, where the poet evokes *his* flames, *his* laughter, *his* sighs. A similar phenomenon marks the other enumeration passage (p. 112), which lists the beloved's features as figments of the poet's memory, underlining their unreality. She is not admired for herself, but seen exclusively in the light of his emotions.

Another sign of this concentration on the inner drama of the lover, and the corresponding suppression of the mistress from the

---

[37] The ballroom is a favorite backdrop for these *coups de foudre*; cf. e. g. Soffrey de Calignon, *Vie et poesies*, ed. Douglas (1874), p. 166: "Je benis, et le lieu, et l'heure et la journee,/ Que je te vis baller le soir d'un hymenee."

[38] For a full enumeration of these themes see Weber, vol. I, pp. 262-90; and Mathieu-Castellani, pp. 57-64.

[39] For examples from Durand's contemporaries, see J. Bernier de la Brousse, *Les Oeuvres Poëtiques* (1618), fol. 10 ro; and S. Du Mas, *Lydie* (1609), p. 109.

poetic discourse, is the vagueness of Durand's portrait of Uranie. Aside from the passages just cited, there are only two further indications of her physical appearance in the entire book, and these are so scanty as to add almost nothing to the picture: on p. 97 the poet evokes "un sein qui la neige surpasse"; and on p. 84 he alludes to the "corail" of Uranie's lips. In any case, the image which emerges from these allusions, and from the more elaborate descriptions in the enumeration poems, conforms completely to Ariosto's portrait of Alcina: blond hair, curly and long; dark eyebrows arched like Cupid-bows; dark eyes; lips of coral; teeth like pearls; an ample breast and a slender neck, both white as snow. In falling back on the stock representation of feminine beauty then current, Durand depicts a fashionable ideal, not an individual.[40]

Remote – if not unreal – the beloved's beauty gives her a supernatural power over the lover. Like other Petrarchists, Durand compares Uranie repeatedly to goddesses, angels, and the legendary beauties of Antiquity. As I noted above, the mistress' name conjures up a celestial sphere far beyond the everyday world: Urania was the Muse of Astronomy in Classical mythology, the embodiment of divine contemplation.[41] In keeping with the heavenly motif, Durand also likens his beloved to Luna; in the paired sonnets on pp. 46-7, for example, he draws a point for point comparison between the two. Uranie is always Diana's equal; when there are differences, the former inevitably has the upper hand:[42]

> L'une [Diane] dans les enfers ne commande qu'aux morts,
> Et la beauté de l'autre [Uranie] a des charmes si forts,
> Que des Dieux et de nous elle engage les ames. (p. 47)

---

[40] See Puleio, "Il ritratto di Alcina e il 'Portrait d'Uranie'"; and cf. Weber, vol. I, pp. 265-8. Cf. also R. A. Sayce's article on "Ronsard and Mannerism: The *Élégie à Janet*," which suggests that the feminine portraits in Renaissance poetry correspond to those which typify the Mannerist style in painting. The same traits reappear in males: cf. the "Mort d'Antinous" attributed to Ronsard, in Raymond and Steele's anthology, pp. 86-7.

[41] By the time Durand was writing, Urania had often figured as the "celestial Muse" who initiates the poet into the secrets of the universe. Cf. A.-M. Schmidt, *La Poésie scientifique en France au XVIe siècle*, pp. 27-33; for an iconographic description of Urania, see Cesare Ripa's *Iconologia* (1603), p. 349. However, her appearance in love poetry is highly unusual: this tendency toward thematic blurring will be discussed in Chapter IV.

[42] For a similarly constructed sonnet which treats the same theme, see Nicolas Le Masson, *Les Premieres Oeuvres* (1608), fol. 43 vo.

In "Ode II" (pp. 91-3) Durand taunts Amor with the news that he has been deposed by Uranie. But when the poet implies that his mistress is "des premiers corps/ L'essentielle intelligence" (p. 91), he steps beyond the usual bounds of Petrarchist exaggeration. In Chapter IV I will suggest that the same type of displaced theological allusion occurs with increasing frequency toward the end of the sixteenth century.

The rustic images of female beauty which characterize the *pastorale* or the many imitations of Ronsard's *Continuations*[43] do not figure in the *Méditations*. Natural settings are evoked, but always without the mistress; Durand prefers the solitary forest to the meadows of bucolic verse. Equally absent are the lush erotic metaphors of the *Song of Songs*, which had exercised a strong influence on Baif and Belleau, among others (cf. Weber, vol. I, pp. 284-6). The old-fashioned form of the *blason*, on the other hand, does survive in the *Méditations*: sonnet X is addressed to Uranie's "belle main";[44] sonnet XIX, to her "beaux yeux." These highlights of single parts of the body do little to render the mistress' presence more vivid: significantly, Durand omits most of the descriptive detail which characterized the earlier *topos*.

In general, the mid-sixteenth century *blason* differs markedly from its late Renaissance descendants. The *Blasons du corps féminin* of 1550[45] aim to eternalize the object of praise, to preserve it forever in a detailed incantation – "sa cage perpétuelle, sa défense contre le temps."[46] By contrast, the "belle main" to which Durand appeals does not exist in isolation; far from inspiring a catalogue of physical details, it blurs indistinguishably into the motion of its acts. To borrow an analogy from the visual arts, Durand's poem demonstrates the Baroque emphasis on movement, whereas the earlier *blason* reflects the ornate, Mannerist immobility of the École de Fontainebleau.[47] Even in the *blason*-like poems of Durand's age which

---

[43] Cf. Marcel Raymond, *L'Influence de Ronsard sur la poésie francaise* (1550-1585), vol. II, pp. 39-47; Weber, vol. I, pp. 281-3; Mathieu-Castellani, pp. 168-74. Durand's "Folastrerie" (pp. 164-8) associates the presence of the beloved with the pleasures of nature, but it obviously does not belong to the bucolic genre.

[44] On this sonnet see Puleio's book, pp. 77-9.

[45] *Poètes du XVIe siècle*, ed. A.-M. Schmidt, pp. 291-364.

[46] Ibid., Schmidt's commentary, p. 294.

[47] See S. Béguin's book on Fontainebleau for the links between the latter and Mannerism. Cf. also the chapter in Mirollo on the hand in Mannerist portraiture and poetry. On applications of the trait of movement in Baroque art to literary

do concentrate on describing a part of the body, a chain of metaphors swiftly digresses from the subject. Durand's sonnet to the "beaux yeux" of the mistress is a prime example of this phenomenon, to which I will return at the end of the book.

In line with Durand's avoidance of directly evoking the mistress, there are very few instances of the "lovely as a rose" or "fading flower" themes (cf. Weber, vol. I, pp. 333-56) in the *Méditations*, as these are motifs which express an ardent concentration on the beloved herself rather than on the plight of the lover. In "Élégie III" the poet praises "Ceste joüe d'oeillets, et de rose, et de lys,/ Où [s]es desirs vivans meurent ensevelis" (p. 112); and in sonnet XXVII he again extolls "Une joüe où l'oeillet dans la rose s'enlasse." But here the flowers are merely ornamental, synonyms for the colors in Uranie's complexion. Nowhere in the *Méditations* does the reader find that equivalence of rose and beloved from which Ronsard drew such splendid effects.

The theme of fading flowers, which inspired some of the most beautiful poems of the sixteenth century, provokes even less of a response in Durand. The only passage in his verse ("Ode I," p. 89) which compares in meaning with such a poem as "Mignonne, allons voir..." does not contain the floral image at all:

Regarde bien qu'en ces beaux jours
La terre est couverte d'amours,
Et les arbres d'un beau fueillage:
Mais qu'aussi l'hyver arrivant
Par sa froideur il les outrage,
Et les emporte par le vent.

De mesme ces jeunes beautez,
Dont les Dieux mesmes enchantez
Adorent les traicts redoutables,
Seront par la course des ans
En hyver aussi mesprisables
Que desirables au printemps.

---

studies, see M. Raymond, *Baroque et Renaissance poétiques*, pp. 39-42. But cf. Steadman's cautionary remark: "One should, for the most part, regard these formal analogies between mannerist and baroque art and the literature of the late or post-Renaissance as suggestions only – as conceits and ingenious correspondences – rather than as scientific evidence."

Cet oeil si beau se cavera,
Ce beau teint se replissera,
Et ceste bouche si vermeille
Qui tire tous les coeurs à soy,
Par l'effect du temps qui sommeille
Ne servira plus que d'effroy.

Que si le temps peut rapporter
Tout ce que l'hyver peut oster,
Nous avons d'autres destinees:
Car les beautez estans un jour
Par la vieillesse moissonnees,
Impossible en est le retour.

In the context of Renaissance literary history, this passage is revealing. By Durand's time the convention of the rose as a metaphor for the mistress – in combination with the *carpe diem* theme – has become so deeply ingrained in the poetic consciousness that it no longer creates any effect of surprise. Here the flower symbol has been deflated to a mere fragment of its former self, a "bouche vermeille." Durand loses the delicacy which the analogy can conjure up, and which underlines the pathetic ephemerality of the beloved's charms. On the other hand, he skirts the temptation to over-daintiness inherent in the theme. The "beau fueillage" which the poet substitutes for the flower lends itself to more violent expressions: winter "par sa froideur *outrage*" the leaves, "les emporte par le vent." The effects of time on Uranie's beauty are described in no uncertain terms, with a kind of sadistic glee: her eye "se cavera," her skin "se replissera," her mouth will inspire nothing but "effroy" – she will become "mesprisable." As Henri Lafay has pointed out (pp. 242-5), the poets of the early seventeenth century take particular pleasure in exploiting the theme of the *vieille*.[48]

Durand's most brilliant and original use of the flower theme occurs in sonnet XXXIX, where he recounts a curious dream:

[48] In its general outlines, Durand's poem remains closer to the traditional *carpe diem* motif, where the vision of old age supports the main argument as a kind of corollary. For similar passages from Durand's contemporaries, see Pierre de Cornu, *Les Oeuvres Poetiques*, ed. P. Blanchemain (1870), pp. 74-5; and Jean Godard, *Les Oeuvres* (1594), pp. 294-5. It will be noted that all three of these poems are odes: the ode was the usual verse form used in treating this motif.

Dieux! que le Songe faict de travaux ressentir!
J'ay creu voir en dormant un jardin plein de roses,
Qui n'estoient point si tost apparemment escloses
Que mon oeil les voyoit en soucis convertir.

J'ay creu voir deux soleils leurs rayons departir
Sur ces mesmes soucis, y faisant mesmes choses:
Car tous deux les faisoient dessecher au sortir
Et reverdir apres quelques petites poses.

Une voix, ce me semble, au profond des deserts
Me disoit, Ce jardin est l'object que tu sers,
Ces roses sont le teint de ta belle Uraine:

Roses qui font produire et croistre tes soucis,
Soucis qui de ses yeux tous les jours esclaircis
Dans leur mesme tombeau soudain prennent la vie.

The abstraction of Petrarchist flower imagery could hardly be taken further than in this poem. The rose garden, a paradise of the senses in Ronsard, is reduced to a mechanical symbol of Uranie's complexion; the rose represents only one trait of the beloved's beauty, rather than a living embodiment of the whole. The plural number points to the same phenomenon: the isolated flower, which shares the mortality of the single human being, is multiplied into an undifferentiated mass of colour and softness. The "soucis" (marigolds) which Durand calls into play are even more removed from organic reality. Their presence in the poem springs from a purely verbal accident: the pun on the word for "cares, worries." [49] Though they die, they are immediately born again – unlike the single flower of the tradition; in the end, they are simply stage props for the poet's inner drama.

The "soucis," unrelated to the mistress' appearance, epitomize the "egocentrism" which I have already noted in Durand's work. He seems far too concerned with the emotions of the lover to focus his attention on the beauty of the beloved, much less to lament her ultimate fate. It is fitting that the flowers of this sonnet should

[49] The pun on the word *souci* is a commonplace of French Petrarchism; for another example see René Bouchet d'Ambillou, *Sidere* (1609), fol. 90 vo, sonnet II.

emerge within a dream,[50] as though he meant to emphasize that they exist only as figments of the poet's fantasy.

Of all the major Petrarchist themes in the *Méditations*, those which center on the lover in the midst of nature recur with the greatest insistence. Henri Weber has formulated the essential scenario: "L'amoureux recherche la solitude dans la nature qu'il rend confidente de ses amours et de ses douleurs; parfois il y trouve comme une sympathie, un apaisement, parfois au contraire l'image de l'aimée le poursuit à travers les bois et les vallons" (vol. I, p. 307). Like his predecessors, Durand portrays himself in a woodland setting, where he confides in the ancient trees, the birds, the winds, the brooks and the nymphs.

Though Durand chooses the forest as his favorite retreat, he does not focus on the delights of nature as they are detailed in certain poems of Théophile and Saint-Amant.[51] For him the woodland setting holds small interest in itself: it is first and foremost a *paysage d'âme*.[52] The gloomy solitude of the forest mirrors the poet's inner state, his sadness and isolation from the beloved; but at the same time, it consoles him in his suffering:

> O Bois, que vous m'estes aimables,
> Que vostre silence m'est doux,
> Si mes ennuis sont incurables,
> Pour le moins les soulagez-vous. (p. 51)

Of course, no amount of consolation can "cure" the lover's woes. In a passage from the "Meslange" – outside the bounds of the love-poem cycle – Durand summons up a reversed image of the forest's significance. The joyous "Stances" on pp. 181-2, discussed earlier in reference to the "happy prison" motif, also contain a reminiscence of the poet's previous ordeal:

---

[50] On Durand's dream sonnets cf. Puleio, op. cit., pp. 67-72.

[51] Cf. Bruzzi, p. 90. In op. cit., p. 93, Odette de Mourgues notes that "Théophile, Saint-Amant, and Tristan consider nature as a succession of landscapes to be enjoyed for their own sake and with some precision; and precision for them consists in putting the stress on concrete details in a landscape." Cf. also the intro. to her *Anthology of French 17th-Century Lyric Poetry*, p. 12.

[52] Cf. Gilbert Delley, *L'Assomption de la nature dans la lyrique francaise de l'âge baroque*, pp. 39-40.

Il me semble qu'encor je me voy dans ces bois,
Courbé sur mes genoux, attendant qu'une voix
Favorable à mon bien vint finir mon attente:
Qu'un bel oeil me conduit au sejour pretendu,
Et me fit voir combien un plaisir attendu,
Arrivant à la fin, rend une ame contente.

By contrast with the "sejour pretendu," the pleasant "prison" of love which the poet now enjoys, the forest represents his experience of exile and absence.

These last two words run like a constant thread through Durand's depictions of the solitary woods. For example, sonnet XXX begins with the following quatrain:

Absenté du bel oeil dont j'adore les loix,
Et cherchant des forests le plus sombre silence,
Je pleignois mon exil d'une mourante voix,
Et contois aux rochers l'ennuy de mon absence.

The *reprise* of the first word at the end frames the stanza, stressing that the poet's exile is confined to the closed circle of his disjunction from the beloved. Earlier I quoted Genot's comments (intro. to his edn., loc cit.) about the self-enclosed circularity of the *Canzoniere*; but if the presence of Laura is painfully heightened by the concentrated "prison" of Petrarch's verse, in late Petrarchism the emphasis is placed on the mistress' absence. Significantly, the "Stances de l'Absence" (pp. 81-2) also have the lonely forest as a backdrop. As I noted above, Bonnefoy has underlined the universal overtones of this poem, which echo those of the "Stances à l'Inconstance." Invoking the theological doctrine that "Tous les maux de l'enfer ne sont rien qu'une absence" (p. 81) from God, Durand extends its application to nature:

Tu confirme cecy, trop amoureux oyseau,
Qui d'un arbre seché fais un vivant tombeau:
Tu plore pour l'absence, et meurs encor pour elle.
Et vous, arbres muets, forests que j'aime tant,
Vos rameaux sans verdeur vont-ils pas regrettant
Les absentes douceurs de la saison nouvelle?

The forest is not only the faithful confidant of the lover, but a living example of the torments he endures along with the rest of creation.

It would be wrong to identify this as "pathetic fallacy," since the poet is not so much projecting his feelings onto nature as trying to perceive some universal law which might explain his suffering.[53]

The opposite is true of a subsequent passage in the same poem, where Durand writes: "Je me plains aux rochers, qui touchez de mes maux/ Semblent plorer pour moy les eaux de leurs fontaines" (p. 82). Even more than most Petrarchists, Durand constantly appeals to the sympathy of nature. The anaphoric sonnet V – which I will examine at length in Chapter II – consists almost entirely of apostrophes to the "Forest," "fidele secretaire" of the lover's complaints. Similarly, in sonnet XXVI the poet invokes the "Petits oyseaux avec qui [il] souspire,/ Chers compagnons, en ce bois ancien" – and I could cite many other examples. Just as the lover considers himself subject to a universal law of nature, so he imposes his own subjectivity on the universe: these are two sides of the same coin, and serve the same purpose of self-dramatization. In the end Nature herself seems to undergo an inner transformation; addressing the "bois pitoyable," Durand proclaims:

> Donc que parmy ces doux ombrages
> Vos oyseaux changent de chanson,
> Et que mes souspirs et mes rages
> Soient leur estude et leur leçon.
>
> Qu'Echo d'une voix incertaine
> Ne responde qu'à mes douleurs,
> Et qu'il n'y ait plus de fontaine
> Qui n'ait sa source de mes pleurs. (p. 52)

Significantly, the mention of Echo and the "fontaine" suggests the identification of the poet with Narcissus, who was in love only with himself. As he weeps into a "fontaine" which reflects his own image, the beloved becomes superfluous.

The sixth "Elegie" (pp. 121-4), the culmination of a series of loosely-constructed plaints preceding the "Discours," also marks the fullest development of the forest motif: the climax of Durand's lament is organically linked with the scene of his "meditations."

---

[53] Cf. Bruzzi, p. 88: "Il sentimento della natura si esprime nel Durand nelle immagini che si generano dal passaggio del sentimento dell'instabilità al concetto dell'instabilità".

The very title of his book implies a contemplative distance from any flesh and blood reality. "...Mes premiers maux n'ont esté que frivolles," he tells Uranie, "Comparez avec ceux qu'en ce lieu deserté,/ Je souffre pour avoir esloigné ta beauté" (p. 122). The construction of the last line is revealing. Supposedly, the lover has removed himself from the *beloved's* presence; but the phrase used by Durand states the contrary, that he had dismissed her from *his* presence. The meditation of the poet proceeds by precisely the same movement – which is the explanation of this sudden reversal of terms. Through the process of self-portrayal he achieves an ever-widening distance from the pretext of his verse, his alleged love for the mistress. Ultimately she is reduced to an imaginary spectator of his inner drama; throughout the latter half of "Elegie VI" (see p. 123) the lover fancies that "les yeux d'Uranie" are observing him:

> Pleust aux Dieux qu'un momment ils peussent estre encore,
> Présens en ces desers, où leur beauté j'adore:
> Pleust aux Dieux, qu'un momment ils voulussent venir
> Assister aux discords que faict mon souvenir...

Vividly Durand evokes the scene which he wants the eyes of Uranie to see before her:[54]

> Ils me verroient tantost au plus creux d'un bocage,
> Le coude my-caché dans la mousse et l'herbage,
> Soustenir de ma main mon front appesanty,
> Comme par la douleur en pierre converty:
> Et tantost contempler la gazouillante course
> D'un ruisseau dont mes yeux semblent estre la source.
> Ils me verroient encor au silence des bois
> Forcer les rochs plus sourds de respondre à ma voix...

Not only must the beloved visualize the lover in his present surroundings, she must measure his sufferings against that of other lovers, stretching far back into time; the rocks and trees bear witness to the unheard-of severity of his ordeal:

---

[54] This passage provides a good example of the rhetorical figure known as *evidentia*: see below, Chapter II.

Ces rochers envieillis qui soustiennent les Cieux,
Ny ses arbres brisez par le poids de leur aage,
N'ont jamais veu d'Amant qui souffrist davantage.

These passages represent the opposite of an "obsession de l'image aimée qui poursuit l'amant": instead, the lover's preoccupation with himself is projected onto a fictional observer. Like the appeal to the forest, the appeal to the beloved only reinforces the centrality of the lyric *je*.

On p. 52 the poet maintains that his sufferings exceed not only those of all past lovers, but of all future lovers as well:

O bois, qui vers moy pitoyable
Escoutez mes cris ennuyeux,
Quelque autre Amant plus miserable
S'est-il jamais plaint en ces lieux?

Non, non, comme il n'en a peu naistre
D'aussi pleins d'amour et de foy,
Je veux croire qu'il n'en peut estre
D'aussi miserables que moy.

Here again the forest serves as a repository, a living testimonial. Just as it preserves the memory of other laments it has "heard," in sonnet V Durand implores it to convey to Uranie a record of his own:[55]

Forest qui toute seule as receu tous mes voeux,
Forest où je veux vivre et mourir langoureux,
Enferme dans ton sein ma complainte eslancée:

Afin que si tu vois ma belle par le sort
Tu luy monstre qu'icy j'ay souspiré ma mort
Plustost qu'en autre lieu souspiré ma pensee.

This sonnet underlines once more a tendency which may be observed in all the "nature poems" of the *Méditations*: a concentration on the sufferings of the poet himself, almost to the exclusion of the

[55] The theme of nature conveying a message to the mistress is frequent in Petrarch and his successors (cf. Weber, vol. I, p. 320). For examples from Durand's contemporaries, see Robert Angot de l'Eperonnière, *Le Prelude poetique* (1603), fol. 6 ro, sonnet XXIIII; and Nervèze, *Les Essais Poetiques*, fol. 10 vo, sonnet XIX.

beloved. The latter is not charmingly portrayed in a natural setting, as Laura[56] and other Petrarchist mistresses so often were (cf. Weber, vol. I, pp. 322-7); Uranie appears only as a witness of the lover's agony. But she is not really "there" even in that capacity. Her image, vaguely outlined, looms with obsessive frequency on the poet's horizon; but she possesses no physical or spiritual reality. Like nature in these poems, she exists only as a function of the lover's self-dramatization.[57]

The bleakness of the landscape evoked by Durand is not unique to his work. As Edwin Duval points out in his book on the early works of Saint-Amant, "in the last three decades of the sixteenth century and the first two decades of the seventeenth, the conventional *locus amoenus* of lyric solitude underwent a minor mutation: the inevitable 'horreur' of the solitary landscape was accentuated to become more explicitly sinister, lugubrious or terrifying – without, however, losing any of its former attraction for the unrequited lover" (p. 19). When Romantics such as Théophile Gautier rediscovered Saint-Amant as a precursor, an eerie "nature poet" like themselves, they were mistaken in assuming there was anything novel about the landscape per se in his poem "La Solitude" (published in 1629). His true originality lay in presenting the desolate scene not as a backdrop for the pining Petrarchist lover, but as a focus for nature imagery which becomes a subject in its own right. "Saint-Amant is not only playing with convention here," Duval notes (p. 21), "he is playing with his reader as well... The force of convention is so great that the absence of the 'lover' is almost tangible."

By the late 1620s, the retreat of the mistress from center stage which I have adumbrated in Durand's verse reaches its logical conclusion: after the Petrarchist beloved, the Petrarchist lover himself vanishes from the scene. Despite its kinship with the past, "La Solitude" is not a Petrarchist poem at all, and for that reason it marks a poetic watershed. Duval rightly concludes (loc. cit.) that the work is

---

[56] Cf. for example the beautiful *canzone* CXXVI, in which Laura is covered with a "pioggia" of spring blossoms (ed. Cudini, pp. 175-7).

[57] Cf. Mathieu-Castellani's remarks on Desportes (p. 238): "Que nous propose-t-on? Un discours, où le 'je' dialogue avec un 'toi', où une voix crée, pour lui répondre, un écho assourdi. Car Diane, Hippolyte, Cléonice, ne sont pas plus réelles ni plus présentes que la nature ou les objets du monde extérieur. La dame est une chaude absence, un beau nom... Elle se confond avec Amour."

a "form of literary play and literary criticism which uses the conventions of lyric to undercut conventional lyric. It is an ingenious blow to the heart of a long but dying tradition." Implicit in the word "dying" is the fact that by this time the process of dissolution was well underway: Durand and others had already prepared Saint-Amant's coup de grâce to Petrarchism through thematic subversions of an equally ingenious but more subtle type. Obliquely, from within the Petrarchist schema, they had been carrying out the program which Saint-Amant would complete: "On every level the conventions of lyric are undercut in order to be infused with a vital and original force, which is in turn undercut, and so on, in what would appear to be an infinite process of lyric deconstruction" (ibid., p. 56).

In other "nature poems" from the early seventeenth century, such as Théophile de Viau's "La Solitude" or Tristan l'Hermite's "Le Promenoir des deux amants," the abandonment of the Petrarchist paradigm is made palpable in a different way, as the happy lovers walk through the tormented landscape of a former age. In this "stroll down memory lane," the old sufferings and frustrations of the *dulce malum* no longer apply to the present. Not only is the poet willingly accompanied by "Corinne" or "Climène" in the "val solitaire et sombre,"[58] but their sensual favors seem to be his for the asking. In Tristan's poem an ancient oak bears the "marques" of outmoded writing; it harbors lyric "plaintes" that now remain unheard.[59] Their exaggerated pathos is symbolized by the image of "sang chaud" gushing forth. The more reasonable lovers of today pass the tree without "cutting its pages" and allowing that torrent of despair to flow:

> Ce vieux chêne a des marques saintes;
> Sans doute qui le couperait,
> Le sang chaud en découlerait
> Et l'arbre pousserait des plaintes.

In the succeeding strophe a nightingale – a time-honored metaphor for the author of verse – is another reminder of the forlorn, unrequited Petrarchist lover who used to haunt these woods:

---

[58] Théophile, in De Mourgues, anth. cit., p. 35.

[59] Ibid., p. 54.

Ce rossignol mélancolique
Du souvenir de son malheur
Tâche de charmer sa douleur
Mettant son histoire en musique.

In both cases, as in the fables of Ovid, the poet of bygone days has been metamorphosed into an inhuman emblem harking back to a legendary past. The singer's "malheur" is but a "souvenir," and his "musique" retraces the "douleur" of an already finished "histoire."

Nowhere is the absorption of the lover in his own fantasy more evident than in the Petrarchist motif of the amorous dream. Here he can fulfil the desires that his diurnal experience thwarts: in his nocturnal visions the beloved is passionate, consenting – but only for a moment.[60] Several passages in the *Méditations* correspond to this classic version of the "songe amoureux," which permits the poet to lead a double life. In sonnet XXI Durand writes:

Veillant, dormant, je suis en semblable malheur:
Le jour par le penser j'entretiens ma douleur,
La nuict par le songer elle est tousjours nourrie...

As this passage illustrates, the second life of dream only reinforces the eternal sameness of the lover's woes; the seductive images which flee at dawn seem to prove the insubstantiality of his fondest hopes. The rhyme of "songe" and "mensonge," conventional in this context,[61] is no accident; in sonnet XX, Durand resumes the lover's fate as follows: "S[e] mentir à [s]oy-mesme, et s[e] paistre de songe."

The "Stances" on pp. 101-2 contain the fullest development of the theme:

[60] On the development of this theme by the Pléiade, see Weber, vol. I, pp. 356-66; on Ronsard in particular, see Grahame Castor, "Petrarchism and the Quest for Beauty...," pp. 91-5, 115-20. On the "songe amoureux" in French love verse 1570-1600, see Mathieu-Castellani, pp. 147-62, 435-55; she notes that "après 1585, le thème connait une fortune prodigieuse" (p. 435). For examples from Durand's contemporaries, cf. d'Audiguier, *Les Oeuvres Poetiques*, fol. 38 vo; Desportes, *Diane*, p. 240; Berthrand, *Les Premieres Idees*, p. 19, sonnet 39; Pierre de Deimier, *Les Premieres Oeuvres* (1600), p. 101. Cf. also the poems grouped under the heading "La Dame en Rêves" in A.-M. Schmidt's anthology, *L'Amour noir: Poèmes baroques* (pp. 99-139).

[61] E. g. cf. Ronsard, *Sonnets pour Hélène*, I: LIV (ed. Laumonier, vol. XVII, p. 244); and Jean Passerat, *Recueil des Oeuvres Poetiques* (1606), p. 329.

J'ay passé maintes nuicts à me plaire en [m]es larmes,
Ne trouvant rien plus doux ny plus delicieux,
Pendant qu'Amour faisoit la garde avec ses armes,
De peur que le sommeil ne coulast en mes yeux.

Mais si par fois ce Dieu, pour t'aller voir (ma Belle),
Cessoit de me garder, pendant qu'il me quittoit
Il mettoit près de moy le Songe en sentinelle,
Qui m'offrait tes beautez, et puis me les ostoit.

O Songe, luy disois-je, ô Songe que j'adore,
Arreste pour un peu, pourquoy t'envole-tu?
Puis je fermois les yeux pour resonger encore:
Mais estant sans sommeil ils estoient sans vertu.

Voila comment j'ay peu profité de mes songes,
Et comment mes plaisirs se sont veuz emportez:
Mais las! si mes plaisirs ont esté des mensonges,
Mes tourmens ont tousjours esté des veritez. (p. 102)

This passage forms a small compendium of the motifs surrounding the amorous dream. In the first strophe, the poet depicts his sleepless nights, tossing and turning in the throes of his passion. Amor denies him sleep for two reasons: dreamless, he might escape his pain for a while in deep unconsciousness; dreaming, he might enjoy the beloved's favors through a fiction almost as "real" as reality itself. But as the second stanza reveals, the latter is a mixed blessing at best. The god Dream is a more cruel master than Amor, for he tantalizes the lover with the mistress' "beautez" only to remove them before full satisfaction can be reached. Unlike other French poets, Durand does not dwell on the image of the beloved, much less describe his pleasures in detail; in the manner of the Italian Petrarchists, he uses the dream mainly as a pretext for an *appel lyrique* (cf. Weber, vol. I, p. 356). When he pleads with "Songe" in strophe three, the object of his oniric pleasures is forgotten: as usual, Durand returns to the dilemma of the lover himself. The pat moral of the final stanza is spoken for him alone: all joys are "songes" and "mensonges"; the lover's suffering is his sole reality.

With the possible exception of this "egocentric" note, all the above is pure convention. Quite the opposite is true of sonnet VI:

Où trouveray-je une onde aussi claire que belle
Pour expier l'horreur d'un songe que j'ay faict?
J'ay pensé sommeillant voir un serpent infect
Qui sifflant vouloit mordre et tuer ma rebelle.

J'ay pensé voir encore, accourant auprès d'elle
Pour la vouloir sauver, un prodige en effect;
Car ce cruel serpent delaissant son project,
Aussi tost d'un enfant a pris forme nouvelle.

Puis il m'a dict, Pauvret, qu'as-tu faict en ce lieu,
Uranie m'ayant resisté, comme Dieu
En serpent je voulois la piquer et surprendre.

Va, de ton trop oser tout seul tu pâtiras,
Sans jamais l'eschauffer tout seul tu brusleras,
Et son coeur sans pitié se rira de ta cendre.

The poet recounts a dream – but is it amorous? Strictly speaking, this is more of a "love poem" than the dream sonnet discussed earlier, with its abstract floral imagery.[62] There Uranie appeared only remotely, by means of interposed symbols: the "roses" of her complexion, the "deux soleils" of her eyes, the "soucis" with which she plagues the lover. In this sonnet she almost seems like an equal of the other two characters, Amor and the poet; but in fact she plays a silent role, while they explain not only their own actions, but hers as well. Considering certain poems of Ronsard[63] or Théophile,[64] where the beloved visits the poet's bed like an alluring succubus, the lack of passion in Durand's nocturnal visions seems remarkable. Here, as in the flower sonnet, the mistress remains distant and disembodied; the only amorous aspect of the dream is Amor himself.

Amor is the most active figure in these verses; no mere symbol, he is split into several *personae*, and undergoes more than one transformation. A "serpent infect" at first, he changes into a harmless child – but this is not the end. As soon as he speaks, he reveals himself to be the mischievous god of old. Showing sympathy for the

[62] As noted earlier, on Durand's dream sonnets cf. Puleio, op. cit., pp. 67-72; she considers them to belong to his "momento manierista."

[63] E. g. the *Sonnets pour Hélène*, II: XXIII (ed. Laumonier, vol. XVII, pp. 264-5).

[64] Cf. the sonnet in vol. II of the *Oeuvres poétiques*, ed. J. Streicher, pp. 202-3.

lover in tercet one, he waxes prophetic in tercet two – not without a hint of *Schadenfreude*, almost of complicity with the poet's enemy. The "Alexandrian" presentation of the dream as a little anecdote[65] serves Durand's habitual technique of tonal modulation. The first tercet represents a tour de force of "conversational style," that much-admired trait of the English Metaphysicals. The word "Uranie" in line 10 has to be drawn out in an anaresis in order to fit the meter; but in effect, the final *e* falls away, giving the verse an unstable rhythm which is further accentuated by the suppressed, or shifted, caesura. The same result is achieved in line 9, where the pause comes two syllables too soon. The enjambment of lines 10-11 brings out the colloquially chaotic syntax of the whole, which matches the playful familiarity of the address ("Pauvret qu'as-tu faict..."). [66] Abruptly changing registers, the second tercet is all solemnity and resounding proclamation. Though the mistress figures in Amor's prediction, the god is addressing the lover, and his pronouncement concerns him alone: as usual, the beloved retreats into the background. By contrast, in sonnet XIX of Ronsard's *Amours de Cassandre*, the mistress delivers the dire prophecy herself.

Durand ignores the Petrarchist tradition in both his dream sonnets; neither of them obeys even partially the conventions of the genre. Rather than a direct encounter with the beloved, Durand's nocturnal visions present a succession of changing images, a world in metamorphosis. [67] They come nearer than the standard Petrarchist conceit to the actual process of dreaming, in which scenes follow one another abruptly and the diurnal order of things is confounded. In a sense both poems approximate the pattern of Freudian dream-interpretation: [68] the dreamer recounts his vision, in the

[65] The "Alexandrian" style depicts the lover and beloved in "conventional roles in anecdotes concerning Venus and Cupid" (I. D. McFarlane, intro. to Scève's *Délie*, p. 29). For other examples in Durand, see sonnets XXII, XXX, XXXVIII, and XLIII.

[66] Such passages as this have led Frank Warnke to assert that Durand "is capable of striking the note of colloquial urgency characteristic of his English contemporaries" (intro. to anth. cit., p. 36).

[67] This is also true of a sonnet by Le Masson (fol. 6 ro) in which the lover is transformed into various animals; but Le Masson's dream fits much more neatly than Durand's into a preconceived framework, that of the "Protean" theme (cf. Rousset, op. cit., pp. 22-4).

[68] Hence Pizzorusso (pp. 42-3) gives a quasi-Freudian interpretation of the ser-

hope of understanding it; the recitation of the dreamed events provokes a decoding of their symbolic message. The difference is that Durand includes the interpretation in the dream itself. In the serpent sonnet, Amor explains the drama of which he himself was a protagonist; in the roses sonnet, a mysterious "voix au profond des deserts" announces the meaning of what has gone before. With the exception of the *Songe* of Du Bellay, these poems have no precedent in their disconnected, truly "dream-like" imagery. Since Du Bellay's work is an allegorical vision of universal *vanitas*,[69] Durand's sonnets remain unique in their lifelike expression of individual dreams (laced though they are, of course, with some of the usual thematic tags).

As opposed to the two sonnets discussed above, Durand's version of the "invocation to Sleep" *topos* – which is closely related to that of the amorous dream[70] – obeys the conventions to the letter. For this reason sonnet XII provides an opportunity to compare his variation on the motif with those of his predecessors and contemporaries in the Petrarchist tradition. The invocation to Sleep lends itself especially well to such a treatment, because it always displays the same easily identifiable traits. Since these stay fairly constant not only from century to century, but also from poet to poet within a given period, the theme invites both diachronic and synchronic analysis.

The invocation to Sleep was one of the most frequently revisited *topoi* of Renaissance love verse. Beset by the torments of an unrequited passion, the poet begs Hypnos to grant him respite from his pain. Why must he toss and turn – he complains – while the rest of mankind reposes in blissful slumber? If Sleep will release him from his plight, the poet promises to honor the god with heartfelt offerings. By the end of the sixteenth century this theme was being rehearsed by scores of Petrarchists all over Europe;[71] the vogue

---

pent sonnet; he asserts that "il serpente è l'immagine originaria del sogno; il significato di questa immagine è erotico" (p. 42). The transformation of the snake into Amor represents the "traduzione cortese" of the dream (p. 43).

[69] See Klaus Ley, *Neuplatonische Poetik und nationale Wirklichkeit*, pp. 337-41, for a discussion of the sources and allegorical design of the *Songe*.

[70] Accordingly, Weber (vol. I, pp. 356-69) and Mathieu-Castellani (pp. 150-2, 435-41) study the two themes conjointly.

[71] Cf. for example L. Baldacci, *Il Petrarchismo italiano nel cinquecento*, pp. 243-244; and Mathieu-Castellani, pp. 147-63.

continued well into the seventeenth century.[72] In fact the sources of the *topos* may be found less in Petrarch than in his Classical mentors and Italian followers.[73]

By the time Durand's *Méditations* were printed in 1611, the invocation to Sleep had known an illustrious *fortune* in France. Rémy Belleau (vol. I, p. 315) and Pontus de Tyard (p. 166) had imported the motif from Italy during the first stage of the Renaissance; their stately, balanced verses are richly studded with Classical allusions. Though presaging the more colorless versions of the following quarter-century, Desportes's sonnet to Sleep (*Hippolyte*, pp. 130-1) published in 1572, still reflects the poetic condensation of the Pléiade. From then until 1600 a number of poets – including Pierre de Brach (*Oeuvres Poétiques*, vol. I, pp. 59-60), Flaminio de Birague (fol. 24 ro), Joachim Blanchon (p. 36), and Jacques de Romieu (fol. 48 vo) – blandly repeat the the *topos* in the customary sonnet-form, with few variations in imagery or technique. In the midst of this monotony, Ronsard injects the invocation theme with new life in his *Derniers Vers*. His starkly urgent plea to Sleep, "Donne moy tes presens..." (ed. Laumonnier, vol. XVIII-i, pp. 178-9), converts the figurative poppy of the *topos* (a traditional attribute of Morpheus) into a medicine which the poet is actually consuming. Similar concretizations infuse the commonplaces with a vivid intensity: the effect is that of revisiting a familiar place under a pitiless and excessive light.

Durand's immediate contemporaries in particular had treated the motif with great diversity and originality. Jehan Grisel (p. 73), Pierre de Deimier (*Premieres Oeuvres*, p. 145), and Nicolas Le Digne (in two examples, *Les Fleurettes*, fols. 71 vo – 72 ro and fol.

[72] The *topos* received one last expression in the graceful extended version by Alberto Lista, "Al Sueño," at the beginning of the nineteenth century; a Romantic, he signals the archaicizing character of his poem by beginning it with an epigraph from Lope de Vega. The text of this literary "throwback" is available most readily in the anthology edited by Menéndez y Pelayo, *Las Cien Mejores Poesías...*, pp. 126-28.

[73] Among the former, Homer (*Iliad* XIV: 224-91), Virgil (*Aeneid* IV: 522-32, V: 835-61), Ovid (*Metamorphoses* XI: 592-649), Statius (*Silvae* V, poem 4), Seneca (*Hercules furens*, lines 1065-76), and Tibullus (*Elegies* II, poem 1). Among the latter: Lorenzo de' Medici, whose sonnet "O sonno placidissimo..." (written circa 1476; see *Opere*, Simone ed., vol. I, p. 81) brings all the Classical sources together for the first time in a unified *topos*; and Giovanni della Casa, whose version of the theme (printed 1558; see *Rime*, ed. Ponchiroli, p. 78) was the most influential in Italy (cf. Baldacci, pp. 243-4).

102 ro) had displayed their inventiveness within the confines of the traditional sonnet, while S. Du Mas (pp. 195-6) and René Bouchet d'Ambillou (fol. 88 ro-vo) had developed the subject in longer strophic forms.[74] In highly idiomatic ways, all these poets had enlarged the expressive range of the invocation *topos*, whether through alterations in style, thematic variations, or insertion of the motif into a fresh dramatic context.

Read against this background, Durand's invocation to Sleep might appear somewhat lackluster at first glance. Unlike Du Mas and Bouchet, Durand does not depart from the usual sonnet-form; nor does his version of the theme display the stylistic brilliance of Deimier's, the thematic variety of Grisel's.[75] Less spectacular in its effects, Durand's poem is on a par with the experiments of his contemporaries – and even, in a certain sense, superior. The very restraint of sonnet XII gives it a hidden force:

Sommeil, dont les destins ont enrichy le monde,
Pour servir de relasche aux desplaisirs soufferts,
Si le galerien qui rame dessus l'onde
Peut reposer par toy dans les coups et les fers:

Si le pierreux peut bien d'une outrageuse sonde
Oublier par toy seul les sentimens divers:
Si le goutteux oublie une rage profonde
A l'heure que tu peux glisser dedans ses ners:

Si l'artisan penible en toy seul se délasse,
Si par toy la douleur d'un jour à l'autre passe,
Pourquoy suis-je tout seul sans toy dessous les Cieux?

---

[74] Both use a six line stanza with rhymes aabccb. The longer form allows them room for complex thematic modulations. In five strophes Du Mas moves from the traditional complaint to Sleep toward a joyous salute to Dawn, identified with the renewed vision of his beloved after a night of absence. In six stanzas Bouchet d'Ambillou shifts from an amorous dream to a painful awakening, then from a lament about absence to an invocation to Sleep. The invocation is couched in the "Alexandrian" style, as an encounter between Morpheus and Amor.

[75] Deimier's sonnet is a tour de force of the "Alexandrian" genre, in which Amor is addressed in a colloquial "style parlé." Grisel addresses Night rather than Sleep, opposing her torments to the joys of Day: but concludes that Day is even worse, since the sight of his beloved will kill him.

Pourquoy du bien commun n'ay-je point jouyssance?
Ha! Sommeil, je t'entends, tu monstre en ton silence
Que la mort, non pas toy, me doit fermer les yeux.

The opening apostrophe to Sleep is simple and straightforward, almost dry. Durand does not engage in the coaxing flattery common to most of his predecessors. Though he praises Sleep, the tone remains distant and formal – quite the contrary of Bouchet's familiarity, for example. The words chosen by Durand to describe the god's good works – "destins"[76] (line 1), "enrichy" (line 1), "relasche" (line 2) – carry no heavy emotional charge; similarly, the human ills which Sleep relieves are merely "desplaisirs" (line 2) – a far cry from the usual Petrarchist hyperboles.

This understated quality governs the diction of the entire poem. It is complemented by a marked reserve in imagery and metrical effects. Eschewing the magical night-evocations of Tyard or Desportes,[77] Durand illustrates the benefits of sleep through four examples drawn from everyday life. The first of these (lines 3-4) may have been vaguely suggested to the poet by the Palinurus episode in Virgil,[78] where the rowers fall asleep on hard benches beneath their oars: "placida laxabant membra quiete/ sub remis fusi per dura sedilia nautae" (lines 836-7). But in the context of the other three vignettes, Durand's concise depiction of the galley-slave seems removed in spirit from a literary allusion. The "pierreux"[79] (lines 5-6) and the "goutteux" (lines 7-8) were doubtless common features of the Court society Durand frequented, and the "artisan pénible" (line 9) could be observed in any Paris street. The inclusion of these figures in an invocation to Sleep bespeaks a unique concern for re-

[76] According to Cotgrave, this word can mean "providence" in the early seventeenth century.

[77] E.g. Tyard: "...la nuit, d'une grande ombre obscure,/ Faict à cet air serain humide couverture..."; "Ja le muet Silence un esquadron conduit,/ De fantosmes ballans dessous l'aveugle nuict..." E.g. Desportes: "Sommeil, paisible fils de la la Nuict solitaire"; "Or que l'humide nuict guide ses noirs chevaux..."

[78] *Aeneid* V (loc. cit.) recounts the misfortune of Palinurus, the helmsman who, overcome by Sleep, fell from Aeneas' ship and was drowned.

[79] The "sonde" mentioned in line 5 was a metal rod which doctors inserted into a wound in order to judge its depth. However, this makes no sense in the context of the "pierreux" who suffers from a kidney or gall stone. Perhaps Durand is comparing the pain of this condition to that of having one's wound explored by an "outrageuse sonde."

alism, not encountered in any of Durand's predecessors, or even in his contemporaries except for Shakespeare.[80]

Here I would distinguish between the drastic literalism of d'Aubigné or the late Ronsard,[81] which takes a hackneyed motif *au pied de la lettre*, and the low-key objectivity of Durand's poem. Its realism does not heighten, by contrast, the effects of a sublime rhetoric; it harmonizes with a global strategy of understatement, which encompasses every aspect of content and form. Ronsard's invocation to Sleep expresses his anguish through exclamatory repetitions and fervent, quasi-religious language; the everyday elements in his sonnet add a note of bitterness and pathetic irony. Le Digne, evoking his migraine by means of a blacksmith metaphor, converts his physical sensations into a dramatic image, underlined through onomatopoeic rhythms and alliterations.[82] In both poets, a flamboyant style exalts the lyric *je*. Both describe their misery from the interior; both remain within the confines of the lyric subjectivity, which a certain type of realism – centered on the self alone – only serves to intensify. The subjectivity of Durand's sonnet is more ambiguous: the poem narrows in on the self, but the final words close around an absence.

This process of abolition is carefully prepared and accomplished by the unfolding structure of the poem. The initial apostrophe to Sleep consists of impersonal generalities. The next two lines depict a human destiny which lies at the farthest remove from the poet's own. Like the galley-slave, the other three sleepers are described without any reference to the lover's torments – though the analogy is obvious enough, given the conventions of Petrarchism. The reader might even be tempted to discern a further parallel between the poet and the toiling artisan, especially since his craft is left unspecified. But this feature is already part of another development, through which the subjectivity definitely does come into the

---

[80] I.e., in the Petrarchist context: such everyday realism was of course the norm in satirical verse, such as that of Mathurin Régnier or Sigogne de Beauxoncles (cf. Lafay, pp. 405-17). On similar aspects in Shakespeare's sonnets see below, the Conclusion.

[81] On d'Aubigné cf. H. Weber, art. cit.

[82] Second quatrain of the first sonnet cited above:

> Je ne puis fermer l'oeil, ma teste est toute plaine,
> D'importuns forgerons, qui forgent à plein bras,
> Et menent plus de bruit, que les Ciclopes d'Athlas,
> Qui battent sans cesser sur l'enclume hautaine.

open. The evocation of the artisan is cut short by the general reflection of line 10, which clarifies the principle of comparison between the lover and his fellow-sufferers. Immediately afterward, the lyric *je* intervenes for the first time: though the tercet fuses poet and artisan by a syntactic bridge, it separates them by antithesis.

The progression from objective generalities and portraits to subjective lament finds its parallel in a rhythmic acceleration, a steadily tightening rhetoric. The quatrains are divided into neatly equal periods of two lines each; but the apostrophe, left suspended, and the repeated "Si" create a mood of expectancy. The syntactic tension culminates in the first tercet, where an abrupt change in periodic structure throws the final "Si" (line 10) into relief. The two succeeding questions – mirror of the two dependent clauses – mark the rhetorical climax of the poem. But they are far from "rhetorical" in the modern sense of the term: unadorned by imagery, plainly direct in diction, these lines come very close to simple prose. Their bareness invests the lover's complaint with a signal power – an austere insistency, free of self-pity.

The final lines confirm the mood of resignation. After the *accelerando*, they form a sudden *rallentando*; the ample, two-verse period is taken up again – but the rhythm is halting and restrained. Numerous half-stops slow the lines to a maximum, and the solemnity is further magnified by the symmetrical placing of the punctuation: in each verse, the retarding effect of the commas in the first hemistich carries over into the second, so it flows smoothly, yet lingers. The metrical weight of the conclusion corresponds to an alteration in theme: the relinquishment of hope in Sleep, and the acceptance of death as the lover's only means of deliverance. As in Seneca's play *Hercules furens*, Sleep prepares the way for Death, teaching man to welcome his ultimate fate: "pavidum leti genus humanum/ cogis longam discere noctem" (loc. cit., lines 1075-6). While Durand clearly builds on the Classical motif of Sleep as the brother of Death, he does not allude to the allegorical kinship directly. Assuming the first printing of the *Méditations* is correct, the word "mort" (line 14) appears in lower case. This avoidance of "Alexandrian" personification adds to the gravity of tone: death almost seems to intervene as a reality, not a mythological figure.

The final verse conveys a mysterious ambiguity. Since the poet has appealed to Sleep personified, death should logically belong to the same imaginary sphere. But Death is not invoked by the lover in turn – as in the *Derniers Vers* of Ronsard,[83] for example; instead, death enters to "close the eyes" of the poet at some unspecified moment in the future. What does this phrase "really" mean? Does it evoke the symbolic gesture of a god? Or does it describe the physical effect of death? No doubt it remains suspended between the two. This fusion of the allegorical and the prosaic gives the entire poem its peculiar density, its presence.[84] When "Sleep" does not answer the lover's prayers, the invocation is revealed to be a fiction; the poet's words have been addressed to an absence. What remains is his reference to the external world, embodied by the four sleepers depicted earlier – and also the objective fact of his own death, which is all that can be read in the silence of the god.

Durand's poem does not dramatize the subjectivity: it moves toward the elimination of the self. In the first part of the sonnet, Durand regenerates the Virgilian (and Statian) opposition between the sleeping world and the lover's tortured vigil[85] through the use of everyday examples; like Statius, he questions Somnus directly, demanding justice. He abandons the decorative attributes of Sleep drawn from these and other Classical sources, particularly Ovid and Tibullus – no poppies, black wings, or Lethean waters appear.[86] In the latter part of the poem, he renews the Senecan motif of sleep as a prefiguration of death. But if the sonnet remains firmly anchored in the tradition, its approach to the given *topos* is unique: here the invocation to Sleep is less a lover's complaint than an exercise in abnegation.

Generally speaking, the most striking aspect of the invocations to Sleep in Durand's time is their eclecticism. Compared with the esthetic equilibrium of the mid-sixteenth century as embodied by

[83] See sonnet IV (ed. and vol. cit., p. 179).

[84] By contrast, cf. the last eight lines of Desportes's "Imitation de l'Arioste au 33. chant" (*Les Imitations de l'Arioste*, ed. Lavaud, p. 486), a passage which may have influenced Durand's conclusion. In Desportes the heavily stressed antithesis between waking and sleeping, life and death, seen purely as physical phenomena, diminishes the impact of the final verse ("...ô mort! haste-toy de me clorre les yeux"). Since sleep is not allegorized, the tension between the allegorical figure of death and the physical reality of death does not arise, as in Durand.

[85] In *Aeneid* IV (loc. cit.), Virgil recounts the tortured vigil of lovelorn Dido, sleepless while the rest of creation slumbers. The passage influenced Statius, who innovates by addressing Somnus directly (see loc. cit.)

[86] See passages cited above. For the Renaissance iconology of Somnus, see Cartari, *Les Images de dieux*...

Belleau, Tyard and Desportes, or the bland conventionality of its final quarter as typified by Brach, Birague, Blanchon and Romieu,[87] the beginning of the seventeenth century is marked by an exuberant inventiveness, a love of variety which precludes the dominance of any single style. As opposed to the previous century, Classical and Italian influences are less plainly evident: the sources of the invocation theme have become thoroughly blended and absorbed. Durand and his contemporaries do not even draw heavily on their predecessors in the French tradition, as Tyard (or Belleau),[88] Blanchon, and others had done. Through variations in verse-form, thematic development, diction, and dramatic presentation, the "poets of 1600" revive the *topos* with expressive vigor – and not by radically literalizing Petrarchist motifs, in the manner of d'Aubigné, the late Ronsard, and the "pétrarquistes noirs." In Bouchet it is the fictional moment of waking rather than the literary theme which is dramatized; in Durand the realistic note generates sobriety, not grotesquerie; and even in Le Digne's evocation of his sleepless migraine, the final *pointe*[89] tips the scale away from the morbidly theatrical.

The stylistic spectrum of the early seventeenth century spans the bantering *préciosité* of Deimier, the Malherbian formality of Du Mas, and the satirical exaggeration of Le Masson. The playful character of his "Nuit d'Amour" (*Premieres Oeuvres*, 13 ro – 14 ro) – which juggles many of the Somnus motifs without actually invoking the god – is easily grasped; but in a wider sense, playfulness is the one quality which links all the "poets of 1600." Throughout the *Méditations*, Durand profits doubly from the stock Petrarchist motifs, using them in the accepted sense and subverting them as well. In the stage of late Petrarchism which the years after 1600 represent, its proponents derive a stimulus to innovation from the very fact that their themes *have* become codified and stereotyped in the extreme. More than ever before, they can assume from the outset that the reader will be thoroughly familiar with the entire canon of *topoi*; this means they can be approached obliquely – subtly refracted through allusion, distortion, inversion.[90] Grisel progressively de-

[87] For all these see loc. cit.

[88] The two versions show marked similarities, but it is impossible to say which was written first, or who was imitating whom.

[89] In the final tercet the poet tells Sleep: "Endors ces forgerons qui battent dans ma teste,/ Pendant qu'ils dormiront, j'auray quelque repos."

[90] There have been many attempts to draw a parallel between such literary de-

negates his ostensible theme; Deimier invokes Sleep in reverse, by telling Amor to leave; in one sonnet Le Digne implores the god to put his headache to sleep rather than himself – in another the lover is curiously fused with Somnus and Love; Du Mas converts the invocation motif into a double apostrophe to Night and Day; Bouchet dissolves it into a multi-temporal sequence, half-memory, half-dream; and Durand invests the symbolic *topos* with a stark reality. Not surprisingly, by 1620 a satirist felt compelled to publish an elaborate and systematic reversal of the well-worn theme.[91]

Adding up the evidence, I would assert that the thematic subversion noted in the *Méditations* could be considered characteristic of Durand's age. Literary *topoi* cannot be re-used without some form of variation; but the "poets of 1600" seem more daring and imaginative in this regard than their predecessors. Mirollo observes that literary Mannerism often entails "exploitation – rather than renovation – of the model or normative tradition. It exploits by giving undue prominence to the model's superficial features, or by upsetting its fine balance through distortion or reversal of an essential feature, thematic or stylistic" (p. 62). But when taken far enough, exploitation itself becomes a source of renovation: the Mannerism of the late Renaissance shades over into the Baroque. As Mirollo points out (p. 162), "literary mannerism does not seem to share with visual mannerism and baroque, or with literary baroque for that matter, a clear stylistic profile of its own. It is not so much an autonomous style as a mode or modulation of the Renaissance literary style that predominated... in the sixteenth century." In other words it is the "deconstructive" element within that style, a meta-level of invention which out-invents its models and ultimately destroys them. With creative brilliance, Durand and his contemporaries push the Petrarchist conventions past their limit, till the tra-

vices and Mannerism in the visual arts. For three different approaches to Mannerism in art, see John Shearman, *Mannerism*; Linda Murray, *The Late Renaissance and Mannerism*; and Arnold Hauser, *Der Manierismus*. For analogies with literature see *French Manneristic Poetry between Ronsard and Malherbe* (*L'Esprit créateur*, VI, no. 4). Among sources already cited, cf. M. Raymond (intro. to anth. cit., especially p. 29), as well as Mirollo and Steadman.

[91] In 1620 Salomon Certon published a sonnet cycle which represents an exact reversal of the invocation to Sleep. The "Premier Alphabeth" of his *Vers Leipogrammes* (pp. 11-22) is entitled "Veille d'une nuict"; throughout these sonnets, which the author claims to have written in a single night (p. 10), the familiar mythological motifs are used to ward Sleep off rather than to invoke him.

dition collapses from within. As I will explain in Chapters III and IV, out of the ruins of that tradition they generate a new poetics: a celebration of inconstancy, both as theme and as style, which signals the end of Renaissance verse.

Returning to Durand's work in particular, the preceding investigation of major Petrarchist themes in the *Méditations* leads to several conclusions. First, along the way I have pointed to a considerable number of "exclusions" in Durand's thematic range. These exclusions all tend in more or less the same direction: toward a suppression of the beloved from the very poems of which she is, supposedly, the inspiration. Second, Durand shies away from the charming vernal images which other Petrarchists readily employ. The flowers, fruits, gardens and meadows which ornament the verse of the Pléiade and later poets are virtually absent in the *Méditations*. The natural settings depicted by Durand are desolate and solitary: the dark forest overhung by cliffs; the woods in winter with their "rameaux sans verdeur," where birds find nothing but a "vivant tombeau" (p. 42). It is as though the beloved, retreating from the poet's vision, had taken with her the freshness and abundance of nature as well.

The desolation of the landscape in Durand's work recalls the stark imagery of d'Aubigné.[92] But despite certain similarities in a few of his poems, Durand does not display d'Aubigné's startling determination to intensify, grimly and single-handedly, a whole gamut of Petrarchist conventions. Instead, Durand contributes to a collective impulse, one which playfully subverts the *topoi* through word-play and jest: only their final implosion breeds the powerful countertheme of inconstancy. In fact – and this is the third conclusion, despite certain exceptions like the sonnet to sleep, throughout the *Méditations* there is a tendency toward abstraction which excludes both the sensuous details of the Pléiade and the concrete morbidity of d'Aubigné. It would be tempting to ascribe Durand's relative dearth of visual imagination to the influence of Desportes;[93] but

[92] Cf. Weber's analysis of the manner in which d'Aubigné converts the bucolic landscape of traditional Petrarchism into an autumnal vision of bareness and desolation (vol. I, pp. 327-33).

[93] Cf. Mathieu-Castellani, pp. 234-5: "Tout se passe comme si Desportes se refusait à voir et observer le monde naturel: ...rien ici ne suggère un contact immédiat avec les choses, une appréhension sensible du monde. Bien au contraire: tout

Desportes specializes in suave musical effects of sheer verbality which render the image secondary, almost redundant, [94] whereas Durand often adopts more jarring rhythms, more adamant tones. The colorlessness of Desportes may have something to do with his neo-Platonic "spirituality": this also finds hardly an echo in the *Méditations*, where the sensuality of the poet's desires is openly expressed, his demands for "jouissance" often appearing undisguised.

In comparison with his predecessors, Durand's most distinctive quality might be termed a negative one. My fourth conclusion harks back to the simple Petrarchist clichés discussed in the first part of this chapter; like them, the more elaborate motifs of Petrarchism which figure in the *Méditations* generally do not undergo a radical transformation: instead they are subtly twisted and undermined. By various verbal tricks, Durand progressively reduces them to a *jeu de mots*. Most of what "happens" in these poems, happens not on the plane of images or of themes, but on that of language itself. Though in the broadest sense this is true of literature as a whole, I would submit that in Durand's work the style often runs counter to the theme, perversely calling attention to itself as discourse. Through turns of phrase, the amorous mythology surrounding the beloved is continually subverted; at times it seems to dissolve altogether, just as her human reality had already retreated from view. To a certain extent, as the following chapters will continue to suggest, this phenomenon seems characteristic of the final phase of Renaissance love verse as a whole.

Beyond that thematic mythology – and, I would insist, beyond the verbal subversions of the text – the "lover" and the "poet" still subsist, even if those roles have been totally fused. In most Petrarchist poems the only love expressed is the love of poetry itself. Repeatedly – and this is the last conclusion – the effacement of the mistress in the *Méditations* corresponds to a focus of attention on the lyric *je* itself, as martyr but also as creator. In the Romantic era it was assumed that Renaissance love poets used the "artificial" clichés of their epoch merely because they could do no better; their conventionality was thought to be inversely proportional to their inventiveness and sincerity. But perhaps the opposite is true: that the

---

indique qu'à la réalité du monde naturel, le poéte préfère la stylisation, et voit dans chaque objet de ce monde un emblème ou un symbole."

[94] Cf. Raymond Lebègue, *La Poésie francaise de 1560 à 1630*, part one, pp. 165-6.

poets of the Petrarchist tradition chose to belong to it, even that they did so *en connaissance de cause*. The superficial advantages of such a choice are obvious: the availability of a rich inheritance of themes and images, the prestige of following in the footsteps of Petrarch or Ronsard, the assurance of a reading-public already well-schooled in the conceits of the genre. Still, in the case of a Maurice Scève – and also, I would maintain, of a Philippe Desportes – the explanation cannot stop there. There are poets more conventional than Durand in the late Renaissance – Déplanches, Blanchon, and Scalion,[95] to name a few; but even they would not have chosen to speak the language of Petrarchism, if it had not corresponded to some essential need. As Terence Cave has written: "The Renaissance lyric is often 'dramatic,' in that the poet's voice is heard through the medium of an adopted rôle: the love-poet writes not as a lover but *as if he were* a lover, so that, through the mimesis of human passion, he may penetrate more deeply into the nature of passion itself, and perhaps participate in one of the fundamental forces of the universe."[96]

[95] See the works by these authors listed in the bibliography.
[96] *Devotional Poetry...*, p. 307.

Chapter II

THE RHETORIC OF REPETITION

Petrarchism is not a monolith, but an endless series of refractions. The preceding analyses underline the fact that even within a well-established tradition, "content" is no stable quantity: thematic elements take on different meanings according to the context; more importantly, they vary with the tone. The *agencement* of changing moods depends on the fundamental devices of literary discourse: in the end, the notion of theme resolves itself into a problem of rhetoric. The analogy between tropes and *topoi* is close. Both sets of conventions maintain an essential identity from poem to poem, poet to poet, age to age – despite all the modulations to which they lend themselves. Just as *topoi* embody a symbolic world which outlives the individual creator, tropes represent the autonomy of language.

The modern Romance literatures participate in an unbroken rhetorical tradition, based on Classical precept and on the imitation of Latin authors; [1] until very recently, composition of Latin verse was the stock-in-trade of secondary schools in France. As I. D. McFarlane has pointed out, apropos the teaching of Latin locution in Paris colleges of the sixteenth century: "It is difficult to imagine that writers brought up in this tradition should have forgotten this training when they came to compose in the vernacular; indeed the onus would be on those who wanted to prove the contrary" (edn. cit., p. 57). It is more than likely that Durand attended one of these colleges in his early youth: as the scion of a wealthy Parisian family,

[1] Cf. I. D. McFarlane, intro. to Scève's *Délie*, p. 56: "French poetry has developed on the basis of a serious attachment to the discipline of prosody and also to the techniques of established rhetoric."

active in royal administration, he would not have been denied the education which behooved his rank.[2] His close connection with Marie de Médicis probably bespeaks a devout Catholicism, or at least an orthodox upbringing. If so, Durand may have learned his Latin from the Jesuits, who were allowed to return to France in 1599, when he was 14 years old. This was the usual age for beginning the concentrated study of rhetoric. The Jesuits brought with them out of exile not only a religious Counter-Reform, but a pedagogical reform as well. One of its chief features was a new emphasis on the imitation of the pagan Classics – rather than the Church fathers – as models of stylistic perfection.[3] But in affirming Durand's familiarity with the art of rhetoric, one need not have recourse to suppositions. Whether he read Ronsard, Desportes, Bertaut, or Motin, whether he listened to the sermons of Bérulle, Coton, or some lesser-known homilist, any young *literatus* of the period would inevitably have been exposed to the practices of ancient eloquence. An examination of some of the devices which abound in Durand's verse affords many insights not only into his own methods of composition, but also into the esthetic preoccupations of his epoch.[4]

Such a study is not only of historical interest: rhetoric has a timeless value. Whatever its imagery or musical effects, simply as

---

[2] If one is to believe Élie Garel, author of *Les Oracles François*, the ballet which Durand devised for Princess Elisabeth in 1615 reflects a vast and arcane erudition. But even if one disallows Garel's symbolic interpretation of the spectacle as overwrought, Durand's works do manifest a familiarity with the Classics, as well as some knowledge of philosophy and theology: cf. e.g. p. 102, lines 43-4, where the phrases "par nature" and "par accident" are used in an Aristotelian (or scholastic) sense; cf. also lines 11-12 on p. 81, which allude to the Catholic doctrine of *damnus*.

[3] Cf. Mariéjol, p. 97; Henri IV carried out a similar reform in the University of Paris: see ibid., pp. 98-100. In *La Pédagogie des Jésuites*, F. Charmot has stressed the Jesuits' encouragement of creativity: "Aucun plan d'études n'a peut-être autant que le *Ratio* poussé professeurs et élèves à se former par la composition littéraire. Dans les collèges, tout le monde doit travailler sans intermittence à quelque oeuvre personnelle" (p. 307). "On commençait par imiter les modèles; mais on tendait à l'originalité: peu à peu, avant même d'être sortis de la longue période d'apprentissage, les élèves devaient s'exercer à mettre en oeuvre leurs inspirations personnelles" (p. 311).

[4] For most Renaissance literary theorists and poets, rhetoric was almost synonomous with poetry. Cf. Alex L. Gordon, *Ronsard et la rhétorique*, p. 25; Robert Griffin, *Coronation of the Poet*, p. 26; and Lee A. Sonnino, *A Handbook to Sixteenth-Century Rhetoric*, pp. 10, 14. In the *Rhetoric of Poetry in the Renaissance...*, J. P. Porter maintains that Ronsard was the first poet to combine "an imaginative grasp of how [ancient] styles could be recreated in the vernacular" with "certain tastes and prejudices of his own time which modified his neoclassicism and led him to... write poems which were not altogether in accordance with his humanist culture" (p. 95).

discourse the poem must employ rhetorical figures, with or without the author's intention. "La figure s'oppose aux manières communes et usuelles de parler," notes Paul Ricoeur, "mais les figures ne sont pas toujours rares; bien plus, le discours le plus rare de tous serait le discours sans figure."[5] Among literary historians and theorists, the latter half of the twentieth century has witnessed a remarkable resurgence of attention to rhetoric.[6] A monument to that renewal of interest is Heinrich Lausberg's *Handbuch der literarischen Rhetorik*, in which the tropes are systematically grouped according to shared characteristics; his categories provide the framework for my reading here.

It would be long-winded and futile to attempt an analysis of all the rhetorical figures used by Durand; on the other hand, a random sample would not reveal how the tropes in a given "family" build upon and complement one another. This chapter concentrates on a single group of devices, the one which offers the most comprehensive view both of the expressive powers of rhetoric in general and of the skill of Durand and his contemporaries in this domain: the figures of repetition. In that rhetoric itself is a constant recapitulation of the same elements across the ages, these are the tropes which epitomize its essential nature. Above all, this genus of figures clearly reveals the esthetic crisis of late Renaissance verse: the climax (and depletion) of the Petrarchist tradition at its fundamental level, that of poetic technique. As J. P. Houston points out in his study *The Rhetoric of Poetry in the Renaissance and Seventeenth Century* (p. 194), Ronsard's *Amours* mark but the "first stage" in a gradual "inspissation of rhetoric": though "not yet a book of baroque style," they represent "the particular kind of rhetorical self-consciousness that was to intensify in the next fifty to eighty years." In this mounting accumulation of effects, the redoubled use of "figures of repetition of sounds and words" plays an obvious and emblematic role.

---

[5] *La Métaphore vive*, p. 191. Cf. Northrop Frye's remark that the notion of "a verbal structure free of rhetorical elements is an illusion" (*The Anatomy of Criticism*, p. 350).

[6] Cf. Paul Ricoeur, op. cit., pp. 172-220. Tzvetan Todorov, one of the founders of modern poetics, has affirmed: "C'est... avec la rhétorique, science générale mais inexistante des discours, que la poétique peut être mise en parallèle" ("Poétique," p. 107).

1. Strict *Conduplicatio*

Of all rhetorical ploys, repetition is the most easily discernible. It can adopt a wide variety of forms, from the simple reiteration of the same word (*geminatio*), to the complex semantic game of serial punning (*annominatio*). In his *Handbuch*, Lausberg divides the large family of repeating figures into two major groups: 1) "Wiederholung gleicher Wörter", and 2) "Wiederholung bei gelockerter Gleichheit."[7] Of the general effect at which both types of repetition aim, he notes: "Die Wiederholung dient der Vereindringlichung, die meist affektbetont ist, auch aber intellektuell ausgewertet wird" (p. 310). The poetry of the early seventeenth century insists on both functions – affective and intellectual – simultaneously. Whatever the original feelings of the poet may have been, in composition a species of abstract argumentation takes over, as though the lyric *je* were pleading a case in court.[8] If the intellectual faculty often won the upper hand, so much the better; for the late Renaissance, reason was not anti-poetic.[9]

Of Lausberg's two basic categories, the repetition of the same words (strict *conduplicatio*) is the more directly emotional. The purest form of strict *conduplicatio* is contact *geminatio*, the repetition of the same word or group of words in contiguity (that is, with-

[7] Cf. p. 310: "Die Wiederholung setzt Gleichheit des wiederholten Wortes voraus. Jedoch ist zwischen strenger Gleichheit and gelockerter Gleichheit zu unterscheiden." Since the terminology of rhetoric is rather fluid, deriving as it does from Classical authors who often conflict in their nomenclature, it should be stated from the outset that I follow Lausberg's classifications throughout.

[8] Many of the poets of the late Renaissance were lawyers and magistrates by profession. Forensic training was part of a lawyer's education, and it is not unlikely that such training further promoted the rhetorical formalism of contemporary poetry. See A. K. Varga, *Rhétorique et littérature*, pp. 86-9; and I. D. McFarlane, *Renaissance France 1470-1589*, p. 417.

[9] Cf. these two precepts from Deimier's *Art Poétique*, published the year before Durand's *Méditations*: 1) "En la Poësie... la raison est si estroictement necessaire, que sans icelle toutes les autres qualitez ou parties qui la doivent embellir... seroient tousjours assez vuides de bonté, à pouvoir faire paroistre du tout excellent et agreable un Poëme où elles seroient esclatantes." 2) "Aussi voit-on qu'une Poësie en qui la raison abondera par tout, sera tousjours estimee et favorablement receuë, bien que toutes les perfections des autres six parties que j'ay dictes ne s'y trouvassent pas." (Cited in R. Fromilhague, *Malherbe*, pp. 126 and 127, respectively.) Cf. Fromilhague's conclusions on the poetic rationalism of both the Pléiade and the "school" of Malherbe (p. 135).

out their being separated by an intervening word or phrase).[10] As Lausberg points out (p. 312), *geminatio* appears most commonly at the beginning of a sentence or verse; true to form, Durand makes frequent use of this position. On p. 52, for example, he answers his own "rhetorical" question ("Quelque autre Amant plus miserable/ S'est-il jamais plaint en ces lieux?")[11] with a double negation: "Non, non... il n'en a peu naistre/ D'aussi pleins d'amour et de foy." The word "non" almost takes on a different meaning, an affectively intensified meaning,[12] once it has been repeated. As Lausberg observes: "Würde es sich um eine völlige, also auch funktionslose Gleichheit handeln, so läge das *vitium* des Pleonasmus vor. Die Gleichheit der Wiederholung impliziert eine affektische Überbietung: die Erstsetzung des Wortes hat die normale semantische Informationsfunktion (*indicat*), die Zweitsetzung des gleichen Wortes setzt die Informationsfunktion der Erstsetzung voraus und hat eine über die bloße Informationsfunktion hinausgehende affektivisch-vereindringlichende Funktion (*affirmat*)." He concludes: "Die Wiederholung ist eine 'Pathosformel'" (p. 311).

Durand's "Discours," the long quasi-narrative poem which ends the *Méditations* proper, includes an expressive instance of *geminatio* as "Pathosformel":

> Helas! combien de fois, par une ruse estrange
> Ay-je d'un autre Amour essayé de chasser
> Cet Amour qui pour toy ne me veut point laisser?
> Mais tout autant de fois qu'au mal qui me possede,
> Mon ame a pour guarir essayé ce remede,
> Autant, autant de fois j'ay recogneu qu'en vain
> L'homme oppose sa force à celles du destin,
> Et que celuy-là seul peut heureusement vivre
> Qui sçait bien disposer ses desirs à le suyvre. (p. 126)

[10] Repetition separated by intervening words is also a form of *geminatio* (cf. Lausberg, p. 312; and see below).

[11] The question is ostensibly addressed to the "Bois" in which the poet is lamenting his fate, so it corresponds to the figure *interrogatio*. But since he himself answers it, the question represents one term of his own inner debate: such a self-interrogation is known as *ratiocinatio*.

[12] Cf. Lausberg, p. 313: "Die *geminatio* ist als grammatische Erscheinung eine primitive Bildung des Superlativs: it. *pian piano, stanco stanco*." It might be said that all *conduplicatio* has a superlative function; in everyday French, the phrase "non, non" often serves this purpose.

I quote the passage in full because the repetition of "autant" serves as a pivot not only for lines 4-7, but for the entire ensemble of question and answer. Here *geminatio* is the climax of a carefully prepared sequence. The plaintive "Helas!" sets the tone, while the phrase "combien de fois" establishes the key syntactical motif. After the headlong double enjambment of the question, made especially effective by the end-word "chasser," the key phrase is taken up again in the first line of the answer, where it occupies the same position as before. The slowing down of verses 4 and 5 through the final commas contrasts with the previous enjambments: this deceleration prepares the *geminatio* of line 6, which amplifies the despairing resignation of the central phrase. The pathos of the line is further heightened by enjambment, acting this time as an accent on the words "en vain." The phrase stands out at the midway point of the answer's temporal flow, equidistant from its end and its beginning. The answer is longer than the question not only in number of lines, but in *haleine*; it seems to be dominated by the sighing rhythms of weary despondency. No matter how many times the poet "recognizes" intellectually the folly of his attempts to escape fate, he never learns his lesson. The expression of this repeated defeat finds its perfect vehicle in the *geminatio* "Autant, autant," the hinge on which both question and answer swing. [13]

Geminatio at the end of a verse is generally rare, [14] and no examples of this device are to be found in Durand's poetry. He does make use of the third possibility, *geminatio* in the middle of the line. In "Elegie V" this occurs off-center, entirely within the second hemistich: "Ha! c'est trop de mal-heur, il faut, il faut quitter/ Ce que je ne sçaurois qu'avec peine arrester" (p. 119) – giving an added sense of urgency to the enjambment of "quitter." [15] More

[13] Similarly, Claude Hopil makes triple repetition the climax and turning point of a whole poem of eleven strophes, the "Vol d'esprit" (Rousset's anth., vol. II, pp. 200-2): "Je le voy, je le voy, je le voy (ce me semble)."

[14] It is all the more striking when it does occur. A moving instance is the last line of *dizain* 18 in Scève's *Délie* (ed. cit., p. 129), where the threefold repetition underscores the poet's helpless torment. For a rousing example of triple repetition at the beginning of a verse, cf. Scalion de Virbluneau, fol. 1 ro: "Alarme, Alarme, Alarme, & au secours..."

[15] In this and the following example from Durand, the repetition lends an almost conversational, or in any case *spoken* tone to the verse. Cf. B. Braunrot, *L'Imagination poétique chez Du Bartas*, pp. 140-1. Cf. also Terence Cave's remarks about the carefully controlled *style parlé* of Sponde (art. cit., pp. 59-60).

often, this form of *geminatio* occupies the exact centre of the verse, the two halves being separated by the caesura. This naturally bestows a chiastic ring upon the verse as a whole. For instance, consider the line: "Depuis si j'ay vescu, j'ay vescu par miracle" (p. 101).[16] Here the *geminatio* engenders a sense of mysterious expectancy: it sets off one life against another, casting doubt on both. The chiastic turn transfers the charge of "par miracle" to "Depuis si" as well,[17] so that at the end of the verse one seems to read it backwards: "I have lived by a miracle, if I have lived since then at all." The rest of the strophe prolongs this sensation of hovering[18] between life and death:

> Depuis si j'ay vescu, j'ai vescu par miracle;
> Ou bien j'eus en naissant plus d'un coeur par le sort:
> Non pour pouvoir jamais croire à plus d'un oracle,
> Mais pour pouvoir vivant souffrir plus d'une mort.

Geminatio need not always be "pure"; it can also appear on either side of an intervening word or phrase, as in Baudelaire's "Entends, ma chère, entends la douce nuit qui marche." As this example illustrates, the interposed word is usually a vocative. Durand employs the device in the "Stances" on pp. 97-9 which begin: "Laissez couler, mes yeux, laissez couler vos pleurs,/ Donnez nouvelles eaux à leur source lassee." The *geminatio* derives additional force from the symmetrical rhythm of the verse, "mes yeux" being precisely balanced by "vos pleurs." Another instance of this type of *geminatio* is found on p. 119, in a line of proto-Corneillian stamp: "Cherche, jeune Tyran, cherche d'autres conquestes." Such a verse reaffirms that the French Classical theatre did not spring up overnight, but was the outcome of a long stylistic evolution in

---

[16] In this case, while the repetition is syntactically necessary, the emphatic central juxtaposition of its terms is not: a good example of the way rhetoric and syntax work in concert. For another instance, cf. Chistofle de Beau-jeu: "Je parle de ce feu, feu divin qui esclaire/ Les plus obscures nuicts, maistre de son contraire" (*Les Amours* [1589], fol. 248 ro, sonnet I).

[17] Cf. Griffin, p. 56: "Chiasmus... allows the poet to intensify the differences and similarities of one or two pairs of grammatical components."

[18] Cf. McFarlane's remarks about the repetition of *mains* in *dizain* 367 of the *Délie*: "the delicate repetition of *mains* introduces a lingering sensation" (intro. to his edn., p. 39); "the recurrence of *mains* introduces that necessary pause which allows the line to make its full impact" (p. 69).

which Durand and many others participated. An arresting reversal of the verb-vocative-verb formula occurs on p. 102: "Songe, luy disois-je, ô Songe que j'adore,/ Arreste pour un peu, pourquoy t'envole-tu?" The redoubled vocative underlines the urgency of the poet's plea, which in turn betrays the rapidity of Dream's retreat.

Closely related to *geminatio* is the figure known as *reduplicatio* (or *anadiplosis*), the repetition of the last word of one verse at the beginning of the next. Most commonly, the repeated word is a proper noun; [19] *reduplicatio* appears under this form in practically all epic poems, where it lends a majestic aura to the hero's name. Durand's "Adventure de Sylvandre," a parody of the solemn epic manner, does not miss the chance to poke fun at this well-worn device (p. 153):

> Appren-moy, grand vainqueur des hommes et des Dieux,
> Qui ravis les esprits par les charmes des yeux:
> Appren-moy de quel traict le bien-heureux Sylvandre
> A peu blesser le coeur de sa belle Cleandre,
> Cleandre dont les yeux, pleins d'amoureux appas,
> N'avoient point plus d'attraits qu'ils avoient de trespas...

The piquancy of the lines derives from the comic (though sexist) contrast between grandiloquent rhetoric and frivolous content: the *reduplicatio* sounds forth the name, not of a stalwart hero, but of a seductive young girl.

Like any other type of *conduplicatio*, *reduplicatio* can easily degenerate into the corresponding *vitium* (Lausberg's term) of pleonasm, unnecessary repetition. Arguably, such is the case on p. 112, where the *reduplicatio* could be said to serve only as filler:

> Ce front demy courbé, digne souhait des Dieux,
> Dont la neige s'oppose aux flames de deux yeux,
> Deux yeux, dis-je, où l'Amour comme un tyran domine,
> Sans qu'il puisse pourtant passer en la poictrine...

An alternate reading would stress the crucial importance of the mistress' eyes to the Petrarchist symbology of love, a significance which

[19] "Am häufigsten findet sich die Anadiplose bei Eigennamen (und auch bei Appelativen) auf der Versgrenze" (Lausberg, p. 314; see his examples on the following page).

is underscored by the emphatic rhetorical device; yet another reading would link this passage to the one just quoted, and bring out the parodic element of exaggeration. In comparison, consider Durand's straightforward use of a loose *reduplicatio* on p. 85 to express the impetuosity of desire:

> ...voyant les attraicts de vos lévres ensemble,
> C'est estre sans raison que ne les baiser pas.
>
> Ouy, je les veux baiser, ces lévres homicides...

These verses might be termed an example of "free chiastic double *reduplicatio*." Both "lévres" and "baiser" are taken up again in the third line, though in reverse order. The *reprise* springs over the boundary between two strophes, aptly translating the poet's haste for fulfilment.[20] Here is ample proof that *conduplicatio* need not always act as a "Pathosformel."

When *reduplicatio* continues in a chain over three or more verses, it constitutes the figure *gradatio*. Durand avoids this device on the whole; it had reached the apogee of its popularity among the Grands Rhétoriqueurs, and in its unadulterated form it must have seemed old-fashioned to poets of the early seventeenth century.[21] All the same, several instances of camouflaged *gradatio* do occur in the *Méditations*.[22] The most blatant appears at the beginning of the "Stances de l'Amour" (p. 103):

> Si l'Amour est un Dieu, que n'est-il sans enfance?
> Ou s'il est un enfant, que n'est-il sans puissance?
> Ou s'il est si puissant, que n'est-ce par raison?

Though *gradatio* is modified here by combination with another rhetorical figure (*derivatio*, the repetition of the same root-word in different cases or parts of speech), the reader has no trouble in recognizing it. The thematic context is decisive here. The use of thinly

---

[20] Cf. the verses of d'Aubigné which use the same figure to evoke quite a different form of love: "Dans le sein d'Abraham fleuriront nos désirs,/ Désirs, parfaits amours, hauts désirs sans absence..." (Rousset anth., vol. II, p. 245).

[21] Except, perhaps, when it was used in a Manneristically exaggerated form: see the sonnet by Du Mas discussed below.

[22] On this count Durand is in perfect accord with the Pléiade's practice of making the traditional figures more flexible and expressive. Cf. Griffin, p. 58.

disguised *gradatio* to link a series of paradoxes on Amor is typical of the period. Sometimes the *gradatio* is fairly overt, as in the lines just quoted; but more often it becomes a semantic chain, as in these verses from Grisel (p. 73):

> Si ce n'est point Amour, qu'est-ce donc que je sens?
> Si c'est Amour, ô dieux! qu'est-ce que sa nature?
> Si bonne, pourquoy donc mortelle est sa pointure?
> Si non, d'où viennent tant de si plaisans tourmens? [23]

Equally elusive is the following concatenation from Durand's "Elegie IV" (p. 117):

> L'espoir naist de fort peu, de l'espoir la poursuitte,
> Et la poursuitte encor tant de flames excite,
> Que celle qui fuyoit se voit le plus souvent
> Poursuivre celuy-là qui l'alloit poursuivant...

A simple readjustment would reveal the true structure of the lines: "De fort peu naist l'espoir, de l'espoir la poursuitte/ De la poursuitte encor une flamme nouvelle,/ De la flamme nouvelle encore une poursuitte..." The chain sequence represents a verbal enactment of the love-chase motif. [24]

Sonnet XXXIX demonstrates an even more refined conversion of *gradatio* from mechanical device into poetic medium. Here are the last four verses of the poem:

> Ces roses sont le teint de ta belle Uranie:
> Roses qui font produire et croistre tes soucis,
> Soucis qui de ses yeux tous les jours esclaircis
> Dans leur mesme tombeau soudain prennent la vie.

These words are spoken to the poet in a dream by "une voix au profond des deserts"; but it is through a transferred *gradatio* that the dream-like confusion of woman and roses is conveyed – or accomplished. By analogy with the repetition of "soucis," that of

[23] For other examples cf. Courtin de Cissé, *Les Oeuvres Poetiques* (1581), fol. 3 ro; La Roque, *Les Oeuvres*, p. 5; Le Masson, fol. 40 ro.

[24] Cf. Braunrot's remark: "...la reprise en écho apparaît comme l'équivalent verbal du mouvement qui anime l'image" (p. 140).

"roses" makes the initial phrase of the first verse glide across the link-word "sont," so that the latter half of the line seems suffused with the meaning of the first.

Metaphorically speaking, the verse just discussed is a kind of *redditio*: the repetition of the same word at the beginning and the end of a line. It may appear inconsistent to introduce this figure into the discussion only now: after progressing from contiguous *geminatio* to cross-linear *reduplicatio*, *redditio* seems like a return to the verse-locked type of *conduplicatio*. But if the main criterion of classification is the aural distance across which repetition occurs, *redditio* represents a more expansive figure than *reduplicatio*. While the latter is normally interrupted by the verse division alone, the former spans all the words within a line. In fact, the effect of *redditio* can extend far beyond the single verse.

The basic principle of *redditio* is the closing of a circle. At its simplest level, it shuts a verse back upon itself, as in "L'Amour n'est à la fin qu'une fuitte d'Amour,/ Et sa possession de la perte est suivie" (p. 105). Here Durand portrays the hopelessness of the lover, caged by Love like the first verse itself: whether he stands or flees, there is no escape, since possession and loss are identical.[25] The meaning of the second verse is already implied by the structure of the first, where the framing words signify sameness and antithesis at once.

Expanded to embrace a whole strophe, as in sonnet XXX, *redditio* can express the ceaseless return of obsessive thoughts:

> Absenté du bel oeil dont j'adore les loix,
> Et cherchant des forests le plus sombre silence,
> Je pleignois mon exil d'une mourante voix,
> Et contois aux rochers l'ennuy de mon absence.

"Absenté" and "absence" are not the same word, though they derive from the same root (once again, the phenomenon of *derivatio*). Durand combines *redditio* and *derivatio*[26] again in the "Stances de l'Amour" (p. 103):

---

[25] For another example of this theme, cf. Beau-jeu, fol. 48 vo, sonnet LXVIII: "Nous ressemblons celuy qui soy-mesme se fuit,/ Qui pensant s'asseurer, au trespas se conduit,/ Et s'empestre aux rets d'une mort plus soudaine."

[26] Cf. these lines from the "Elegie III," p. 113: "...Et sortans de la terre en soldarts convertir/ Et puis aussi soudain r'entrer comme sortir..."

Foible divinité, qui ne reçoit son estre
Que du bien ou du mal que le desir fait naistre,
Et qui sans nous en nous ne peut avoir de lieu,
Qu'à bon droict sur ton dos on a planté des aisles,
Ne pouvant commander qu'aux légères cervelles,
Dont la raison s'envole aussi tost que le Dieu.

The demolition of Amor's prestige culminates in the carefully prepared final *pointe*; by the time it has been reached, the word "Dieu" can only sound ironical.[27] The effect is heightened by *redditio* with the initial phrase, which had set the stage for the ultimate conceit well in advance.[28] Note in passing the well-turned *geminatio* of line 3: "sans nous en nous"; it succinctly conveys the self-destructive, and self-induced character of passion.

The second quatrain of sonnet XX contains a specimen of hidden *redditio* (and concealed *gradatio* as well):

Voir mon espoir changer d'effect et de pouvoir,
Voir envoler le bien que je pensois avoir,
Voir mes supplices vrais, et mes délices feintes...

The figure would probably not strike the reader's attention, if it did not occur twice in succession. The play on words set in motion here goes beyond *derivatio*; it approaches the etymological game of *annominatio*, a device which will be examined later on. This poem, which consists almost entirely of infinitive phrases, could be called an example of "syntactic *conduplicatio*." Sonnets constructed on the same principle are frequent in the late Renaissance.[29] In fact, Sonnet X from Durant de la Bergerie's *Imitations* (1610 edn., fol. 28 vo) is so close to Durand's in theme and structure that one of them may have provided the model for the other. The insistent repetition

---

[27] This is a good example of what Odette de Mourgues has called the *précieux* awareness of "the divergence between the convention and the reality," or "the discrepancy between the larger field of actual experience and the limited précieux world" (op. cit., pp. 136-8). For a similar passage cf. Bertaut, who also maintains that Love is only a weakness within ourselves (*Les Oeuvres poétiques*, ed. Chenevière, p. 374): "...quoy que la terre vante/ Les vains miracles de ses coups,/ Les traits dont il nous épouvante/ Sans nous ne peuvent rien sur nous."

[28] "Nothing is less unexpected or startling than the last *trait* or *chute* which ends the précieux poem" (de Mourgues, p. 129).

[29] Besides the two cited here, cf. Papillon de Lasphrise, *Les Premieres Oeuvres Poetiques* (1599), p. 242, sonnet XCIIII.

of "Voir" at the beginning of each verse (which is why the third has been included here) represents still another form of *conduplicatio,* one which also helps to establish the embedded *redditio.* This is the most familiar of all redoubling figures, anaphora (X.../ X.../ X...).

Anaphora (in Latin, *repetitio)* was a popular figure throughout the sixteenth century,[30] but it became more ubiquitous and exaggerated as the century drew to a close. Helmut Hatzfeld asserts that extended anaphora is one of the hallmarks of Mannerism in late Renaissance poetry.[31] Whereas *redditio* closes off the intervening words in a self-contained unity, anaphora simply punctuates their open-ended flow. Durand turns this figure to advantage in a number of poems. Sometimes he limits anaphora to a single repetition, as at the end of "Elegie V" (p. 121):

> C'est tout-un, je ne veux, ny ne puis m'en desdire:
> Il faut mourir pour elle, et se plaire au martyre,
> Il faut prendre en l'aimant plaisir à m'enflamer,
> Ainsi qu'inevitable il me la faut aymer...

In the previously quoted passage, the repetitions verged on the mechanical; here the recurrence of "Il faut" springs organically from the sense and rhythm of the whole, translating the lover's surrender to his inevitable fate.[32] (The lines are further strengthened by a double *derivatio*, based on the roots of *plaire* and *aimer.*) Another *repetitio brevis* appears on p. 128, in a passionate moment of the "Discours":

> Bouche, mon seul desir, seul objet de mes voeux,
> Bouche pour qui j'estime et respecte mes feux,
> Tu me tins ces propos pleins de douceur extreme...

[30] Ronsard shows a special predilection for it; cf. Gordon, p. 115: "Les anaphores abondent dans la poésie de Ronsard et constituent un trait dominant de son style". For numerous examples, see his entire section on *anaphora*, (pp. 114-21). Similarly, in his study of Du Bellay, Griffith observes that "aside from antithesis... the most recurrent figure in *L'Olive* is anaphora" (p. 106).

[31] This is in line with his general theory that literary Mannerism represents an excessive elaboration of tropes and figures which had been used with moderation during the High Renaissance (see art. cit., pp. 229-30).

[32] The construction "il me la faut aimer," impossible in modern French, seems especially apt here, as it puts emphasis on "la" while suggesting "il me le faut."

Continuing through more than two lines, anaphora ceases to act as a glorified *geminatio*. In the "Adventure de Sylvandre" Durand employs an extended anaphora to express the hero's indecision about whether to confess his love to Cléandre (p. 156):

> Ore il veut l'aller voir pour luy dire ses maux,
> Ore il desire en soy conserver ses travaux,
> Ore il veut descouvrir son amoureux martyre,
> Ore il le veut celer, et mourir sans le dire,
> Et demeure suspens deçà delà porté,
> Comme un vaisseau sur mer par deux vents agité.

As I mentioned earlier, the "Sylvandre" epyllion parodies the conventions of Classical epic; in this passage, the rhetorical technique for conveying inner agitation is lifted straight from sequences in Virgil and Ovid, among others.[33] Anaphora marks the successive twists of the will with imitative abruptness, while at the same time propelling the rhythm jerkily forward; these prosodic effects reinforce the image of a ship being buffeted about on a stormy sea.

An entirely different tone governs the following lines from the "Discours" (pp. 129-30):

> Pour aimer seulement ne vient pas mon soucy,
> Mais il me vient d'autant que ton coeur m'aime ainsi:
> Tu m'aime, et tu me peux voir languir au supplice,
> Tu m'aime, et tu peux bien negliger mon service,
> Tu m'aime, et tu peux bien consentir à ma mort,
> Tu m'aime, et tu peux bien, voyant mon triste sort,
> L'empirer de refus?[34]

---

[33] Cf. for example *Metamorphoses* VIII: 462-74; like Durand, Ovid couples anaphora with the conventional marine simile for doubt. For a similar use of rhythmic effects to convey inner inconstancy, see Jean Loys, *Les Oeuvres Poetiques* (1613), p. 91: "[Amour] leur verse imposteur maint enfiellé breuvage:/ Or de joye & plaisir, & ores de servage,/ Les faisant or'contens, ores desesperer."

[34] On the elision of "aime[s]" in this passage, cf. Kr. Nyrop; *Grammaire historique de la langue française* (1899), vol. I, p. 230: "Les poétes élident quelquefois à la finale un *e* féminin suivi de *-s*. Cette négligence est surtout propre aux poètes du XVe et XVIe siècles; elle se trouve plus rarement au moyen âge et dans les temps modernes. Malherbe... en citant le vers de Desportes: 'Tu t'abuses toi-même, ou tu me porte[s] envie,' blâme sévèrement cette licence, mais Deimier proteste: 'On dit *tu pense* et *tu penses* ... comme de mesme, *tu donne* et *tu donnes*... comme aussi en tout autre terme de pareille nature' (*Académie de l'Art poétique*, 1610)."

The withering irony of these verses flows from the exposure of Uranie's inconsistency; her actions stand in flagrant contradiction to her words, reduced to a single affirmation, "Je t'aime." Every time the poet flings these words back in her face, they diminish in credibility, by contrast with the loveless indifference which she displays.[35] Far from being hollow sound and fury, anaphora is indispensable to the poetic argument.[36] According to Hatzfeld (pp. 230-231), the anaphoric repetition of whole phrases (rather than single words) is a another trait of literary Mannerism; it also occurs in the next two examples from Durand given below. Other instances include the first sonnet (p. 1) in Jean Déplanches's *Oeuvres Poetiques* of 1612, which is constructed around the phrase "Je vay semer"; and the first sonnet in Bernier de la Brousse's collection (p. 1), which is dominated by the anaphoric phrase "J'ourdis." The device was such a prevalent feature of the late Petrarchist *maniera* that it provoked a funny parody by J. de La Borderie in his *Les Préludes...* (p. 54).

Quite diverse in tone from the accustory passage just cited is another anaphorical sequence, also from Durand's "Discours" (p. 127):

> Ton oeil a bien peu voir combien j'ay combatu
> Pour deceler l'ennuy dont j'estois abbatu,
> Combien j'ay sceu plutost endurer que me plaindre,
> Combien j'ay sceu mes cris d'un silence contraindre,
> Combien j'ay sceu long temps luy cacher ma langueur,
> Et combien j'ay celé les regrets de mon coeur...

Here the repetition conveys the continuous and heroic efforts of the poet to conceal his love.[37] The purpose of this build-up is both to dramatize the fierceness of his passion, and to excuse the confession which finally did take place despite himself (ibid.):

---

[35] Cf. the passage in "Elégie I," where Durand uses anaphora in accumulating proofs of *his* fidelity (p. 108, lines 86-93); it is amusing to find him turning the same rhetorical figure to opposite ends. Notice also the delicate chiastic balance of line 93, with its echoing *annominatio* ("doux-douleurs"). (On this figure see below.)

[36] Cf. Griffin, p. 60: "When [Du Bellay's] anaphora is harmoniously paced with the poem's theme it becomes the very expression of an idea."

[37] Curiously, the verb "deceler" in this passage appears to mean the opposite of what it literally says. At any rate, it prepares from afar the switch from "j'ay sceu" to "j'ay celé," which is all the more surprising because the repeated "combien" leads one to think that the whole phrase will remain the same as before.

Je me voy, ce me semble, encor pasle et timide,
Commencer le discours de ma flame homicide:
Je me voy, ce me semble, encores tout tremblant
Te descouvrir l'ennuy qui m'alloit bourrellant,
Et pense voir encor ton bel oeil plein de flame
Asseurer d'un sous-ris la crainte de mon ame...

I have cited the above passage in full because it illustrates another form of anaphora cultivated by Durand: initial repetition across intervening lines. The device is relatively obvious here, since only one other verse separates the first "Je me voy, ce me semble" from the second. (Less evident is the partial reappearance of the phrase in line 5.) The *reprise* lends a greater immediacy to the description, as though the poet were conjuring up the scene before the reader's eyes as well as his own. A similar vision-linked anaphora dominates the second part of "Elegie VI," in which the poet appeals to Uranie's sympathy by picturing his agonies as seen through *her* eyes (p. 123). In fact, she is absent, "but if your eyes *could* see me," he insinuates,

Ils me verroient tantost au plus creux d'un bocage,
Le coude my-caché dans la mousse et l'herbage...
Ils me verroient encor au silence des bois
Forcer les rochs plus sourds de respondre à ma voix...
Ils verroient pourmener un corps inanimé...

– and so on through three more repetitions of "ils verroient," separated by numerous verses describing the poet's plight. This passage exemplifies the rhetorical figure known as *evidentia*, which Lausberg defines as "die lebhaft-detaillierte Schilderung eines rahmenmäßigen Gesamtgegenstandes durch Aufzählung sinnenfälliger Einzelheiten" (p. 399). *Evidentia* (Gk. *enargeia*)[38] was a favourite courtroom device, used to provoke sympathetic participation on the part of the jury; I have already alluded to the importance of the judiciary influence in French Renaissance literature. The ploy is complicated here by the fact that the speaker is himself the subject of the depiction he is framing for the "spectator": that is, he makes Uranie pic-

[38] Cf. T. Cave, "*Enargeia*: Erasmus and the Rhetoric of Presence in the Sixteenth Century." For a similar use of *evidentia* see La Roque, *Les Oeuvres*, p. 17, sonnet XXXII.

ture him in his grief, while he in turn views himself through her eyes – as he would have her see him, with pity and remorse. At a further remove, the reader re-experiences these retreating planes of vision as a *composition en abîme*. In "Elegie VI," anaphora contributes decisively to the imaging process.[39]

Among the looser forms of anaphora are strophes which begin with the same phrase, as in "Ode I" (p. 88), where the first three stanzas repeat the initial word "Maintenant," throwing into relief the advent of spring.[40] The evocation of nature also provides the subject of Durand's most thorough-going exercise in the figure, sonnet V; this poem is the most elaborate example of strict *conduplicatio* ("Wiederholung strenger Gleichheit") in all his verse:

Forest de mes Amours, fidele secretaire,
Forest où mes douleurs Echo va racontant,
Forest où les oyseaux vont mon mal recitant,
Forest où mon malheur me permet de me plaire:

Forest où mon ennuy m'a rendu solitaire,
Forest où les Zephyrs vont sans cesse habitant,
Forest où les rochers vont le Ciel supportant,
Forest où cent ruisseaux ont leur cours ordinaire:

Forest qui toute seule as receu tous mes voeux,
Forest où je veux vivre et mourir langoureux,
Enferme dans ton sein ma complainte eslancée:

Afin que si tu vois ma belle par le sort
Tu luy monstre qu'icy j'ay souspiré ma mort
Plustost qu'en autre lieu souspiré ma pensée.

Within the limited space of a short form like the sonnet or *dizain*, rhetorical figures stand out more sharply than in an elegy or ode; relative to the compact sphere of the poem, their weight deter-

---

[39] This is a good example of the poet's applying even to himself that aesthetic of "taking one's distances" which André Chastel has identified as a signal trait of "l'esprit de 1600" in art (see his *La Crise de la renaissance 1520-1600*, p. 192). Cf. Cave, *Devotional Poetry*, pp. 276-83, on the increasing inter-penetration of visual and literary arts toward the end of the Renaissance in France, a tendency which comes to a head in the first decade of the seventeenth century.

[40] In his "Gaieté," P. de Cornu uses anaphora on the same word and in the same thematic context (see the Blanchemain edn., pp. 108-9).

mines unavoidably its discursive shape. At the same time, the brief stanzaic form has an internal logic of its own: this too increases in strength by inverse proportion to the poem's length, so that the shorter form will always "bend" rhetorical devices to fit its own requirements more markedly than the longer form. Such a process of mutual transformation can be readily observed in the sonnet above. Anaphora appears in the guise of a drawn-out invocation; the woodland backdrop of the poet's laments becomes the object of a vow, which is simultaneously a declaration of friendship and trust toward the forest itself. The theme could not be more conventional; handled by Ronsard with mastery, it runs through the works of most Petrarchist poets. Durand personifies the forest in a typical outburst of "pathetic fallacy" – or so it would seem. Each repetition of "Forest" deepens the impression of intimacy, just as each line adds something to the poet's portrait of his "friend." Anaphora is effective not only because of repetition, but because of variation; repetition throws into relief the accompanying *change* from verse to verse.

The first quatrain strikes a balance between evoking the forest and reciting the poet's woes: "mes Amours," "mes douleurs," "mon mal," and "mon malheur" are counterpoised by "fidèle," "Echo," "oyseaux," and the invocation itself. The second quatrain shifts heavily to the forest side of the scale: after the first verse the poet's feelings give way completely to a stylized description of the woods. In the first tercet the lover's preoccupations dramatically reappear, and it becomes clear what his intentions have been all along: not to praise the forest, but to use it as a vehicle for his own laments, as a pitiful appeal to the beloved. It is no accident that the last member of the anaphoric sequence is the most emotional: "Forest où je veux vivre et mourir langoureux." It marks the point at which the poet drops the mask of pastoral solitude, addressing his mistress *by means* of the bucolic sounding-board. Despite the anaphoric invocation, center stage continues to be occupied by the lyric *je* itself.

While it would be impossible to convey this poetic "message" without recourse to anaphora, the sonnet form still directs the poem's discursive flow. At first glance it would seem that the rhetorical figure had vitiated the sonnet structure, effectively transforming it into a dizain followed by a quatrain. That this is not the case has already been shown by reference to the varying foci of interest – forest or self – that govern the two quatrains, both of which, in turn, differ conceptually from the tercets. But I would go one step further, and suggest that the division outlined above is implicit in the cumulative tension of the anaphora itself: that the first tercet possesses a stanzaic integrity not in spite of, but because of, the previous eight repetitions of "Forest." By the time the tercet is reached, any further repetitions of the word must either fall into singsong or shift to a higher level of intensity; instead of letting the poem subside into deflation, Durand opts to augment the energetic charge.

This illustrates a more general principle. After a string of dependent clauses the reader has a stronger sense that "something has to give" than would be the case with a poem such as sonnet 20 from book III of La Ceppède's *Théorèmes* (ed. Rousset, pp. 385-6), with its anaphoric independent clauses ("L'amour a ces haliers à son chef attaché:/ L'amour fait que sa Mère à ce bois le void pendre," etc.) Given the context, La Ceppède is clearly using the device to obtain what Odette de Mourgues has called "[a] stiffen[ing of] the rhythm into the rigid and robust homophony of litanies" (op. cit., p. 63). In Durand's sonnet, a feeling of suspense is created through the steadily increasing expectation of the main clause; anaphora heightens the tension by making one listen for the final cadence which will end the repetitions. If extended tropes present a danger to the coherence of shorter forms, they can also provoke a more vigorous solution.

All the same, in the late Renaissance intensity is not always the object. In their "deflationary" mode, Durand and his contemporaries thicken[41] rhetorical devices precisely in order to call attention to the verbal surface of their verse, as pure discursive construct. This radical reductionism is flaunted in a sonnet by Du Mas (p. 115):

<table>
<tr><td>Le Ciel,</td><td></td><td>destine.</td></tr>
<tr><td>L'honneur,</td><td></td><td>ravit.</td></tr>
<tr><td></td><td>le veut qui mon ame</td><td></td></tr>
<tr><td>L'espoir,</td><td></td><td>seduist.</td></tr>
<tr><td>Amour,</td><td></td><td>domine.</td></tr>
</table>

[41] Cf. Houston's remark, quoted earlier, about the increasing "inspissation of rhetoric" as the Renaissance draws to a close.

Du divin,		mine.
D'un bel oeil,		suit.
	vient ce desir qui me	
Du parfaict,		nuit.
D'une main		espine.
Oeil		violent.
	qui n'a trait qui ne soit	
Main,		excellent.
Trosne,		presence.
Phare,		claireté.
	d'Amour inhonore ta	
Ange,		beauté.
Astre,		puissance.

Here strict *conduplicatio* shrinks the poem's structure (and thematic content) to a mere skeleton. The sonnet form itself – the quintessential vessel of Petrarchist verse – has been vitiated to the point that the tercets split into a couplet followed by a quatrain. Such a piece represents the *reductio ad absurdum* of the late Renaissance tendency toward the Manneristic exaggeration of rhetorical figures, particularly the figures of repetition. As "metamimesis," [42] the poem traces a portrait in miniature of the poetics of the age. It jokingly displays the corrosive technique of the final stage of Petrarchism, which undermines the very tradition that it exploits, both formally and thematically. In the end, excessive reiteration opens out – emblematically – on empty space: the hollowness of a depleted discourse.

2. Freer Forms of *Conduplicatio*

Until now this chapter has been principally concerned with the devices in Durand's verse which belong to the first of Lausberg's

---

[42] I borrow this term from Howard Felperin. By contrast with mimesis, the depiction of "reality," metamimesis portrays concepts through style or complex metaphor. For example, in his discussion of Shakespeare's sonnets (p. 193), Felperin notes that the "dark lady" may be equated with poetry, in "the 'metamimetic' project of representing nothing other than linguistic difference itself."

two categories of *conduplicatio*, "Wiederholung strenger Gleichheit." The second, "Wiederholung gelockerter Gleichheit," is a freer, more complex domain of rhetorical expression. The simplest form of "loosened" *conduplicatio* is *derivatio*, it can be succinctly defined[43] as the repetition of the same stem in different parts of speech or verbal inflections: vie-vivre, mourir-mourant, aime-aimer, joye-joyeux, triste-tristement, etc. The examples in the *Méditations* are almost numberless, and there would be little point in trying to give a full account of them all. In any kind of writing or speech, *derivatio* arises as a matter of course.[44] Even so, this commonplace linguistic feature can become a surprisingly powerful poetic medium; a few samples will demonstrate how Durand employs it.

The main function of *derivatio* is to emphasize the *meaning* of a root, as it persists despite all changes in morphology. In the line "Un sein pour qui l'amour fait aimer tous ses traits" (sonnet XXVII), for example, the idea of love reaffirms itself; love can focus on one trait of a person, though to love is to love the whole. The semantic reminder may also be expressed negatively, as in the verse: "Elle oyt tout sans l'oüyr comme une idole vaine" (sonnet XXVIII); "Uranie" gives the impression that she is hearing the poet's plaints, but she cannot really be *hearing* them if they do not affect her. Shifting from noun to verb lends greater vividness to the basic denotation of a stem. In these verses from the "Stances de l'Absence": "L'absence d'un bel oeil, mon vainqueur et mon Roy/ Absente aussi mon coeur qu'il a pris pour le suivre" (p. 82), the repetition of "absence" as a verb gives the concept an active force of movement, which is accentuated by the enjambment.[45] The absence of the beloved absents the lover from himself, just as a king cannot leave his palace without emptying it of his entourage; like the metaphor just evoked, *derivatio* reactivates the latent powers of

[43] For a detailed definition, see Lausberg, pp. 328-9.

[44] Cf. Lowry Nelson, *Baroque Lyric Poetry*, p. 153: "It can be safely said that none of the rhetorical devices used in Baroque poetry is entirely new; all of them, in one form or another, could be matched in Antiquity, in the Middle Ages and in the Renaissance. They seem, in fact, to be common aspects of spoken language."

[45] Cf. Grisel (p. 62), who underlines the transition from noun to verb by means of a clever rhyme:

O fortune! si jamais
Icy des biens tu me fais,
Je te prie que ta roüe
Plus à mon malheur ne roue...

a word. As here, it can even revive the meaning of a hackneyed *topos.*[46] The root-word does not have to be an abstract notion like absence for this vivifying process to occur; for instance, consider the following example from a sonnet addressed to Amor: "Car ta mere Venus ne receut sa naissance/ Que des flots qui sans foy flottent au gré du vent" (sonnet IX). Here rhythm and alliteration conspire with *derivatio* to set the waves in motion.[47]

If *derivatio* is hyperbolic, *annominatio* is expansively metaphoric. Whereas the former intensifies a word-stem "vertically," hammering home its basic meaning, *annominatio* extends the stem "horizontally" to embrace a wider semantic range than before, even plunging it at times into self-contradiction. In fact the oxymoronic type of *annominatio* stands as a hallmark of the poetry of Durand's age. It is a figure eminently suitable for expressing the antithetical *dulce malum* of Petrarchan love: or in the words of Durand, "Bonheur de mon malheur, mon plus aimé soucy" (sonnet XLIII).

As the hyphen in "Bon-heur" indicates, the two halves of the word were only beginning to become inseparable in 1611; during the sixteenth century, "heur" usually stood alone.[48] "Bon-heur de mon malheur" provides a clear example of the more common variety of *annominatio* known as "organic": an extension of meaning which retains the same etymological root in both words. "Inorganic" *annominatio*, on the other hand, juxtaposes two or more words of disparate origin which merely sound alike, such as "douleur" and "douceur" (cf. p. 112, lines 7-8). Inorganic *annominatio* resembles punning or *calembour* (though without the humorous connotation), while organic *annominatio* shades off into simple *derivatio.*

The difference between the two is sometimes elusive. For instance, take these lines from "Elegie III": "Qu'esperant, mon espoir soudain desesperé/ N'espere point de tresve en mon mal enduré"

---

[46] Similarly, B. Baddel uses a double *derivatio* to imitate the cyclical movement of Petrarchist "death in life": "Mourir mille fois, & en mourant vivant,/ Et en vivant mourant, & du mourir revivre..."

[47] Cf. I. D. McFarlane, "Aspects of Ronsard's poetic vision," pp. 29-30, where he speaks of Ronsard's "portrayal of undulating succession by means of repetition ('onde sur onde,' 'flot... flot')," remarking that "this helps to give a certain swaying movement to the verse, and is a device that recurs throughout Ronsard's writing, from the *Amours* down to the last poems."

[48] Cf. the lines of Scève: "Mais toy, qui as (toy seule) le possible/ De donner heur à ma fatalité..." (ed. McFarlane, p. 378); and ibid., p. 193: "L'heur de nostre heur enflambant le désir..."

(p. 113). "Esperant," "espoir," and "espere" all belong to the same *derivatio*, based on the unaltered concept of hope. "Desesperé" adds a discordant note to the quartet, despite its etymological kinship with the other words. While they all stress the fundamental meaning of "espoir" by repeating it in different forms, "desesperé" introduces another sense altogether, linked only through negation with "espoir." This example stands on the threshold between *derivatio* and organic *annominatio*, which leads through surface similarity to a deeper correlation.[49]

The device of negating a word-stem through organic *annominatio* adroitly lends itself to the Petrarchist *Leitmotiv* of inner contradiction. In the same breath, the lover affirms and denies his joy; and the entire "philosophy of love" which dominated Western poetry for three centuries can be evoked by a single phrase. For example, consider the verse on p. 77 which addresses Uranie: "Beauté qui me donnez ceste mort immortelle." An astonishing number of concepts converge in the last two words: the death in life which the first glimpse of the beloved inflicts upon the lover; the unending renewal of that death, and its "undying" continuance in the lover's constancy; the strange immortality imparted by love as a rebirth into *vita nuova*; the suffering of the lover, who undergoes the pains of death not once but a thousand times; his joy in that suffering – these are motifs which were separately discussed in the chapter on Petrarchist themes. By the complex allusive power of *annominatio*, all of them reside in a single phrase (or none of them, since too much repetition effaces *topoi* in the end).

Organic *annominatio* is not confined to expressing *dolendi voluptas* alone. Durand uses it on p. 130, at the climax of the "Discours," in a completely different context. After refuting Uranie's claim that the "loix d'honneur" of society prevent her from yielding to his advances, the poet exclaims:

---

[49] For another example of *derivatio* combined with organic *annominatio*, cf. these verses by d'Audiguier (fol. 35 ro): Fair l'Amour alors qu'il me défait,/ Et tout défait, l'Amour mesme défaire;/ Le défaisant, le rendre plus parfait,/ Le parfaisant l'éprouver plus contraire.../ It will be noted that this passage also makes use of *gradatio*. For a simpler instance of organic *annominatio* cf. Deimier, *Les Premieres Oeuvres*, p. 101: "Alors je m'esveillai ravy de voir ma belle,/ Mais ce triste resveil esveilla mes douleurs."

Humaines loix? helas! mais plustost inhumaines,
Renversez-vous ainsi la puissance des Dieux,
Si le peché d'aimer est si delicieux?

He goes on to elaborate a hierarchy of laws, in which those of nature and the gods override the petty conventions of human society. Again, this theme of love's natural and divine right against conjugal fidelity belongs to the stock-in-trade of Petrarchist poetry, [50] but Durand contrives to give it a distinctive twist. A few lines later he addresses Uranie as an "inhumaine beauté": this is a *reprise*, intended to focus the full import of the *annominatio* on the person of Uranie herself, so that she alone must answer for universal cruelty and injustice.

The organic type of *annominatio* is limited to variations on a single word-stem, the different offshoots of which are etymologically related. The other type, inorganic *annominatio*, brings into play not just one root-meaning with its various forms, but any number of words – no matter how inconsistent – linked only by a punning, external similarity. This device can be seen at its most obvious in such lines as the following, where the two members of the figure are identical twins: "Je fuis une inconstance et *suis* une beauté,/ Fuyant l'esprit je *suis* par le corps arresté" (p. 120, my italics). It goes without saying that in the first line, the lover is not claiming that he himself is "une beauté"; but readers who examine closely their reasons for recognizing the verb as "suivre" rather than "être" will be surprised at their complexity. It is not simply a matter of common sense: "The poet would defeat his own cause if he claimed to be handsome, since Uranie could accuse him of vanity." The ear registers *suivre* because it stands as an antonym to *fuir*, and the poetry of this period normally proceeds by antithesis. [51] The opposition "fuis"-"suis" derives added force from the monosyllabic rhyme

---

[50] On the particular popularity of the "*honneur* vs. *amour*" theme in the late Renaissance, see Janik, pp. 129-30. For extensive developments of the *topos*, see Amadis Jamyn, "Contre l'Honneur," in *Oeuvres poétiques*, ed. Ch. Brunet (1878-9), pp. 203-7; and La Valletrie, "Le Faux Honneur des Dames" (a cycle of eighteen sonnets), in *Les Oeuvres Poetiques* (1602), fols. 17 ro-21 vo.

[51] Supposing the same lines turned up as a lost fragment of Mallarmé's *Hérodiade*, their potential meaning would radically shift. In the conclusion to his *La Création poétique au XVIe siècle*, Henri Weber places antithesis among the three or four cardinal characteristics of Renaissance poetry, alongside its distinctive types of rhythm, imagery and personification (see vol. II, pp. 742-3).

of the two words, and from their analagous position in both the rhythmic and syntactic structures of the verse (second word and first accented syllable of the hemistich; first-person singular verb of an independent clause). All these aspects of the "suis" in line 1 communicate themselves to its twin in line 2; the repetition of *fuir* in another part of speech (*derivatio* again) facilitates the passage of the charge, as does the echoing *i* of "esprit." These parallels only serve to accentuate an underlying dissonance: the second "suis" participates in a different rhythmic, syntactic, and semantic pattern from that of the previous line. Still, thanks to *annominatio*, the resonance of *suivre* lingers in the second verse, so that the motion of pursuit curiously fuses with the immobility of capture, of passive arrest.[52]

Unintentional? Innocent internal rhyme? Compare another, not dissimilar case of *annominatio*, but one where the transfer I mean is drawn out in successive shifts rather than arriving suddenly, with the added jolt of homonymic contrariety. Addressing his "amoureuses pensees" in "Elegie III" (pp. 113-14) Durand complains that they are like the teeth sown by Cadmus:

> Car me representant les torts et les injures
> Du bel oeil qui m'a pris, ce sont dents et tortures
> Que vous faites germer en mon coeur plein de feux...

"Torts" and "injures" combine because of their semantic kinship; but they merge aurally in "tortures," and so they fuse in meaning once again, though by a different process than before. "Tortures" not only represents a phonetic union of "torts" and "injures": because of that union, it also partakes of their semantic charge. In this sense, through *annominatio*, it comes to *mean* them as well as itself; and vice-versa. I would go even further, and suggest that "dents" participates in the same semantic interchange, owing to its syntactic

[52] See I. A. Richards' lecture on the "Interinanimation of Words," in his *Philosophy of Rhetoric*, pp. 47-66. Of "some forms of poetry," he remarks: "We know [little] about the behaviour of words in these cases – when their virtue is to have no fixed and settled meaning separable from those of the other words they occur with. There are many more possibilities here than the theory of language has yet tried to think out. Often the whole utterance in which the co-operating meanings of the component words hang on one another is not itself stable in meaning. It utters not one meaning but a *movement* among meanings" (p. 48).

and rhythmic position (as partner of "tortures," and as analogue to "torts"). The principle of "transferred *annominatio*" is essential to the interpretation of poetry in any period, but especially when considering an era as conscious of rhetorical nuances as the late Renaissance. Two more examples will confirm Durand's fondness for the device, and his skill in using it.

The "Stances" on pp. 76-7 appeal to the Titans in Hàdes to compare their torments with the poet's:

> Ombres qui dans l'horreur de vos nuicts eternelles
> Gemissez sans repos vos fautes criminelles,
> Quittez pour un petit vos manoirs gemissans,
> Et venez asseurer qu'en sa pleine fatale
> L'enfer n'a point de peine à mes peines egale,
> Ny point de feux aussi comme ceux que je sens.

This forceful opening stanza makes the most of several rhetorical devices: direct *invocatio* ("Ombres"); *derivatio* coupled with *redditio* ("Gemissez-gemissans"); *geminatio* ("peine-peines"); and hyperbole. But the strophe hinges on the *annominatio* of lines 4 and 5; by means of it all the horror of Hades, the "pleine fatale," communicates itself to the "peine" of the following verse, which then expands into the plural, unnumbered "peines" suffered by the lover.

To conclude, here is a still more subtle piece of verbal modulation. The first of these two lines has already been mentioned as an instance of *geminatio*: "Laissez couler, mes yeux, laissez couler vos pleurs,/ Donnez nouvelles eaux à leur source lassee" (p. 97). By now it should be readily apparent how the *annominatio* of "laissez-lassee" builds on the rhetorical charge of the *geminatio*. By an effect of *redditio*, "lassée" harks back to the flow of tears released in the previous line, while underscoring the superhuman demands which the eyes have already met. Along this circular frame, the threefold *annominatio* marks out the cyclical renewal of the lover's pain.

These last two examples point to a more generalized phenomenon. I noted above that Helmut Hatzfield has identified accumulated or exaggerated tropes as a typical trait of literary Mannerism in the late Renaissance;[53] I also remarked that in his compre-

---

[53] On this subject cf. also M. Raymond, intro. to anth. cit., pp. 27-42, where he lists some of Hatzfeld's precursors.

hensive study of rhetoric in the sixteenth and seventeenth centuries, J. P. Houston alludes to the "inspissation" of figures as a hallmark of the transition from Renaissance style to Baroque. It might be possible to draw a distant analogy between extended anaphora and the elongated lines of Mannerist painting; or perceive, in the piling up of tropes, a parallel to the extravagant visual arts of the Baroque. In any case, Durand and his contemporaries show a predilection for accentuating and compounding rhetorical devices, especially the figures of repetition. The "reductionist" sonnet by Du Mas, examined earlier, epitomizes this trend in the domain of strict *conduplicatio*; it is equally discernible among the tropes of "lossened" reduplication.

One of Salomon Certon's Latin epigrams provides a lapidary illustration: "Foemina, flamma, fretum, furtim, fera, funera fundant,/ Tantis torturus tu tria tota time" (p. 181). In this elegiac distich, a complex network of interlocking sounds sharply contrasts the sources of danger with their fearful victim: reverberating *annominatio* and alliteration seem to fuse each line into a huge, composite word.[54] Appropriately, Certon uses the imposing full hexameter to express the threat; its sonorous measures are dominated by *m*'s and *n*'s. By contrast, the halting abbreviated line, with its stuttered *t*'s, aptly translates the sensation of fear.

A more extended union of verse-form and rhetoric can be found, once again, in Du Mas's *Lydie* (1610). By contrast to the *reductio ad absurdum* of Petrarchism in the sonnet cited above, his "Sonnet de Paroles Monosyllabes" (p. 125) demonstrates that virtuosity can enrich thematic content as well as undermine it:

Beaux yeux à qui je suis, que vos traits me sont doux,
Doux le ret qui me tient, & le raiz qui me luit,
Luit à moy, luit à tous, luit au coeur de la nuit:
Nuit où je suis sans jour, nuit où je suis sans vous,

Vous tout le loz du Ciel, & le plus beau de nous,
Nous que vos yeux ont pris: ou vit un feu qui nuit,
Nuit à qui ne vous sert: nuit à qui ne vous suit.
Suit de coeur & qui tout, n'est à vous plus qu'à tous:

[54] In this rich elaboration of repeating devices, Certon was following Classical precedent; cf. e.g. Lucretius, book III, line 869: "mortalem vitam mors cum immortalis advenit."

Tous ceux-la n'ont rien veu, qui n'ont veu ce beau sein,
Sein que les dieux ont faict, & si blanc & si plain,
Plain est le flot qui dort, il est tel & tout plein,

Plein de noeuz & de lacs où je suis, où je vis,
Vis donc lis, clair & pur, & ces vers que tu lis,
Lis les des yeux du coeur, & les pren de ma main.

This poem forms a virtual compendium of all the types of *conduplicatio* discussed in this chapter: *geminatio* ("Luit... luit," "Nuit... nuit"); *reduplicatio* in chain sequence, or *gradatio*; *redditio* ("Plain [55]... plein"); *derivatio* ("tout... tous," "vis/Vis," "lis/Lis"); and above all, *annominatio* ("ret... raiz," "Plain... plein," etc.). (Cf. also the chiasmus in line 9.) Du Mas achieves one of his most subtle effects in line 13, where he breaks abruptly with the syntactic pattern of the previous verse. The invocation to the lily ("Vis donc lis...") seems to merge with the echoing phrase "ces vers que tu lis," so that the beloved is implicitly identified with the verses. That this is not an over-interpretation seems clear from the final line, which exhorts the mistress to take the poem, like a flower, from the lover's hand.

Uninterrupted *gradatio* and multiple variations on the vowel *i* weave Du Mas's sonnet into a delicate, seamless unity. The most important repeating device in the poem should not be forgotten: as stated in the title, all the words employed are monosyllables.[56] As much as any other, this feature helps to create the gentle murmuring monotone which is the sonnet's chief distinction; but it is not a form of repetition commonly subsumed under the term *conduplicatio*. The definition of the figure might be further extended to include syntactic redoubling, a device which also adds to the effect: throughout the poem, parallel constructions relay one another in a softly lapping undulation. I suggested earlier that sonnets composed of a string of infinitive phrases – increasingly common toward the end of the Renaissance – exemplify this syntactic type of *conduplicatio*.[57] The same could be said of *vers rapportés*, a rarefied

[55] The word *plain* (now archaic) is a homonym of *plein*, not an alternate spelling; it means "even, unified, smooth" (cf. L. *planus*).

[56] For another "Sonnet en monosyllabes" see Papillon de Lasphrise, *Les Premieres Oeuvres Poetiques* (1599), p. 200.

[57] Cf. also the many imitations of Laugier de Porchères's "Sonnet sur les Yeux de Madame de Beaufort" (discussed below, Chapter IV); their repeated negations combine *gradatio* with a series of syntactic parallels.

form much favored by Durand and his contemporaries: in each line the same parts of speech are repeated three or four times.

Vers rapportés embody another kind of reduplication: one which takes place at the level of meaning. A skillful exercise in the genre, like those of Du Mas (p. 114) or Durand (sonnet XVIII, given below), neatly divides into three or four self-sufficient poems-within-a-poem, each of which reiterates the sense of the whole:

O Amour, O penser, O desirs pleins de flame,
Une Dame, un object, un brasier que je sens
Me blesse, me nourrit, conduit mes jeunes ans
A la mort, aux douleurs, au profond d'une lame:

O Amour, O penser, courez tost à Madame,
Addressez, racontez, monstrez comme presens
A son coeur, à son ame, à ses yeux tout puissans
Mes passions, mes maux, les douleurs de mon ame:

Poussez, faites voir, forcez sa resistance,
Sa beauté, sa rigueur, et sa fiere constance
A pleindre, à souspirer, à recognoistre mieux

Les douleurs, les ennuis, les extremes supplices
Que j'ay, que je nourris, que je tiens pour delices,
En aimant, en pensant, en desirant ses yeux.

With the typical ambiguity of late Petrarchism, such poems both "inflate" and "deflate" the semantic charge. Here the magnified cesuras create a panting rhythm which dramatically conveys the desperation of the lover and the urgency of his desire; the tripling of the plea heightens the impact of the whole. At the same time, read from another perspective, the multiplication of parts devalues the emotional seriousness of the plaint, emphasizing the brilliance of sheer artifice. The image of the mistress, and that of the poet, are decomposed into a chain of abstractions. Similarly, the sonnet form is undermined to the point that it literally breaks apart; though by doing so, it calls attention to itself *as* form. In other words, the same extreme devices serve paradoxically both to reinforce and to "puncture" the poem at every level. The ultimate result is to shift the focus radically from thematic content to verbal play, to parade the sonnet as an object made (and unmade) by language. Reverting to the sense of the word in late Renaissance love verse, the poem – not the mistress – is emphatically revealed as the poet's true "objet de désir."

An eccentric offshoot of the semantic variety of *conduplicatio* is the *calligramme*, a verse-form which enjoyed considerable popularity in the late Renaissance. In this genre the poem reproduces its subject so exactly that the distinction between *mot* and *chose* almost vanishes: the theme is blatantly literalized on the page, while the reified words becomes an insistently visual thing of beauty (*calligramme*). Grisel's non-paginated work includes numerous *calligrammes* of various shapes; an especially elaborate example is Jacques de Romieu's poem in the form of a pyramid (fol. 48 ro). Similarly, in emblematic poems, the text, image, and motto triply mirror one another. The most peculiar type of visual repetition of all may be found in Certon's *Vers Leipogrammes*, where in each successive sonnet of his three "Alphabeths" a letter of the alphabet is completely omitted throughout the poem. Like the skeletal sonnet by Du Mas cited in section 1, this is a striking illustration of the "emptiness" toward which excessive devices converge, a typographic portrayal of their derisive hollowness.

Though the reduplication of verbal content in visible shapes goes beyond the realm of rhetoric per se, syntactic and semantic repetitions accompany virtually all types of literal *conduplicatio* as a matter of course. Again, Durand and his contemporaries characteristically take these natural features of speech to their extreme conclusion. A large-scale example of the trend is Jean Le Blanc's *La Neothemachie Poetique du Blanc* (1610), where reiteration at all levels forms the very substance of the work. The title is already an instance of punning *annominatio*: the poet's name is also his theme; the author is the work. The first 152 pages of the book are taken up by one long set of variations on the notion of whiteness; here is a sample (pp. 149-50):

L'air est blanc, & l'onde agitee,
Blanches les voiles des vaisseaux,
Leucothé blanche, & Galathee,
Les Cygnes blancs, & les ruisseaux.
La neige, le marbre, & l'albastre
Sont blancs jusqu'à l'extremité:
La craye, la chaux & le plastre,

Et blanc le metal argenté.
De blanc les heureuses journees
Furent peintes antiquement;
Les vierges de blanc sont ornees
Au jour de leur enterrement.
. . . .
Blanche est l'innocence, & nostre ame
Quand elle vient dedans le corps:
Blanche est son ombre, & son fantasme,
Blanche quand elle sort dehors.

In these lines *conduplicatio* on the word *blanc* cannot be disentangled from the thematic (non-)development, with its endlessly repeated evocations of whiteness. As in Du Mas's monosyllabic sonnet, recurring parallel constructions blend the poem's diverse elements into a unified discursive flow. Here as throughout the *Neothemachie Poetique du Blanc*, semantic and syntactic redoubling go hand in hand with literal *conduplicatio*, mutually echoing and enriching one another. In fact, these intertwining devices seem to constitute the work's only *raison d'être*. The ultimate pun of its title is that the *Neothemachie* expresses a poetic blankness; like the "ame" of the lines just quoted, the meaning which emerges from the echoes is nothing but an "ombre blanche."[58]

Chapter I described the entire history of Petrarchism as a series of variations on a set of conventional themes. Within any given work, or even within a single poem, these *topoi* echo back and forth in constant cross-references; similarly, on a larger scale, they reverberate from poet to poet and from century to century. In the love verse of the Renaissance, repetition is a thematic as well as a rhetorical principle; Petrarchism represents a *conduplicatio* writ large. This holds true from the outset, as the master's example proves: Petrarch founds his poetry on an elaborate *annominatio*. The name "Laura" lends itself to numerous puns – "l'aura," "lauro," "l'auro," "l'oro," etc.; throughout the *Canzoniere*, these words create a dense polyphony of internal echoes (cf. Friedrich, pp. 196-201), persua-

[58] For other poems on whiteness, see Le Digne's "Stances. Sur le Blanc" (fols. 67 vo-69 ro), and Jamyn's "La Louange du Blanc," (edn. cit., pp. 284-8). An obvious later parallel is Gautier's "Symphonie en blanc majeur"; and of course, the supreme development of the motif is chapter 42 of *Moby Dick*.

sively underlining the lover's obsession with the beloved. But the identity between *topos* and figure goes still deeper: in a Petrarchist context, repetition corresponds to the cyclical renewal of the lover's passion and despair. These inevitable recurrences, these compulsive returns to a fatal point of origin, determine the entire movement of the *Méditations*. It is no accident that the beginning and the end of the book's sonnet-cycle trace a vast *redditio*, the last verse of the last sonnet rejoining the first verse of the first:

> Languissant nuict & jour en un égal martyre,
> Voicy ce que mon coeur a tousjours medité... (p. 39)
>
> Et que je suis tousjours en un egal martyre. (p. 74)

In a passage quoted in the previous chapter, Genot remarks that the *Canzoniere* enacts an "existence circulaire"; ultimately, that enactment takes place on the level of words. The figures of *conduplicatio* epitomize the way in which poetic systems "close back" on themselves by means of a circular reiteration. In most cases – unlike that of the verses just cited – the very techniques which create an impression of closure also prolong the movement of the work: reduplication both rounds out and continues its development. The repetition which takes place in poetry does not trace a *closed* circle; like a spiral, it displays circularity and open-endedness at once. A final example from the *Méditations* will make this principle clear.

Few would dispute the importance of repetitions of the simpler type, "Wiederholung strenger Gleichheit," since these stand out with undeniable insistence. The other category, "Wiederholung gelockerter Gleichheit," may at first seem less vital to poetry, especialy as it moves into the more elusive ranges of inorganic *annominatio*. On the contrary, I would maintain that elaborations of free *conduplicatio* constitute the really indispensable class of poetic instruments. Exact repetition can become mechanical; the test of the poet is in the placement of the repetitions and the variations on what comes between them, not in the mere fact of repeating.[59] The artistry expended in handling straightforward *geminatio* is immea-

[59] Cf. Odette de Mourgues's discussion of the Ronsard's lifelong predilection for exact *conduplicatio*, and the expressive variety which he draws from the device ("Ronsard's later poetry," pp. 289-90).

surably multiplied in forging the minute, significant links of *annominatio*. Rhyme itself, the most-employed and least-discussed device in traditional poetry, is best understood in the context of subtly altered reiteration.

As a case in point, consider the following passage from Durand (p. 154), taken almost at random:

> L'assemblee finit, et d'un instant tous ceux
> Qui s'estoient là treuvez s'en retournent chez eux,
> Fors ces nouveaux Amans, qui par miracle estrange
> Avoient faict par leurs yeux de leurs coeurs un eschange,
> Qui s'estans mis à part ensemble à deviser
> Sentoient à chaque mot leur coeur se diviser,
> Leurs yeux mal asseurez, leur incertain langage,
> Leur estoient des tesmoins de leur futur servage,
> Et leur ardent desir les faict si fort troubler,
> Que pas un en souffrant n'ose se deceller.

None of the rhymes in this excerpt from the "Adventure de Sylvandre" [60] is particularly salient; as far as sheer virtuosity is concerned (*rime riche, couronnée*, etc.) they are all fairly weak. But it is the pairing of words semantically which justifies rhyme, not the dazzle of gratuitous technique. The pairing of "ceux" and "eux" stresses the uniqueness of the lovers as contrasted with all the others at the "publique assemblee" (p. 153). The rhyme of "estrange" with "eschange" can be compared to Ariel's

> Nothing of him that doth fade
> But doth suffer a sea change
> Into something rich and strange.

In both instances, the rhyming adjective instills a noun of process with an overtone of wonder; in the example from Durand, "change" is implicit in the "exchange," which sparks a dual metamorphosis. The last three rhymes trace the growth of an amorous

---

[60] Like the passage quoted earlier, the present one is modeled on Desportes's "Eurylas" (*Élegies*, pp. 199-200, lines 110-36). Cf. in particular: "Chacun sent aussitost ceste blessure estrange./ Ils font sans y penser de leurs coeurs un eschange..."; "Ses yeux mal asseurez, son inconstant langage,/ Monstrent les passions qui troublent son courage." However, by compressing the episode and using the rhymes with a lapidary deftness, Durand improves on Desportes's more diffuse example.

transformation: as they speak, the lovers' hearts "divide" with every word, so that "deviser" fuses with "diviser" in more than an aural sense – to speak *is* to be torn. The wavering of their voices and gazes already portends their mutual enslavement: their language *is* their servitude, a "langage-servage." Since the desire which overwhelms them is what they dare not divulge, their turmoil both impels them toward and keeps them from confessing; "troubler" and "deceller" are doubly merged, as equivalents and antipodes.

Rhyme is essentially a form of inorganic *annominatio*; the fact that this rhetorical figure is woven into the very fabric of Western technical conventions attests to the decisive weight of *annominatio* in the poetic tradition. This is particularly true in the late Renaissance, when discourse unfolds largely through the use of successive antitheses. Opening the *Méditations* at any page, the reader finds such rhymes as "delice"-"supplice," "fuitives"-"captives," "clarté"-"obscurité," etc.; or if the pairs do not form antonyms, they often consist of quasi-synonyms: "songes"-"mensonges," "douleur"-"malheur," "cordage"-"servage," etc. The rhyming of opposites allows the poet to synthesize thesis and antithesis, without destroying their semantic contrariety; the linking of quasi-synonyms underlines their similarity, while bringing out subtle distinctions between the two. Like all other figures of repetition, rhyme incorporates both sameness and difference. Even contact *geminatio* obeys this law: the second appearance of the word implies an intensification of meaning over the first. Reiteration creates a field of tension between the like and the unlike; that tension acts as a dynamic force, impelling language forward while preserving its continuity.[61] Especially in a poetics of set conventions such as Petrarchism, this "spiral" progression occurs on a historical plane as well: like the figures of rhetoric handed down by the tradition, its literary *topoi* turn around, and away from, a central point of identity. Durand and most of his contemporaries prolong the Neoclassicism of Desportes; in this guise, late Renaissance verse temporarily regains the

[61] Cf. I. A. Richards, pp. 130-1: "So far from verbal language being a 'compromise for a language of intuition' – a thin, but better-than-nothing, substitute for real experience – language, well-used, is a *completion* and does what the intuitions of sensation by themselves cannot do. Words are the meeting points at which regions of experience which can never combine in sensation or intuition, come together. They are the occasion and the means of that growth which is the mind's endless endeavour to order itself."

stylistic poise and moderation of *L'Olive* and the *Sonets pour Hélène*, but only at the price of what may seem to modern readers a monotonous blandness, an artificial pallor. At the same time, the "poets of 1600" already show definite signs of the "extreme patterning and enumeration" which Houston (p. 173) considers typical of the Baroque. Agents of transition, they announce "things dying, and things newborn." Here again, their use of tropes mirrors their use of Petrarchist themes: recapitulation leads to redundance, and surfeit paves the way for innovation. Like the thematic content of constancy to the beloved, the rhetorical form in which it is cast tends toward ceaseless reiteration. Antithesis follows antithesis, restatement retraces restatement – edging gradually, ineluctably, toward the final emptiness of exhaustion and disenchantment. Inconstancy occurs on an artistic plane at the end of the Renaissance: the outworn passions are discarded, and poetry moves on.

PART TWO: POETRY OF CHANGE

CHAPTER III

THE THEME OF INCONSTANCY

In his reminiscences of Durand, Guillaume Colletet already singled out the "Stances à l'Inconstance" as "toutes merveilleuses" (p. XVI); the renewal of interest in Durand in the last forty years was originally sparked by this poem alone. Unfortunately, their enthusiasm for the "Stances" has led some critics to dismiss his other verse from serious consideration. To do so is to misunderstand the "Stances" themselves, which take on their full meaning only in relation to the *Méditations* proper, with their emphasis on constancy. Of these poems Yves Bonnefoy writes in his "Préface" (p. III): "Les *Méditations*, c'est l'envahissement d'une poésie qui ne se voulait peut-être d'abord qu'un jeu facile... par un doute quant au fondement des représentations, des valeurs qui ont survécu à la grande crise dont Machiavel ou Montaigne ont été les catalyseurs. Et en cela déjà ce livre [est]... un signe de plus de l'affaiblissement de la foi jusqu'à hier consentie à ce réseau symbolique qui depuis si longtemps médiatisait l'absolu."

Durand's love poem cycle is emblematic of late Petrarchism as a whole: an echo-chamber of ingrown discourse, where repetitive tropes and vitiated *topoi* reverberate along a narrow enclosure, simultaneously magnified and emptied of meaning. The "Stances..." mark a liberation not only from "Uranie" – the Muse of Astronomy, and the name given by the poet to his mistress – but from the fixed stars and rigid constellations of the language which enshrined her. Similarly, the rise of amorous inconstancy as a prevalent theme reveals its larger significance only when considered against the backdrop of the literary evolution which preceded it. While related motifs had previously appeared, particularly in Ronsard and Desportes, the invocation to the goddess Inconstancy does not emerge as a fully-fledged, iconoclastic *topos* until the beginning of the seventeenth century. It is legitimate to assert, as Jean Rousset and others have done,[1] that the inconstancy motif forms a hallmark of the period in which Durand wrote; but the historical development of the theme, especially as it implies a radical departure from the high-flown idealism of the Petrarchist tradition, has not received the attention it deserves. To this diachronic perspective I would add a synchronic one: the inconstancy invoked by Durand differs notably from the inconstancy extolled by Lingendes – and both, in turn, offer an alternative to the constancy on which a poet such as Sponde insists. The amoral posture, the displaced religious tone, and the universal scepticism of the "Stances à l'Inconstance" reveal a deepening rift in the former "réseau symbolique," a disintegration of conventions and ideals which heralds the end of Renaissance verse.

1. The Praise of Inconstancy (1550-1600)

In its origins, Petrarchism is a poetry of constancy, an exercise in spiritual devotion. The *Canzoniere*, which has its roots in the medieval lyric, celebrates the poet's fidelity – even beyond death – to a chaste and unapproachable beloved; despite their stylistic experiments, Petrarch's Italian followers remain true to his quasi-religious conception of the lover's role (cf. Friedrich, pp. 159-61, 309-28). On this point as in general, the first Petrarchists in France display a high degree of orthodoxy. Scève's *Délie, objet de plus haute vertu* (1544) and Du Bellay's *Olive* (1549) propound a neo-Platonic contemplation of the mistress' beauty;[2] the vulgarity of amorous inconstancy is clearly excluded from such a vision. Though somewhat more direct in their sensuous evocation, the first *Amours* of Ronsard (1552) do not even contain the word *inconstance*, much less advocate its practice.[3]

---

[1] Cf. Morel, p. 74; Rousset, *La Littérature...*, pp. 32-50; Boase, intro. to Sponde, pp. 113-14; Mathieu-Castellani, "La Poésie amoureuse... d'après les recueils collectifs (1597-1600)," p. 16 – and also *Les Thèmes...*, pp. 315-16, 403-9.

[2] Cf. I. D. McFarlane, *Délie* edn., pp. 41-2; on Platonism in *L'Olive* cf. Spitzer, art. cit.

[3] Cf. A. E. Creore's helpful *Word-Index to the Poetic Works of Ronsard.*

Hardly had a "pure" Petrarchism been introduced into France than the counter-influence of Italian anti-Petrarchism made itself felt: in 1552 Du Bellay composed his satirical poem "A une Dame" – republished in 1558 as "Contre les Pétrarquistes";[4] it marks his definitive break with Petrarchism. Though not anti-Petrarchists in the full sense of the term, many other French poets subsequently reject an important tenet of Petrarchist orthodoxy: the lofty character of the beloved. Ronsard undermines it first with his countrified portrayal of Marie, then with his bitter evocation of Hélène. The un-Petrarchan notion of the mistress' intentional cruelty[5] finds its culmination in the "love" verse of d'Aubigné. Along with minor figures like Béroalde and Nuysement, he exploits a vision of the beloved which the *Sonets pour Hélène* only mildly touch upon (cf. Mathieu-Castellani, pp. 319-48). In their works of the 1570s and 1580s, the execration of the mistress seems complete: she is denounced as a Hecate, hellish and demoniac. Why should the lover maintain his constancy towards her?

This is precisely where the greater subtlety of Ronsard becomes apparent. Whether heavenly or infernal, the beloved of d'Aubigné or Béroalde remains a goddess: though the lover denounces her, her dominion over him never slackens. Despite their violent imagery, these poets continue to respect the most hallowed of Petrarchist conventions, attachment to a single mistress. Ronsard already flies in the face of that principle in his *Continuation des Amours* of 1555, in which the humanization of the beloved is matched by a more down-to-earth portrait of the lover. The *Continuation* prolongs the previous collection only by its title: the abandonment of Cassandre for Marie marks a clear departure from the Petrarchist ideal of life-long fidelity.[6]

Ronsard defends this plurality of loves in the long elegy "A son livre"[7] of 1556, which Laumonier has called "[une] pièce... capitale

[4] Ed. Chamard, vol. IV, pp. 205-15; vol. V, pp. 69-77.

[5] Petrarch's Laura is "cruel" only in the sense that she is indifferent to the lover's pleas; after her death she becomes a figure of divine goodness, who beckons the poet to a higher spirituality (cf. Friedrich, pp. 202-7; and Genot, intro. to the *Canzoniere*, pp. 37-8).

[6] Ronsard had precursors in this change of mistresses, most notably Pontano and Baïf (cf. Lebègue, pp. 56-7); however, it was Ronsard who constructed a poetic program around the celebration of successive loves.

[7] *Oeuvres complètes*, ed. Laumonier, vol. VII, pp. 315-25; all subsequent references are to this edition of Ronsard, unless otherwise stated.

pour l'étude de l'évolution d[e son] génie":[8] here he endorses amorous inconstancy – but without switching to the satirical counter-conventions of anti-Petrarchism.[9] By placing it at the end of the *Nouvelle Continuation des Amours*, Ronsard signalled the importance of the poem himself. More than a justification of the *Amours de Marie*, it represents a conspicuous *prise de position* toward the Petrarchist tradition. For the first time, anti-feminist motifs and libertine frivolity take their place in a love poem cycle which elsewhere extols the mistress' virtue and the lover's devotion in the most orthodox terms. This does not necessarily imply a new literary doctrine to replace Petrarchism: instead Ronsard appears to juxtapose or alternate, for various kinds of poetic effect, two incompatible sets of *topoi*. In a sense, he already manifests that "thematic inconstancy" which will characterize the work of Durand and his contemporaries.

With the *Continuation* and *Nouvelle Continuation*, a uniquely French variant of Petrarchism comes to the fore; by justifying inconstancy, Ronsard significantly widened the thematic range of amatory verse. His personal declaration of independence will later settle into a *topos*. That Ronsard was its ultimate source seems evident, given the neo-Petrarchist fidelity[10] celebrated by Desportes, whose influence dominated love poetry after 1572. From then until 1600, when the praise of inconstancy enters its apogee, several minor poets – chiefly Trellon and Habert – keep the thread of continuity intact; but the real innovator had been Ronsard.

The repercussions of Ronsard's example were soon to be felt throughout the entire range of French poetry: a case in point is Agrippa d'Aubigné. The manuscripts first published a century ago contain a long-winded allegory in couplets;[11] in the prayer which

[8] Ibid., p. 325, note 3.

[9] Like the anti-Petrarchists, Ronsard makes fun of the Petrarchan legend, rejecting the notion that the poet could have loved Laura for thirty years "sans avoir rien" (line 50). However, he does not disclaim love altogether, or treat it merely as a subject for racy jokes. In lines 139-50, he claims to respect feminine virtue, and expresses the desire to "trouver une amye/ Qui nous ayde à passer cette chetive vie" (lines 147-8). This and other passages are far removed in spirit from the comic sarcasms of anti-Petrarchism.

[10] That Desportes shifted from "Diane" to "Hippolyte" or "Cléonice" does not change the stance of neo-Petrarchist fidelity *within* each love verse cycle; however, in his final love poems a strong reaction against the ideal of constancy does make itself felt (see below).

[11] Ed. Réaume and de Caussade, vol. III, pp. 225-34.

closes the poem,[12] d'Aubigné entreats Inconstancy to make him as faithless as his mistress. In purely formal terms, this invocation marks a new departure: for the first time, Inconstancy is incarnated as a goddess, rather than figuring merely as a quality of behavior – whether that of the poet, the mistress, society, or nature. Such a personification does not occur in Ronsard or the other Pléiade poets. With Inconstancy deified, the ancillary theme of offerings *ex voto* also arises. As in the invocation to Sleep, the lover will repay the kindness of the goddess with sacrifices of those things which are dear to her. Unlike Somnus, Inconstancy does not possess attributes laid down by an ancient tradition; she is a creature of the late Renaissance. The imagination enjoys free rein: inconstancy can be seen in everything that is mobile, changing, or ephemeral. D'Aubigné promises to immolate autumn leaves, the air of a ringing bell, a weathercock, soap bubbles, feathers, sea-water, a chameleon, etc. The temple he vows to build for the goddess provides a good occasion for paradox:[13] a monument is raised to the transitory; and as a final tribute, the poet has the edifice go up in flames. All these motifs will later be widely exploited in France.

Depite the similarities with future poems, d'Aubigné does not make a "doctrine" out of inconstancy, as later poets tend to do. Even in the invocation just mentioned the lover is begging for release from his constancy, not thanking the goddess for a liberty he already savors, as in Durand's "Stances à l'Inconstance."[14] In any case, though his manuscripts may have been circulated privately, d'Aubigné's influence on younger poets cannot compare with that of Philippe Desportes, who superseded Ronsard as court favorite in the 1570s and 1580s. At first glance, the neo-Petrarchism of Desportes seems like a complete restoration of the Italian tradition which Ronsard had partially rejected.[15] For the most part, this evaluation stands. But in composing love poem cycles for a plurality of

[12] These closing lines are reprinted in Rousset's *Anthologie*, vol. I, p. 63.

[13] The popularity of the inconstancy theme in the late Renaissance may be attributed in large part to the vogue of the *paradoxon*: cf. Ellrodt, part II, pp. 330-51.

[14] In another long piece (ed. cit., vol. III, pp. 235-40) d'Aubigné celebrates the triumph of constancy. In an "Ode" from the *Printemps*, the poet does claim to practice inconstancy; but as Jean Rousset asserts, "la dernière strophe nous prie de n'y voir que 'paradoxe pour rire'; on s'en serait douté, connaissant D'Aubigné pour ce qu'il est, en poésie: amant constant et 'immobile'" (see *Anthol.*, vol. I, p. 261 [note to text on p. 64-6]).

[15] Cf. Mathieu-Castellani, pp. 209-11, 212-13.

loves – "Hippolyte," "Diane," and "Cléonice" – Desportes subtly furthers the erosion of Petrarchist values which Ronsard had begun. The later works of Desportes also include poems which express that erosion of values more openly. The title of his *Diverses amours* (1583)[16] is significant; here again Desportes follows the recent precedent of Ronsard, who had added a section of *Amours diverses* to the 1578 edition of his works.[17] Thematically, however, Desportes's collection represents an original departure, both from the practice of his predecessors and from his own earlier production. In contrast to the standard Petrarchism of his love verse cycles, the *Diverses amours* frequently decry the mistress' inconstancy; and there are even poems in which the lover declares his own infidelity.

The most remarkable of these is an invocation to Inconstancy in sonnet form:

> Franc du triste servage où j'ay tant supporté,
> Qu'un seul des maux souffers me transit quand j'y pense,
> Je t'en vien rendre grace, ô deesse Inconstance!
> Devant à ta faveur l'ame et la liberté:
> Un songe imaginé, que l'on dit Fermeté,
> M'avoit si bien pipé par sa belle apparance,
> Qu'abhorrant tout secours j'embrassoy ma souffrance
> Et renforçoy les fers dont j'estois arresté.
> Celle en fin qui servoit à mon feu de matiere,
> Oubliant ses sermens et changeant la premiere
> M'a fait voir que la foy n'estoit qu'un nom trompeur:
> Et mon ame aussi tost de toy favorisée,
> A rompu ses liens, sa prison a brisée,
> Et de toute constance a delivré mon coeur.[18]

Desportes' invocation differs from d'Aubigné's in two ways. The first is formal: whereas d'Aubigné's invocation serves as coda to a longer work, Desportes's entire sonnet is constructed around the

[16] The *Diverses amours* was the last of Desportes's love verse collections to be significantly expanded: in 1583 the poet grouped seventy-six pieces under this heading, thirty-six of which had not been published before (cf. Lavaud, p. 302).

[17] In the 1578 edition Ronsard clearly seeks to accentuate the difference in tone between the *Amours de Cassandre* and the *Amours de Marie*; many of the poems deleted from these two collections find their way into the *Amours diverses*. On this "profond remaniement" see Weber, intro. to Ronsard's *Amours*, pp. LX-LXIII.

[18] First published in 1583; *Diverses amours et autres oeuvres*, ed. Graham, p. 86.

invocation. The second is thematic: d'Aubigné prays to be delivered from his constancy, while Desportes thanks Inconstancy for the freedom he already possesses. In both these respects, later poets will develop their invocations in the manner of Desportes; this is hardly surprising, given his influence on the younger generation. More unexpected is the fact that the sonnet does not derive from an Italian source,[19] like most of his later love verse.[20] As Ronsard paved the way for the praise of inconstancy, so Desportes laid the groundwork for the invocation *topos*.

Only two years after the publication of Desportes's sonnet, a close imitation already appears in the *Dernieres Amours* of Isaac Habert. Still, for one reason or another, none of the poems cited thus far constitutes an invocation to Inconstancy as it will be formulated after 1598. Ronsard does not even put *inconstance* in the vocative, much less portray it as a goddess. D'Aubigné does personify Inconstancy, but his invocation is only part of a longer poem; he is still seeking release from a single beloved, not celebrating his total freedom. Like him, Desportes and Habert remain close to the attitude of Du Bellay's "Contre les Petrarquistes" or Jodelle's *Contr'Amours*: their break with the mistress signifies a complete abandonment of love, not the exuberant pursuit of various lovers.

In a less satirical form than in Du Bellay and Jodelle, the anti-Petrarchist rejection motif found great favor in the latter part of the sixteenth century.[21] Here Claude de Trellon is a key transitional figure: while his verse contains that same motif in its more traditional guise,[22] in other passages he illustrates the difference in tone be-

---

[19] In his edn. Graham does not list any Italian or other source for the poem (cf. loc. cit.).

[20] On Desportes's increasing reliance on Italian models, cf. Lavaud p. 314. A similar invocation, addressed to "Liberté," also seems to have been "invented" by Desportes himself (see edn. cit., p. 77).

[21] It was powerfully employed in one of Ronsard's last sonnets: "Amour, je pren congé de ta menteuse escole..." (ed. Weber, p. 478). It seems characteristic of Ronsard that he does not utterly condemn love, even here; in the last line, after evoking his various mistresses, he concedes: "Si elles m'ont aimé, je les ay bien aimees."

[22] A typical example may be found in his *Oeuvres* (1595), fol. 244 vo; but significantly, it bears the title "Adieu à l'Amour mondain." It is typical of Trellon's generation that this poem appears in a section of religious works, *L'Hermitage*. At the end of the century a phase of devotionalism succeeds the former predilection for amatory verse: after the Pléiade and the early Desportes, religious themes predominate. But the latter are increasingly mixed – as here – with *topoi* drawn from the profane tradition; this trend toward "thematic inconstancy" will be discussed in the following chapter.

tween the *contr'amour* type of revolt against Petrarchism and that of the subsequent "poets of inconstancy." Rather than saying farewell to love altogether, they resolve to continue their affairs – not only without fidelity to the mistress, but "sans passion" (cf. Mathieu-Castellani, pp. 315-16).

Trellon's thematic pose differs profoundly from that of his predecessors and immediate contemporaries. The change may be observed in the sonnet "J'avouë que je suis inconstant & volage..." (op. cit., fol. 176 vo):

> J'avouë que je suis inconstant & volage,
> J'avouë, je le suis, mais non pas tant que vous:
> Tesmoing, vous me monstrez un jour fort bon visage,
> Un autre jour vos yeux sont tous plains de courroux.
>
> J'avouë, je le suis, nous le sommes tretous.
> Et qui dit le contraire il farde son langage,
> Jamais la loyauté ne loge avecque nous,
> L'inconstance tousjours guide nostre courage.
>
> J'avouë que le change est mon Prince & mon maistre,
> J'aime le changement, je le luy fais paroistre,
> La nouveauté me plaist sans fin je l'aimeray.
>
> Je ne le nie pas par tout je le confesse:
> Mais vous qui l'adorez plus que moy, ma Maitresse,
> Vous le desavouëz comme s'il n'estoit vray.

Here Trellon revives the Ronsardian injunction to "aimer en cent lieux"; the influence of the *Continuation des Amours* reveals itself not only in the content of the poem, but in its distinctly Ronsardian *style bas*: Desportes could not possibly have been the model here. Despite this literary allegiance, Trellon goes much further than Ronsard had done in exalting change: in lines 6-8, he denies that human beings are capable of any type of constancy; in lines 9-11, he claims inconstancy as the "guiding" principle of his life. He does not retract that claim in other poems like Ronsard, who sets strict limitations on mutability. Whereas Ronsard confines inconstancy to the amorous sphere, condoning it only under certain conditions, Trellon gives it free rein. The anaphora of "J'avouë" underscores the urgency of his avowal: the poet seems impelled to bear witness to his creed, as though he were propagating a sardonic gospel.

In 1583 Desportes had given the invocation to Inconstancy its conclusive form; in 1595 Trellon provides an important part of the *fond*: a cynical "philosophy" of chronic infidelity, of "Amour sans passion," presented under the guise of psychological realism. Though he consigns his inconstancy poems to the *Meslanges* section of his *Oeuvres*, outside his conventional love verse cycles, even these contain such lines as the following (fol. 130 ro):

> Ces sots, ces jeunes gens qui lisans a tout heure,
> Mes escrits vont jugeant par mes discours de moy:
> Ne sont ils pas bien fols d'y adjouster leur foy,
> Car ce n'est rien en fin que fainte, & que painture...
> Pour servir mes Amis j'irois dans le trespas,
> En ce qui est d'Amour qu'on ne s'y fie pas:
> Car je n'aime rien tant qu'a faire mes affaires.

In these verses from the *Amours de Felice*, the poet's claim to an assiduous readership is not just an idle boast; it alludes to a revealing tendency of the era. Trellon's poems were in fact read and appreciated by many "jeunes gens." In her article on the collective anthologies (1597-1600), Mathieu-Castellani has noted the popularity of "Trellon..., dont le succès va grandissant, et qui témoigne d'un goût trés vif pour le 'réalisme' en matière amoureuse" (p. 10).[23] By openly declaring the falsity of his Petrarchist motifs *within* a Petrarchist love poem cycle, Trellon delivers the coup de grâce to Petrarchism as a spiritual discipline – and as a serious literary discipline as well. The disruptive pose of the faithless lover is matched by that of the faithless poet: thematic hollowiness itself becomes a theme, in the very midst of the themes which it discredits.[24] The *topos* of inconstancy converges with a distinctive form of poetic instability. As subsequent developments will demonstrate, not all of Trellon's

---

[23] For an example of Trellon's lasting influence, cf. Lespine, op. cit. (1623), p. 81:

> Qui veut bien heureux vivre,
> Exempt de passion,
> L'inconstance il doit suivre,
> Et n'avoir dans le coeur aucune affection;
> Prenant pour son contentement
> Tout ce qui tient du changement.

[24] For a similar and much longer "deconstructive" passage in Trellon see op. cit., fol. 194 vo.

younger readers were "sots"; many understood and absorbed his message. With a deepened insistence, the poets of Durand's generation will also underline the insubstantiality of literary motifs.[25]

The erosion of Petrarchist values which Ronsard had begun comes to a head around 1600; in the wake of Trellon, a new thematic stance asserts itself. For poets like La Roque, Motin, Durand, and Lingendes – to name only a few – the mistress no longer merits the slightest respect: since she has been inconstant in love, the poet will follow suit – "inconstance payée d'inconstance."[26] What had earlier been an extreme – such as Desportes's joy at being "liberated" by his faithless mistress – becomes the normal tone of an entire thematic genre. The beloved is accused of every imaginable vice, from deceit to depravity; in the "Stances à l'Inconstance," she is virtually cast aside like a useless object. It would be hard to imagine an attitude more remote from the quasi-religious cult which the beloved had inspired in Petrarch and his followers. On the other hand, Durand and his contemporaries notably depart from the tradition of anti-Petrarchism, in that they *include themselves* in their accusations: like Ronsard, the later "poets of inconstancy" represent infidelity as an aspect of human nature. Rather than repudiating love altogether, in the manner of Jodelle or Du Bellay, they pass on to the next love-affair. For them as for Ronsard, neither lover nor mistress can be expected to imitate the inhuman (and thus apocryphal) purity of Petrarch and Laura. Whether early seventeenth century poets were conscious of the fact or not, Ronsard had freed them from the absolutes of Petrarchism and conventional anti-Petrarchism alike.

Still, the limits of Ronsard's experiment are also manifest. For example, the internal inconstancy of the individual human mind never comes to full and positive expression in his writings. On the contrary, throughout his works the notion of an inner instability is repeatedly rejected in favor of a "Stoic" constancy. The same is true of the external dimension: Ronsard generally disclaims inconstancy in its larger, universal sense; at best, it is an unfortunate state which men must endure in the sublinary sphere. He places hope in the

---

[25] This tendency toward thematic vitiation, already discussed in passing, will be examined at greater length in Chapter IV.

[26] The title of a poem by La Roque, first published in the *Muses francoises ralliées de diverses pars* (1599), pp. 250-1; reprinted in Rousset's *Anthologie*, vol. I, pp. 68-9. Cf. Le Digne, fol. 122 ro: "Si elle veut changer pour degager sa foy,/ Je chercheray du feu pour ma chandelle esteinte."

ability of the sage to surmount these vicissitudes, and to accede to a Platonic vision of permanence: his break with the amorous constancy of Petrarchism does not imply a sense of total disjunction.[27] By contrast, the poets of Durand's generation adopt a stance of radical doubt, deriding the capacity of human reason and the notion of a cosmic order. While Ronsard's works evoke inconstancy on a variety of levels, they are dominated by counter-*topoi* from the central traditions of the Renaissance – Christian, neo-Platonic, Stoic – which ultimately reaffirm the integrity of man, as the microcosm of an ordered universe. In the later "poets of inconstancy," instability and change emerge as the overriding principles of the human mind and the world: microcosm and macrocosm disintegrate into the same chaos.[28]

Though Trellon's doctrine of "Amour sans passion" makes him a precursor of the invocations to Inconstancy published after 1598, two further conceptual elements of the latter are absent in his work: the union of the poet with cosmic change and the subtly implied parody of sacred verse. Trellon proclaims the inner instability which Ronsard had denied, but he does not expand his vision to include the external world. It is this universal dimension of the invocations to Inconstancy which gives them a vaguely "subversive" undertone. They are a sign of the times: in large part, they assimilate a commonplace of the period in which they were written, a cliché which transcends the sphere of amorous verse.

From the end of the sixteenth century to the middle of the seventeenth, the theme of inconstancy recurs with extraordinary frequency, in literature both sacred and profane; the world picture which it reflects has often been considered characteristic of the age.

---

[27] Cf. e.g. the "Hymne de l'Eternité," which affirms his yearning for a state of permanence; and compare the passage in the *Odes* (vol. II, p. 4) where he decries the inconstancy of his fellow men, or the lines in the "Hymne de la Mort" (vol. VIII, pp. 172-3) where he laments that stability is denied us in the sublunary realm.

[28] Cf. Mathieu-Castellani, p. 406: "...l'inconstance, si elle apparaît comme l'élément le plus visible de cette nouvelle psychologie amoureuse, mieux, de cette métaphysique amoureuse, n'est pas l'essentiel. Elle masque même, plus qu'elle ne révèle, un certain nombre de choix 'premiers'. Le poète baroque est, d'abord, celui qui choisit le multiple contre l'un, l'existence contre l'essence, la division, la contradiction, contre toute logique... L'univers mental de l'homme de la Renaissance s'effrite et cède sous les assauts de cette logique implacable qui refuse la logique."

Like the universe of which he is a part, man is swept away in the ruin of time; his internal inconstancy corresponds to the most fleeting phenomena of nature, "vapeur, fleur, torrent."[29] For a devotional poet like Sponde or Chassignet, man's only hope is to renounce the earth and seek the permanence of God's grace, conceived as something beyond the realm of human thought. Drawing on the same images of flux and decay, the verse of other poets, such as Durand or the *libertins*, never adumbrates an otherworldly solution. Whereas the Christian authors judge only the sublunary sphere to be inconstant – in this not far removed from medieval concepts of *vanitas* – a novel tendency makes itself felt in the "Stances à l'Inconstance" and similar works of the late Renaissance: in them inconstancy is joyously embraced as the "propre de l'homme."[30] In seeking the sources of this receptive attitude toward inconstancy as a principle of being, one need look no farther than Montaigne. His influence on the "poets of inconstancy" has never been methodically studied, but it can hardly be doubted.[31] Unlike the devotional poets, Montaigne does not repudiate the instability of earthly existence – either external or internal. Despite his early admiration for the constancy of the ancient Stoics, he increasingly accepts inconstancy as an integral and even desirable part of our nature. One of the final additions to the *Essais* recommends the inconstancy of wind as a positive model for man:

---

[29] Cf. the poem "Hélas! Qu'est-ce de l'homme..." from Jean Auvray's *Pourmenade de l'Ame devote* (1633), reprinted in Rousset's anth., vol. I, pp. 45-6; cf. also the other poems which Rousset groups under the heading "l'inconstance noire" (pp. 31-60).

[30] This is the thematic tendency which Rousset has dubbed "l'inconstance blanche" (cf. the poems grouped under this heading in ibid., pp. 61-112), as opposed to "l'inconstance noire." But it is obvious that both tendencies belong to the same period, and that they are inseparably related. In fact the boundaries between "black" and "white" inconstancy are often rather "gray": frivolity may mask a deep-seated tragic sense, traces of which appear in many of the "inconstants blancs."

[31] Between 1595 and 1650, as A. Thibaudet has pointed out in his edn. of the *Essais* (p. 22), sizeable editions of Montaigne were issued about every two years; no educated person can have remained impervious to the general enthusiasm. Moreover, certain works reveal his influence quite directly. In *La Littérature de l'âge baroque...* (p. 46) Jean Rousset singles out as a prime example of this influence the two strophes from Durand's "Stances à l'Inconstance" which begin "Nostre esprit n'est que vent..." On echoes of Montaigne in Durand and Pierre Motin, cf. also A. J. Steele, anth. cit., p. XIX.

> Moy qui me vente d'embrasser si curieusement les commoditez de la vie, et si particulierement, n'y trouve, quand j'y regarde assez finement, à peu pres que du vent. Mais quoy, nous sommes par tout vent. Et le vent encore, plus sagement que nous, s'ayme à bruire, à s'agiter, et se contente en ses propres offices, sans desirer la stabilité, la solidité, qualitez non siennes.

It would be easy to cite similar examples.[32] By their imagery and the "philosophy of life" which they suggest, such passages strongly foreshadow the inconstancy poems of Durand and his contemporaries.

The praise of inconstancy as they develop it assumes a distinctive rhetorical form which has nothing to do with Montaigne. Its roots may be found in the genre of the mock encomium,[33] versions of which abound throughout the sixteenth century. The best-known is Erasmus' *Moriae Encomium*, where he accentuates the inherent ambiguity of the genre by having Folly celebrate herself: "Stultitia loquitur." But I would also point to Ronsard's ironic hymn to wealth, or Panurge's panegyric of debts in Rabelais.[34] When it is not merely burlesque – as in Francesco Berni's *capitoli* – the mock encomium serves a double purpose: on one level, the praise of dubious abstractions can only appear sardonic; but on another level, the satirical tone allows the author to say iconoclastic things with impunity. He can always excuse himself with the words: "It was all in good fun." Though this is true of any kind of humor, the mock encomium is especially equivocal, because it presents itself as outright praise rather than simple persiflage.

Like Erasmus – and unlike Ronsard or Rabelais – Durand and other "poets of inconstancy" depict a personified abstraction. Though *Inconstance* is more explicitly a goddess than Folly, she does not speak on her own behalf, like her Spenserian counterpart Mutabilitie: instead, she is worshipfully invoked by the poet. It

---

[32] For the passage just quoted, which Montaigne inserted during the last revision (1589-92), see edn. cit., p. 1078. For another example see p. 589.

[33] On the mock encomium in Antiquity and the Renaissance, see Ellrodt, part II, pp. 333-40.

[34] Panurge intones a panegyric of debts through two whole chapters of the *Tiers Livre*; in Ronsard's "Hynne de l'Or" (ed. Cohen, vol. II, pp. 260-74) part of the irony is that a professedly poor poet should celebrate the glories of wealth. Both Rabelais and Ronsard make brilliant use of the shifts of tone which such an ambivalent stance permits.

could be argued that this attitude of adoration is what sets invocations to Inconstancy apart from previous examples of the mock encomium. Tongue in cheek, the poet appeals to the embodiment of a universal principle; his encomium is also a prayer. But the deity he praises represents the exact opposite of the "Prime Mover"; she stands for the instability and change of the sublunary world. Like Mutabilitie in Spenser's powerful *Cantos* of 1609,[35] *Inconstance* often threatens to supplant the higher order. The date of that work indicates the pan-European apogee of this unprecedented allegorical figure in the opening decade of the seventeenth century. Significantly, both "Incostanza" and "Instablitià" are represented for the first time as goddesses in Cesare Ripa's *Iconologia* of 1603;[36] they had not appeared as such in previous mythological handbooks, like the highly popular one by Cartari. Without entering into the debate about period styles, I can think of no better argument for associating these years with the rise of the Baroque, understood as an emphasis on rapid movement and constant metamorphosis.

In reading their invocations to Inconstancy, one must always keep in mind that Durand and his contemporaries were nourished on devotional verse which tirelessly decried the instability of earthly existence: the images drawn from nature – wind, fire, feathers, and so forth – had long been employed as emblems of worldly transience and futility before they were converted into symbols of lighthearted love. Poems in praise of inconstancy may thus be read as the secular reverse of a religious obverse; they sharply contrast with a devotionalism which disdains the present in favor of the future, and this world in favor of the next.[37] Though it is tempting to overemphasize the "subversive" aspect of invocations to Inconstancy, they usually keep within the bounds of a playful ambiguity. All the same, a solemn note is sometimes heard in these harmless variations on a theme; it reaches its climax in Durand's "Stances à l'In-

[35] Spenser's two *Mutabilitie Cantos* recount the attempt of Mutabilitie to usurp the universal dominion of Jove. In the end she is "overruled" by Nature. For commentary on the underlying meaning of this struggle see S. P. Zitner's intro. to his edn. of the work, pp. 14-21, 50-2.

[36] Inconstancy and her attributes are elaborately described on pp. 225-6 (note also the illustration, which figures on the cover of the present study), while Instability is more briefly depicted on p. 237.

[37] On the spiritual awakening of the period and its stylistic ramifications, see Clément, *Une poétique de crise: poètes baroques et mystiques (1570-1660).*

constance," which Yves Bonnefoy has called "un hymne au Verbe, qui prend la place de Dieu." [38]

2. The Invocation to Inconstancy

In the late Renaissance the rise of the inconstancy theme is paralleled by a burgeoning "thematic inconstancy," a blurring of the boundaries between the serious and the frivolous, the sacred and the profane. This fusionary tendency finds its archetype in the work of Cardinal Jacques Davy Du Perron: ecclesiastical politician, learned theologian, and accomplished devotional poet, Du Perron was also a famous author of amatory verse. His love poems appear repeatedly in the collective anthologies; a favorite among them was "Le Temple de l'Inconstance," a suite of *stances* first published in the *Muses francoises ralliées* of 1599, [39] and much too long to be reproduced here.

While the motif of an altar or temple of Inconstancy was not new (cf. the poem by d'Aubigné discussed earlier), Du Perron's originality consists in developing the theme throughout an entire poem, containing several elements which will later recur in Durand's "Stances à l'Inconstance." Above all, Du Perron does not shy away from exploiting the religious associations summoned up by the image of a shrine: the mistress will be its priestess, the lover its "Templier," and the "sainct Temple" will be full of the "encens" of "mille faux sermens." Though he is careful to stress the Classical models for this place of worship – the priestess is a cross between the Cumaean Sibyl and the Delphic Pythia – certain phrases carry an ambiguous undertone: for example, "viendront adorer," "La Deité qu'adorent les Amants," "Le sacré nom"; and especially "le coeur touché de repentance," "je viendray souvent/ Offrir mon coeur par un sainct sacrifice" – expressions which recall the devotional fervor of the Counter-Reformation. [40] The audacious twisting of such cross-generic references is symptomatic of the period.

---

[38] Preface to edn. cit., p. VII.

[39] On pp. 213-14. The slightly altered version of 1618 is reprinted in Rousset's anth., vol. I, pp. 70-71.

[40] Cf. Marion Praz's essay on Counter-Reformation imagery in Crashaw (*The Flaming Heart*, pp. 204-63).

Du Perron's central conceit revives an age-old *topos* which ultimately derives from the later Middle Ages: that of the "temple of Love."[41] Against the background of this venerable French tradition, Du Perron's verses reveal their full significance. The use of sacred allusions to celebrate a loyal love can be justified, because of the analogy with devotion to God; the same religious language, when used to evoke a "shrine of Inconstancy," seems decidedly more problematic. Without wanting to exaggerate, I would maintain that such a conceit not only represents the reversal of an ancient *topos*, it also turns on their head some of the traditional values associated with the theme.

It is more than likely that Durand was familiar with the "Temple de l'Inconstance" – if not directly influenced by it. The third stanza in particular –

> Tout à l'entour je peindray maint image
> D'erreur, d'oubly, & d'infidelité,
> De fol desir, d'espoir, de vanité,
> De fiction, & de penser volage.

– seems to have captured the younger poet's imagination. Like Du Perron's temple painting, the "tableau fantastique" of the "Stances à l'Inconstance" will portray a mixture of abstractions: "L'oubliance, l'espoir, le desir frenetique,/ Les sermens parjurez, l'humeur melancolique..." (lines 43-4). Another detail which reveals Durand's familiarity with "Le Temple de l'Inconstance" is his recasting of Du Perron's final apostrophe: "Fille de l'air, Déesse secourable,/ Qui as le corps de plumes tout couvert..." (lines 37-8). In the "Stances à l'Inconstance" Durand concentrates these two lines into a single phrase: "fille de l'air de cent plumes couverte" (line 36); this is a typical example of the poem's energetic compression.

---

[41] The motif may be traced from the *Roman de la Rose* (cf. the initiation sequence lines 634 and ff.) through Jean Lemaire's *Temple d'Honneur et de Vertus* to the "Temple de Cupido" described by Marot in *L'Adolescence Clémentine* (edn. cit., pp. 25-41) – which corresponds in every detail to a Gothic cathedral. But even here the moral purpose of the lover remains unchanged from that expressed in the *Roman de la Rose*: he pursues "Ferme Amour," constancy to a single mistress. Marot's poem does not contradict what Saulnier (loc. cit.) identifies as his "prépétrarquisme": as in Petrarch, the beloved is a mirror-image of divine stability and permanence.

Despite the religious overtones of his tribute, Du Perron does not allow Inconstancy a universal dominion, as Durand and others will do. He prudently stresses that she is a "Deité qu'adorent les Amants" (line 27); apart from a reference to "les ondes de la mer/ Les vents, la Lune" (lines 14-15), he limits her sphere to that of "tout Amant... variable" (line 40). In other words, the Inconstancy celebrated by Du Perron, while more generalized than that of Trellon, remains closely associated with amorous infidelity. Quite different is the goddess invoked by S.-G. de La Roque in a sonnet from his *Amours de Narsize* (1609):[42]

Puissante Deité, redoutable Inconstance,
Qui par tout l'Univers dissouts nos lyaisons,
Fille unique du temps, Royne des Horisons,
Qui mesmes des rochers brave la resistance.
En fin le grand Soleil aime ton inconstance,
Et se plaist de le suivre en diverses maisons:
Comme l'An a courir par ses quatre saisons:
Mesurant de leur tour l'une et l'autre distance.
Par ton mobile accord sont les cieux emportez,
L'air, la terre et la mer s'en treuvent agitez,
Rendant leurs actions d'une suitte inégale.
Hé donc? puis que par tout on voit reigner ta loy,
Pour me guerir des traicts d'une amour desloyale
Respand ton influence aujourd'huy dessus moy.

Not until the final tercet does La Roque bring in the amorous aspect of inconstancy: his poem celebrates change as a cosmic principle, not as mere infidelity. Like the devotional poets of the period, he conceives the world to be a domain of perpetual motion, where the sun, the seasons, the heavens, the earth, the sea are "emportez" and "agitez" by the ceaseless progression of time, which undermines even the resistance of solid rock. In this sonnet, as in Durand's "Stances," the power of Inconstancy seems to rival that of the Godhead. By using Alexandrines, La Roque obtains a greater rhythmic sweep than Du Perron's light decasyllabics allow; coupled with the thematic expansion, this metrical dilation almost creates the impression of a sacred hymn, ample and majestic. The opening line, with its vigorous sonority, recalls the initial verse of the

[42] Included in his *Oeuvres*, p. 202.

"Stances à l'Inconstance": "Esprit des beaux esprits, vagabonde Inconstance..." Durand's poem was published only two years after La Roque's; perhaps Durand had the older poet's verse in mind.

Apart from this metrical detail, the "Stances à l'Inconstance" show little evidence of La Roque's influence. Certain broad similarities obviously pertain: the universal vision of inconstancy as the central principle of nature, and the hymnic solemnity of the versification. On these counts Durand definitely belongs to the "family" of La Roque rather than Du Perron. But the psychological inconstancy repeatedly analyzed by Montaigne, and which finds a slight echo in Du Perron (cf. the verses quoted earlier), is virtually absent from La Roque's variation on the theme. As far as the human element is concerned, La Roque thinks only in terms of amorous infidelity; though he widens the outer dominion of Inconstancy to include all of nature, he does not allow her inner reign to reach its Montaignian dimensions, as a fundamental trait of the mind. By contrast, in the "Stances à l'Inconstance," inner instability and external change form a continuous whole; like Montaigne, Durand considers the one to be a reflection of the other, both equally a part of the universal "mutation et branle" (*Essais*, edn. cit., p. 589).

An even more obvious difference between La Roque's sonnet and Durand's *stances* lies in the verse form itself. As noted earlier, Du Perron's decasyllabics complement the lightness and frivolity of his poem, whereas La Roque's Alexandrines create a solemn, hymnic effect. In both cases, the metrical possibilities are well exploited. On the other hand, La Roque's use of the sonnet-form raises questions which are both complex and problematic. To this reader at least, after the majesty of the preceding lines, the request of the final tercet sounds trivial, anticlimactic. This *chute* is introduced through the sudden use of "conversational style," launched by the colloquial phrase "Hé donc?" The effect is furthered in the rest of the tercet by suppressed caesuras, rhythmic unevenness, and loose, casual syntax. Like the opening invocation, this is still direct address, but it has shifted from hyerbolic worshipfulness to flippant familiarity. While it is dangerous to second-guess intentions, it could be argued that the poet wished to convey this sense of disproportion – such "deflating" tricks are current in the period, and can often be observed in the *pointes* which end a sonnet. In any case, the fall of tone achieved here is certainly consonant with a parodic strategy, that of the mock encomium: if Du Perron hints at irony through lightness, La Roque implies it by means of anticlimax.

In the "Stances à l'Inconstance," Durand gives the hymnic potential of the invocation to Inconstancy its full scope: not only through the thematic expansion noted above, but also through the choice of the meter and stanzaic form which perfectly embody that expansion and allow it to flourish. Like La Roque, he opts for the Alexandrine, with its broadly flowing rhythm; but like Du Perron, he casts his poem in *stances*, which permit an unlimited extension. By combining Alexandrine with *stance*, he obtains the ideal breadth and length for his theme. Still, it would be specious to attribute the choice to Durand's personal taste alone. Though the five-line strophe chosen by Durand was less common than the six-line variety, *stances* in Alexandrines were common at the time – apart from the sonnet, this verse-form is probably the most characteristic of the age. In his *Geschichte der Ode and der Stances...* Dieter Janik has traced the rapid rise of the latter's popularity at the end of the sixteenth century (see pp. 127-38). By the early seventeenth century, Alexandrine *stances* were easily the most current of longer strophic forms.

No matter how strong the conventions, it is always possible for the poet to transform the inherited materials. This principle has often been illustrated in studies of Ronsard and Du Bellay, whose virtual translations of an Italian original frequently surpass the model in craftsmanship and expressive power. At the end of Chapter I, I showed how a stock theme like the invocation to Sleep lends itself to highly divergent variations, owing to an evolution in the global style of the period as well as to individual diversity within that style. Durand's "Stances à l'Inconstance" offer a particularly striking example of this process of transformation: not only are the theme and versification strictly conventional, the poem is a virtual recasting of a work by Pierre Motin. Despite this ostensible lack of "originality," Durand completely activates a potential which remains only latent in Motin: the "Stances à l'Inconstance" are like a translation, not from one language to another, but from diffuseness to intensity. Suddenly, the inconstancy theme takes on its full meaning; and in a single poem, Durand crystallizes the predominant insight of an epoch.

Motin's lengthy "Inconstance," which wends its way through fifteen six-line stanzas, first appeared in the *Muses francoises ralliées* of 1603;[43] its date of publication precedes that of Durand's "Stances à l'Inconstance" by eight years. Given that in 1603 Motin, a frequently published poet, was thirty-seven years old, and Durand, at eighteen years of age, had not yet published at all, it is safe to assume that "Inconstance" antedates the "Stances à l'Inconstance" in composition as well. The general similarities between the two poems are hardly unexpected. Both address Inconstancy as the supreme goddess of the universe, promising the poet's joyous submission to her law of constant change; both celebrate infidelity as the only way of freeing oneself from the pains of love, arguing that if women are incorrigibly unfaithful, then men must follow suit; both employ the motifs of atomistic flux, the *tableau fantastique*, Aeolus, and the instability of thought. These thematic parallels can easily be ascribed to the conventions of the genre; but the literal resemblance between certain passages is too close to be dismissed as mere coincidence.

Some examples:

MOTIN: [Toy] Qui habites par tout & n'as point de sejour...

DURAND: Deesse qui par tout et nulle part demeure...

MOTIN: L'on y verra la mer & les ondes esmeuës,
L'arc avec ses esclairs, son tonnerre & ses nuës,
Le feu prompt & leger vers le Ciel aspirant...

Des fantosmes, des vents, des songes des Chimeres,
Sablons tousjours mouvans, tourbillons & poussieres...

DURAND: Les femmes et les vents ensemble s'y verront.

Les sables de la mer, les orages, les nuës,
Les feux que font en l'air les tonnantes chaleurs,
Les flammes des esclairs plustost mortes que veuës,
Les peintures du Ciel à nos yeux incogneuës...

MOTIN: Et si je le pouvois, j'y peindrois ma pensée,
Mais elle est trop soudain de mon esprit passée,
Car je ne pense plus à ce que je pensois.

---

[43] I use the text as reprinted in *Le Cabinet des Muses*, vol. I (1619), pp. 67-72.

DURAND: Je peindrois volontiers mes legeres pensees,
Mais desja le pensant mon penser est changé;
Ce que je tiens m'eschappe, et les choses passees
Tousjours par le present se tiennent effacees...

MOTIN: Et si pour tour le monde il n'est qu'une seule ame,
L'Ame de tout le monde est le seul mouvement.

DURAND: Si la terre pesante en sa base est contrainte,
C'est par le mouvement des atosmes divers...
Et les saisons font voir que ta Majesté saincte
Est l'ame qui soustient le corps de l'Univers.

MOTIN: Le Ciel m'est un exemple à ma flame legere,
Est-il rien de plus beau & de plus inconstant?

DURAND: [Deesse]...qui fais que les Cieux se tournent à toute heure,
Encor qu'il ne soit rien ny si grand, ny si beau.

Not only do these snippets illustrate the close textual similarities between the two poems: I would submit that they also reveal a disparity in verbal concentration. Such reactions are inevitably subjective to some degree: there is no real way to "demonstrate" that the simpler songs from Shakespeare's plays are richer in poetic texture than an advertising jingle, in the way a scientist can prove a principle of physics. I am not even making a relative value judgment, because I recognize that Motin's diffuseness creates an illustrative effect all its own, which only becomes apparent in the full text (like Du Perron's, much too long to be reproduced here). It is always unfair to compare single verses taken out of context, because their impact may depend on a global poetic strategy. Certain lines and passages in Motin's poem probably serve the same function as that of the final tercet in La Roque's: a drop from exaltation to banality underlines the irony of the mock encomium. In fact Durand employs a similar technique in the central passage of the "Stances à l'Inconstance." Given the predilection for intensity of expression in the twentieth century, it is not surprising that this is the one poem by Durand which has found favor with most readers; but for the same reason, many of them have found the "lowering of poetic tone" in that particular passage a disappointment. I will return to this topic in the following section.

Motin's careful preparation of an ultimate "puncturing tactic" may be readily observed in the first strophe of "Inconstance," where an array of rhetorical devices lends the opening invocation an air of hymnic grandeur:

> Toy qui gouvernes seule & le Ciel & la Terre,
> Qui faits diversement le repos & la guerre,
> Qui habites par tout & n'as point de sejour.
> Je te revere, ô Saincte, & Deesse inconstance,
> Arbitre des humains contraire à l'esperance,
> Et la fidelle seur de Fortune & d'Amour.

The emphatic *Toy* launches the apostrophe with solemn formality, and its momentum is carried forward by anaphora ("Toy qui.../ Qui.../ Qui...") and parallel construction (three dependent clauses). The hieratic tone is further enhanced by the three symmetrically paired opposites, which unfold in triadic expansion; the last and longest of them occupies all of line 3. Expanding progression also characterizes the vocatives and appositions of lines 4-6; in line 4, the passage from "Saincte" to "Deesse" marks a semantic intensification.

If all these features increase the magnificence of the invocation, other factors do just the reverse. On closer inspection, the antonyms of the first lines seem jeeringly mechanical. Had it been metrically possible, Motin might have been tempted to couple "paix" with "guerre" – the usual antonyms – just as he had joined "Ciel" with "Terre"; but by inserting the vaguer word "repos," he makes the conventional dichotomy fall even flatter. The adverb "diversement" underlines the diffuse, meandering quality of the lines. The rhyme of "guerre" with "Terre" further vitiates their intensity, since the pairing provides neither antithesis (even in the mild form of a standard dichotomy) nor reinforcing parallelism. The same countercurrents reappear throughout the poem – for example, take line 76: "Ainsi je m'affranchis de martel & de flame." The blacksmith image is so desultory that it reads like an incongruous juxtaposition of objects. Motin often achieves a similar effect by introducing a colorless expression at a moment of climax: for instance, the phrase "fidelle soeur" in line 6 above, which ends the grandiose first strophe on a sardonically banal note.

These "puncturing" devices could be ascribed to a simple lack of competence; but given the tradition of the mock encomium, one must judge them carefully. Motin plays not only with flatness, but also with exaggeration: it is the essence of satire alternately to inflate and deflate its subject. The overblown apostrophe of line 4, for example, underscores the irony of the panegyric. Similarly, the long *enumeratio* which spans strophes 6-7 (see below) crowds so many objects together that the accumulation loses its force, subsiding into derision. Even without the high-flown rhetoric, the things listed possess a humor all their own.

The strophes (5-8) in which Motin develops the *tableau fantastique* motif arguably constitute the most effective passage in his poem, and it is no accident that Jean Rousset singled them out for inclusion in his anthology (vol. I, pp. 72-3). It is here also that Motin most directly influenced Durand's version of the invocation to Inconstancy:

> Je veux dans un tableau la Nature pourtraire,
> J'y peindray la Fortune & le change ordinaire
> De tout ce qui se void sous la voute des cieux,
> L'Amour y sera peint d'une forme nouvelle,
> Non comme de coustume, avec une double aisle,
> Je luy en donne autant come Argus avoit d'yeux.
> L'on y verra la mer & les ondes esmeuës,
> L'arc avec ses esclairs, son tonnerre & ses nuës,
> Le feu prompt & leger vers le Ciel aspirant,
> Girouettes, moulins, oiseaux de tous plumages,
> Papillons, Cerfs, Dauphins, & des Conins sauvages
> Qui perdent de leurs trous la memoire en courant.
> Des fantosmes, des vents, des songes des Chimeres,
> Sablons tousjours mouvans, tourbillons & poussieres,
> Des pailles, des rameaux, & des fueilles des bois,
> Et si je le pouvois, j'y peindrois ma pensée,
> Mais elle est trop soudain de mon esprit passée,
> Car je ne pense plus à ce que je pensois.
> Je veux qu'en ce tableau soit ma place arrestée,
> Aupres de moy tirez Achelois & Prothée,
> Faisant comme semblant de me ceder la leur,
> Et lors si de mon coeur apparoist la figure,
> C'est trop peu de couleurs de toute la peinture,
> A peindre sa couleur qui n'a point de couleur.

Far more than Du Perron had done, Motin jumbles together the most unlikely objects and abstractions; whereas the former's "painting" remains sedate and contained, that of the latter resembles the broad ceiling-frescoes of Baroque art. As in such a fresco, symbolic figures ("Amour," "Prothée") and teasing details ("pailles," "Papillons") emerge from a turbulence of atmospheric effects ("esclairs," "nuës," "tourbillons"). The picture also contains odd half-images which could only be rendered by words: for example, the striking evocation of animals "Qui perdent de leurs trous la memoire en courant" (line 36). This type of language occupies a peculiar no man's land between the abstract and the concrete. It does not, as in the familiar process of metaphor, establish a continuity between the two; instead, they are simply swept along together in an on-going verbal motion.

The blurring effect which Motin creates by such means provides the perfect medium for his theme: his poetic technique also reflects the instability of sublunary existence. Throughout the poem, disconnected metaphors of the type just described appear alongside highly conventional similes like that of lines 23-4, where the lover's liberation is compared to Theseus' escape from the labyrinth: "Et par toy qui me sers comme un fil à Thesée,/ J'eschappe du Dedale où j'estois esgaré." At times Motin renews hackneyed mythological allusions by unexpectedly juxtaposing them: in lines 28-30 for example, he depicts an Amor who possesses as many wings as the eyes of Argus. Thematic richness alternates inconsistently with flatness; and in the end, deflation triumphs. After accumulating the images of his *tableau fantastique*, Motin seems to erase them: he concludes that there is no way to paint his changing thoughts (lines 40-2) [44] or to portray his inconstant heart: "C'est trop peu de couleurs de toute la peinture,/ A peindre sa couleur qui n'a point de couleur" (lines 47-8). On one level, these Montaignian lines are a form of hyperbole; but they resolve into the negative notions of colorlessness and loss of direction. Here again, the words waver teasingly between the concrete and the abstract, between image and blankness, between exaggeration and denial.

The inconstancy of Motin's poetic language is mirrored in the looseness of the poem's larger structures. Each strophe virtually

[44] Motin develops this conceit at length in another poem, the "Stances" included by Rousset in his *Anthologie* (vol. I, p. 91). For other examples of this Montaigne-inspired *topos*, which is highly characteristic of late Renaissance verse, see ibid., pp. 92-7.

reads like a distinct paragraph in a rambling treatise: strophes 2-4, for instance, could be rearranged in any permutation without seriously altering the sense of the whole; one strophe does not call for the next. Only after strophe 5 does one encounter some development of argument and imagery across the barrier of stanzaic separation. Though strophes 5-8 derive a certain coherence from the *tableau fantastique* motif, it would be wrong to assume that this episode represents a turning point. The "painting of thoughts" theme which is introduced in the middle of strophe 7 does prepare the shift to astrological musing in strophe 9 by focusing on the inconstancy of the poet's own mind; yet the rest of the poem wanders on as before.

Without seeking a continuity of argument between each stanza, can any rough structural divisions be discovered in "Inconstance"? Strophes 1-4 could loosely be called an apostrophe, in that they consist of verses addressed to Inconstancy. The relative cohesion of *stances* 5-8 has already been discussed. Strophes 9-15 might be said to form a third section, since they evoke the amorous inconstancy of the poet and of lovers in general. But this would be stretching the point. The consistency of both the first and the third "sections" is so slight as to be negligible; the strophes of the third in particular have little in common but inconstancy itself. The poem drifts to its conclusion without ever fixing on anything, like the flotsam and jetsam of its imagery. As the random bits and pieces succeed one another, they seem to cancel out what went before; in a sense, they demonstrate what Motin says in the penultimate *stance*:

> Non, mon ame est tousjours une table d'attente,
> Et mon coeur un mirouër qui tousjours represente
> Un pourtraict aussi-tost pour un autre effacé. (lines 82-4)

Maintaining a stream of whimsical vagueness through ninety lines is an achievement all its own: "metamimetically,"[45] Motin expresses inconstancy through the formless divagation of the poem itself. He aptly evokes the dissolving shapes of clouds in the last two verses: "Le Ciel m'est un exemple à ma flame legere,/ Est-il rien de plus beau & de plus inconstant?"

---

[45] See the definition in Chapter II, note 42.

Like Motin, Durand also sets out to illustrate the principle that – in the former's words – "L'Ame de tout le monde est le seul mouvement" (line 54). "Inconstance" portrays that movement in playful gusts; Durand's "Stances à l'Inconstance" convey it as a surging, continuous swell. The difference between the two is typified by the fact that Motin closes his poem with a light-hearted question, while Durand ends his with a powerful affirmation of "change immortel."

The eleven strophes of the "Stances" can be divided into three distinct sections: the invocation of universal Inconstancy in 1-3, the portrayal of human inconstancy in 4-7, and the sacrifice to Inconstancy in 8-11 – though the final stanza also occupies a place apart. In the first three strophes, the hymnic character of the "Stances à l'Inconstance" immediately captures the reader's attention:

> Esprit des beaux esprits, vagabonde Inconstance,
> Qu'Æole Roy des vens avec l'onde conceut
> Pour estre de ce monde une seconde essence,
> Reçoy ces vers sacrez à ta seule puissance
> Aussi bien que mon ame autrefois te receut.
>
> Deesse qui par tout et nulle part demeure,
> Qui preside à nos jours, et nous porte au tombeau,
> Qui fais que le desir d'un instant naisse et meure,
> Et qui fais que les Cieux se tournent à toute heure,
> Encor qu'il ne soit rien ny si grand, ny si beau.
>
> Si la terre pesante en sa base est contrainte,
> C'est par le mouvement des atosmes divers;
> Sur le dos de Neptun ta puissance est dépeinte,
> Et les saisons font voir que ta Majesté saincte
> Est l'ame qui soustient le corps de l'Univers.

S. A. Varga observes that "ce qui nous frappe tout d'abord, c'est le ton grave, l'allure solennelle de ce poème" (p. 254), and Pizzorusso speaks of its "ampio respiro poetico" (p. 45). Tardieu asserts that "la ferveur du ton, le vocabulaire ('Seconde essence'... 'ta Majesté saincte', etc...), le *tempo* majestueux de cette sorte de prière lui donnent, par moment, l'allure d'une poésie sacrée" (p. 193). Undeniably, the "Stances à l'Inconstance" begin with a solemnity of tone normally reserved for religious verse; the deflating effects which typify the mock encomium are used sparingly, if at all.

As Yves Bonnefoy remarks (p. III), “voici d’un coup l’abstraction s’évapore, les mots retrouvent un poids et la parole une gravité qui démentent le vide là même où... l’idée en est formulée de façon aussi précise qu’illimitée...”

A grave music inheres from the outset in the prosodic density of Durand’s poem, which is particularly rich in vocalic colour. S. A. Varga has noted the “résonance sonore des voyelles nasales an, on” (p. 255) in the initial strophe. In *Le Vers français* (p. 282), Maurice Grammont claims that such vowels generally create a tendency toward “lenteur,” especially when they are “sombres.” Without subscribing wholesale to his fanciful theories, I can admit a certain relevance here. Throughout the stanza, the first hemistich of each verse begins on the upbeat, emphasizing the more sprightly movement of its *voyelles claires*; while in each of the second hemistichs, the reassertion of the *sombre* tonality seems to produce a *rallentando*. A masterly example of this appears in the last verse, where the unstressed expression “Aussi bien que mon” suddenly come to rest on the long *a* of “ame,” throwing the substantive into relief as well as bringing out the final *voyelle sombre* of “autrefois.” The entire poem is full of similar phonetic subtleties, but it would be tedious to analyze them all in detail; besides, they take on their true value only in conjunction with rhetorical and thematic elements.

The aural condensation of the “Stances à l’Inconstance” does not impede their flow; on the contrary, it combines with the onrushing rhythm to create an irresistible momentum. Its force can already be felt in the virtual suppression of the caesura in lines 2-6; throughout the poem, the verse rarely falls into two distinct hemistichs – instead, each line traces a single, overarching movement. This steady, large expansion no doubt contributes to what Pizzorusso calls the “ampio respiro” of the poem; but it would lose its impact without the syntactic reinforcement, which parallels the prosody on another plane. Durand refrains from making immediately explicit, as does Motin, the direct address to Inconstancy: like La Roque, he delays the rounding out of the grammatical structure – even though the poem’s title foreshadows it. His first three lines are really an extended vocative; but only at the word “Reçoy” does this become completely obvious. The resulting ambiguity gives the invocation a mysterious quality of suspense: that “holding of breath” – and its subsequent release – seems to join all the elements of the strophe into a single respiration. The next two stanzas achieve the same effect on twice as large a scale: both are subsumed into one syntactic and rhetorical movement. The vocative "Deesse," with its multiple dependent clauses, maintains all of strophe 2 in a state of postponed completion. Judging by the punctuation of the original edition, a full stop at the end of line 10, that completion never takes place; but it seems clear that the tension carries over into strophe 3, where it is partially relaxed by the appearance of an independent clause.

This redoubled apostrophe, in which the second and third stanzas form a rhetorical enlargement of the first, endows Durand's opening invocation with a dynamic unity. By way of contrast, one may compare it to the corresponding passage in Motin's "Inconstance": while strophe 1 of the latter begins an invocation to the goddess, strophe 2 already strays off on the ancillary theme of the constant lover's woes; strophe 3 pays more attention to Amor than to Inconstancy, and strophe 4 – though it hails her once again – mainly concerns the poet's own quest for enlightenment. In the "Stances à l'Inconstance," prosodic, syntactic, and rhetorical cohesion are complemented by thematic rigor. In the first three strophes Durand never deviates from his hymn to the goddess of change, which gradually builds up to a resounding climax; above all, he avoids the discordant subjective note introduced by Motin. Inconstancy is celebrated as the offspring of the two most capricious elements, air and water (line 2);[46] her powers appear to be second only to God's ("seconde essence," line 3). Like Him, she is omnipresent but unlocalized (line 6), "presiding" over man from the cradle to the grave (line 7). She occupies no distinct place because she represents the very principle of movement, whether that of human wit (line 1) and desire (line 8), or that of the heavens themselves (lines 9-10). In the final strophe of the invocation, Durand places all of creation under her empire. Reflecting the current popularity of Lucretian theories,[47] he asserts that even the earth

[46] As Varga has pointed out (p. 255), the theme of amorous inconstancy being "born" of the sea also appears in sonnet IX of the *Méditations*; but there the analogy with the birth of Venus is made much more explicit. Cf. La Fontan, *Les jours et les nuicts* (1606), fol. 36 ro: "on nous asseure à tous que le sexe fragile n'a rien de constant que l'inconstance, non sans cause nous auroit on peint Venus fille de la mer, si ce n'est pour nous representer que ses nieces estoient comme les ondes tousjours roulantes, tousjours courantes & perpetuellement agitees des vents de leurs legeres opinions..."

[47] Cf. Eleonore Belowski, *Lukrez in der französischen Literatur der Renaissance*.

consists of atoms in motion (lines 11-12). Inconstancy also reigns over water, the second heaviest of the elements (line 13); by pushing the point, the reader can find the other two as well. Like the waters of the ocean, the aerial sphere fluctuates (line 14): weather changes with the seasons, which signal the passing of the year. Line 15 identifies Inconstancy with "l'ame qui soustient le corps de l'Univers," possibly a distant allusion to the empyrean fire. The references to time will be taken up in the following section of the poem; the four elements will reappear more clearly in section three.

In the opening invocation Pizzorusso perceives a direct reference to the Catholic liturgy: "L'Inconstanza è salutata e celebrata come una Divinità, come la 'seconda essenza' ('internum principium ex quo modi isti exsurgunt et cui insunt') di un mondo dominato dal movimento" (p. 46). By making Inconstancy the "ame de l'Univers," Durand comes close to substituting her for God Himself.[48] Bernd Rathman points out that the idea of a "seconde essence" of the Deity, associated with the generation of movement, may have its source in the Hermetic tradition.[49] In lines 4-5 the poet offers up his psalm to the goddess ("vers sacrez à ta seule puissance") in return for the saving grace his soul has received from her. Before leaping to Warnke's conclusion that such lines comprise a "blasphemous application of Eucharistic imagery" (p. 35), the reader should recall that the extravagance of the invocation is perfectly in accord with the conventions of the mock encomium. Along with the hyperbolic "inflation" of the genre comes an equally characteristic "deflating" touch: the first phrase of the poem is a play on words, and its tribute to Inconstancy as the quintessence of wit cuts her cosmic dimensions down to size. Even so, most critics who have written about the work agree that the overall impression created by the opening is one of sacredness and grandeur. If not blasphemous,

---

[48] Cf. Ode II, where Uranie is indirectly identified as "des premiers corps/ L'essentielle intelligence" (p. 51).

[49] Cf. this passage from Hermes Trismegistus (quoted in Rathmann, p. 37): "L'Intelligence, le Dieu mâle et femelle qui est la vie et la lumière, engendre par la parole une autre intelligence créatrice, le Dieu du feu et du fluide... La pensée créatrice, unie à la raison, enveloppant les cercles et leur imprimant une rotation rapide, ramena ses créations sur elle-même et les fit tourner de leur principe à leur fin comme entre deux limites inaccessibles, car là où tout finit, tout commence éternellement." Jamyn propounds a similar male-female cosmogony in his "La Louage du Blanc," edn. cit., pp. 285-6.

the religious allusions are at least ambiguous. Durand will echo them again in the final verses of the poem.

Like the three strophes of the invocation, strophes 4-7 compose a distinct rhetorical and thematic section:

> Nostre esprit n'est que vent, et comme un vent volage,
> Ce qu'il nomme constance est un branle retif:
> Ce qu'il pense aujourd'huy demain n'est qu'un ombrage,
> Le passé n'est plus rien, le futur un nuage,
> Et ce qu'il tient present, il le sent fugitif.
>
> Je peindrois volontiers mes legeres pensees,
> Mais desja le pensant mon penser est changé;
> Ce que je tiens m'eschappe, et les choses passees
> Tousjours par le present se tiennent effacees,
> Tant à ce changement mon esprit est rangé.
>
> Aussi depuis qu'à moy ta grandeur est unie,
> Des plus cruels desdains j'ay sceu me garantir;
> J'ay gaussé les esprits, dont la fole manie
> Esclave leur repos sous une tyrannie,
> Et meurent à leur bien pour vivre au repentir.
>
> Entre mille glaçons je sçay feindre une flame,
> Entre mille plaisirs je fais le soucieux;
> J'en porte une à la bouche, une autre dedans l'ame,
> Et tiendrois à peché, si la plus belle Dame
> Me retenoit le coeur plus long temps que les yeux.

This middle section is divided into two symmetrical parts of two stanzas each. The first part continues the general reflections of the preceding invocation, focusing this time on the inconstancy of human thought; in strophe 5, the lyric *je* appears more as a prototype of that inconstancy than as an individual agent. The introduction of *je* in this more general sense provides a smooth transition to the second part of the section, in which the abstract principles receive their practical application in the poet's amorous life.

I have already noted that the "theoretical" half of the passage points to a Montaignian influence – not necessarily a direct one, since (more or less) philosophical variations on this theme were common at the time. Varga calls it "une démonstration paradoxale, philosophique et lègére à la fois" (p. 256); but it also has a tinge of melancholy. Contemporary readers would have been especially sensitive to such undertones, since they were used to encountering similar reflexions in devotional laments over earthly transience.[50] The cunningly emphatic rhymes ("volage"-"ombrage"-"nuage," "pensees"-"passees," etc.) and the marked antitheses ("aujourd-huy"-"demain," "tient present"-"sent fugitif," "se tiennent effacees," etc.) are joined with an airy, rapid prosody, in which *p*'s, *t*'s, and *voyelles claires* predominate. Again I would not want to rely too much on such questionable categories, but the "clear" timbre here contrasts appreciably with the *sombre* phonetics of the preceding section. Despite its lightness of touch, Yves Bonnefoy rightly stresses the centrality of this passage in Durand's "théorie du langage" (p. VIII), "devançant les principes d'incertitude de la physique moderne ou les inquisitions déconstructionnistes. Toute pensée dépend des mots qui la pensent, on ne peut l'interpréter qu'en révélant ou apercevant l'excès du signifiant, comme nous dirions, sur la chose, autrement dit ce qu'a d'illusoire le signifié" (p. VII).

Pizzorusso remarks reproachfully that "il tono poetico si abbassa" (p. 47) in strophes 6-7, where the poet evokes his amorous inconstancy: but in fact the lowering of tone should not be understood as a negative factor. As I have repeated throughout this book, when poets persist in employing a certain procedure, there is some reason to assume that it represents a strategy, not a deficiency. These strophes stand at the crux of the "Stances à l'Inconstance," and their frivolity deflates the tension in a way which is typical of the late Renaissance. They manifest a "poetics of inconstancy" which delights in abrupt shifts of style and perspective. Here the "puncturing" tactic also works well in the context of a mock encomium. All the same, the gay irony is loaded: words like "manie," "Esclave," "tyrannie," "repentir," and "peché" color the passage

---

[50] Cf. for example these lines from Le Blanc's "Poeme, sur la vicissitude des choses mondaines" (part II, p. 13):

> De mesme qu'une vague est d'une autre poussee,
> Comme une autre survient esgalement pressee
> D'une qui luy succede, & qu'une autre arrivant
> Pousse encore derechef celles qui vont devant:
> Le temps d'un pied semblable empoudre sa carriere,
> Le present fugitif met le passé derriere,
> Et, suyvi du futur qui talonne ses pas,
> Un autre court apres qui jadis n'estoit pas.

with a hint of seriousness, even despair.[51] The last two words in particular bring the (ir)religious undercurrents closer to the surface. Durand's poem does not subside into random subjective motifs, like the latter half of Motin's "Inconstance"; instead he concentrates the theme of amorous inconstancy into a brief personal accent, placed between two larger visions. In a sense, strophes 6-7 illustrate the dictum "reculer pour mieux sauter," as the subsequent stanzas amply prove. But in their central position, they also represent a "hollow heart," an emblem of declining Petrarchism as a whole; as such they contribute to a deeper design, which reveals itself only in the poem's closing lines.

The third and final section of the "Stances à l'Inconstance" consists of four strophes. In contrast to those of section two, the strophes of section three do not fall into obvious subdivisions; as in section one, they form an overarching phrase. It is as though the rhythmic momentum which reached its first high point at the end of strophe 3 were taken up again and carried to an even greater climax; after the fervent invocation to the goddess, the still more fervent sacrifice:

> Doncques fille de l'air de cent plumes couverte,
> Qui de serf que j'estois m'a mis en liberté,
> Je te fais un present des restes de ma perte,
> De mon amour changé, de sa flame deserte,
> Et du folastre object qui m'avoit arresté.
>
> Je te fais un present d'un tableau fantastique,
> Où l'amour et le jeu par la main se tiendront:
> L'oubliance, l'espoir, le desir frenetique,
> Les sermens parjurez, l'humeur melancolique,
> Les femmes et les vents ensemble s'y verront.

[51] For a similar passage where this is not the case, cf. Du Pin-Pager, *Les oeuvres poétiques* (1630), p. 104:

> ...que c'est vivre heureux que vivre sans maistresse,
> Estre absolu sur soy, gouverner ses desirs,
> Cueillir sans rendre compte un monde de plaisirs,
> Sans soupçon que jamais on vous nomme infidelle
> Si l'humeur vous en dit courtiser la plus belle,
> Luy dresser des autels luy consacrer des voeux,
> Ores baiser ses mains, or prendre ses cheveux,
> Feindre de passion autant que l'esperance
> D'accomplir vos dessins vous donne d'asseurance.

Les sables de la mer, les orages, les nuës,
Les feux que font en l'air les tonnantes chaleurs,
Les flammes des esclairs plustost mortes que veuës,
Les peintures du Ciel à nos yeux incogneuës,
A ce divin tableau serviront de couleurs.

Pour un temple sacré je te donne ma Belle,
Je te donne son coeur pour en faire un autel,
Pour faire ton sejour tu prendras sa cervelle,
Et moy je te seray comme un prestre fidelle,
Qui passera ses jours en un change immortel.

The structure of the final section resumes and expands the double apostrophe of the first. In strophe 8 the poet invokes Inconstancy once again, offering up his "amour changé"; in strophes 9-10 he presents her with another ex-voto of thanks, the "tableau fantastique." The redoubled construction (one stanza to two) corresponds exactly to that of the poem's opening invocation. In strophe 1 the poet had also made a gift to the goddess: "Recoy ces vers..."; and the listing of her attributes in strophes 2-3 is mirrored by the *enumeratio* of the painting's motifs in strophes 9-10. But in the final section Durand adds a third member to the series, raising the tension another degree. The reduction from two strophes back to one might lead the reader to expect instead a fall in intensity; but after the enumeration of nouns in strophes 9-10, the seven verbs of strophe 11 act as a last burst of energy, toward which the preceding images converge. In the final stanza, the poet heaps up further offerings to Inconstancy in rapid succession: they include not only his beloved, but also himself.

Here one touches on another level of intensification which the third section brings to the poem. In strophe 1 the poet affirms that he has received Inconstancy into his soul (line 5), but his invocation keeps in the main to an "objective" celebration of her powers; only in section two (strophes 4-7) does a "subjective" element come to the fore, especially in the playful avowal of amorous inconstancy. In the final section the objective and subjective spheres are fused at a higher plane of perception. Just as the poet has accepted Inconstancy into his heart, he is now received into hers; merged with her powers, he occupies the center of a world in flux. The final section brings into play the entire spectrum of reality, external and internal;

in an apotheosis of the "poetics of inconstancy," the trivial mingles with the sublime, and the inanimate with the divine.

The thematic progression builds up to its climax with well-ordered gradualness. It begins with the frivolous remains of the poet's love: his abandoned passion ("flame deserte," line 39) and its "folastre object" (line 40) compose his lowest sacrifice to Inconstancy. These phrases pointedly negate the double shibboleth of the Petrarchist ideal, the lover's burning adoration of an "objet de plus haute vertu." The former "serf" (line 37) can now present a better gift: his ex-voto portrays the aimless sorrows and deluded hopes (lines 42-3) he has renounced; like the votive paintings hung in churches, the "tableau fantastique" (and the poem itself) illustrates the sickness as a memorial to the cure. The first half of the description (strophe 9) consists almost entirely of human, "subjective" elements, which range from the light-hearted to the serious. Paradoxically, invisible abstractions are visibly depicted; in this context, innocuous expressions assume a disquieting concreteness: "l'amour et le jeu *par la main se tiendront*" (line 47), "Les femmes et les vents *ensemble s'y verront*" (line 50). In a sense, this type of imagery represents an extreme development of *ut pictura poesis*, an esthetic ideal which enjoyed great favor in the Renaissance. But such phrases also introduce a note of comic mockery. The insubstantial is made substantial; and conversely, the substantial becomes insubstantial. Reification equals erasure. Love is only a game, and women are not just capricious as the wind – they exist in the same sense as wind, reduced to an elusive feature of nature. This paired equivalence is underlined by the phrases "par la main" and "ensemble," by the virtual suppression of the caesura in both lines, and by the fact that they rhyme with each other.

At the end of strophe 9, the word "vents" already signals the transition to the second half of the "tableau fantastique" evocation, which harks back to the cosmic imagery of the poem's beginning. Here again, there is a significant shift in register: from the lower elements to the higher.[52] In the opening invocation, fire appeared very indirectly, at best; but in strophe 10, it is the heaviest element, earth, which retreats into the background. Water, the next heaviest

[52] On the symbolic importance of the four elements in late Renaissance literature, see E. M. W. Tillyard, *The Elizabethan World Picture*, pp. 68-73. For a pronounced example of their use as images in love verse, cf. Le Masson, fol. 8 ro.

element, had also figured prominently in the first invocation, where Inconstancy was called the daughter of "Æole Roy des vens" and "l'onde" (line 2). But in the final section of the poem she is hailed exclusively as the "fille de l'air de cent plumes couverte" (line 36). Both water and earth are represented in strophe 10 by a single phrase, "Les sables de la mer" (line 46); after this brief allusion, the lighter elements take full possession of the scene. Steadily the vision rises from "orages" – which still imply a passage between ground and sky – to "nuës," which sail completely clear of the earth. In this realm of air the "feux" (line 47) and "flames" (line 48) of lightning introduce the final element with a vengeance; the near suppression of the caesura in both lines seems to emphasize the swiftness and energy of fire, while the repetition of the same image in different words creates a strange semantic "flash."

The last two verses of the strophe carry the vision even higher, to the empyrean sphere of "peintures du Ciel à nos yeux incogneuës" (line 49): as enjambment adds its hastening effect to that of the weak caesuras, the rhythmic sweep attains its climax. As at the end of strophe 9 a key word, "divin" (line 50), announces the shift to the central theme of the succeeding stanza: the union of the self with the divine. "Dieu est mort," writes Bonnefoy (p. x) of these lines, "c'est bien ce que disent déjà les *Stances à l'Inconstance*, mais le divin lui survit, c'est simplement ce qui paraît, disparaît, se métamorphose: ce qui 'est', pourquoi pas, du moment que les mots ne feignent plus que cette apparence ait substance." Further on I will return to the question of the religious overtones, which are best discussed in reference to thematic trends. On the intratextual level, Bonnefoy is justified when he asserts, in the continuation of the passage just cited: "Qu'est-ce que la poésie? demande Durand. Aller si près des choses impermanentes du monde que cette impermanence même se découvre substance, se fasse joie; et de ce fait le poème sera la nouvelle écriture sainte." At the end of the "Stances," the "peché" of a deluded belief in constancy is finally redeemed by faith in Inconstancy: the beloved is an altar, the poet is a priest – and by analogy, his verses assume the role of a liturgical text.

Strophe 11 can be compared to the closing cadence of a musical work: the onward rush comes to a halt with a series of chords. They are figured by five resounding verses in which the caesuras are still unstressed, but where the end of each verse is strongly marked: not only by the regular punctuation, but by the five-fold rhyme on *el(le)*. This rhyme is the prosodic master stroke of the poem. The thematic elements of the preceding two sections are fused in the third; rhythmically and tonally as well, the final section combines the solemn momentum of section one with the rapidity of section two. But the last strophe of the poem creates its own frame of reference, both thematically and prosodically. A precedent for its masculine-feminine rhyme on the same sound can be found only in strophe 5; since the latter concludes the first half of the second section of the "Stances," it stands at a midway point between the end of the poem (strophe 11) and its beginning (strophe 1). In relation to these two stanzas, the first and the fifth, strophe 11 takes on its full meaning.

Like those of strophe 11, the rhymes of strophe 5 are accentuated by regular end-punctuation in the original edition. The principal themes of section two as a whole converge in strophe 5: amid philosophical reflections on the inconstancy of human thought, the lyric *je* makes its first pronounced entry into the poem – though without the "personal" tone it will assume in the next two stanzas. The repetitive rhyme seems to symbolize the monotony of constant effacement, perpetual loss of track: a jejeune version of *aporia*. Despite the light-heartedness of treatment, this ceaseless round of emptiness – which consumes past, present, and future – cannot help but strike an undertone of futility, almost despair.[53] But the opening invocation had already announced the conversion of that vapidity into a positive force: line 5, which comprises the only allusion to the lyric *je* previous to strophe 5, proclaims the infusion of a godlike Inconstancy into the poet's soul.

In its dominant theme, strophe 11 refers back to strophe 1: once again, the *je* is united with the deity. Now the multiple recurrence of the nominative pronoun – as opposed to the weak pronominal adjective of line 5 – alters the balance of the union. The self no longer passively receives the divine (cf. "receut," line 5): it actively participates in the powers of the universe. Strophe 11 also harks back to strophe 5, by its metric similarity and by its "subjec-

[53] Mathieu-Castellani makes a sharp distinction between "l'inconstance noire" and "l'inconstance blanche" (see pp. 403-9, 508), denying that poets of the latter tendency (such as Durand, in her grouping) possess a "conscience tragique du monde" (p. 508). But the ultimate affirmation of the "Stances à l'Inconstance" must be understood against the background of "le desir frenetique,/ Les sermens parjurez, l'humeur melancolique" (lines 43-4) which are evoked in the poem. Cf. Bruzzi's contention that wherever it appears in Durand's verse, "la metafora della dissolvenza configur[a] nell'instabilità un senso tragico della vita" (p. 96). In fact, the tragic also forms only one aspect of the poet's vision.

tive," repeated use of *je*. In 5 the inconstancy of the mind is conceived as loss and effacement, while in 11 the poet willingly embraces that inconstancy, so that loss itself reemerges as a form of possession.[54] Because he embodies a universal principle, his emptiness becomes a plenitude: his own subjectivity is now "l'ame qui soustient le corps de l'Univers" (line 15). Even the frivolity of his amorous adventures is transformed – and here the importance of strophes 6-7 to the overall design reveals itself. The lover's sacrifice of his "folastre object" (line 40) assumes an almost macabre tone: the mistress is dismantled like a doll. But at the same time, she is hallowed. The human, virtually absent in section one, predominant in section two, merges in section three with the inanimate and the divine. The final strophe takes this development to its extreme conclusion: the human "subject" is "objectified" (as a "temple," an "autel"), but the reduction implies a consecration, as though the "subject-object illusion" had given way to a superior awareness.

Within that higher perception, the trivial can be experienced as the divine: its medium, the poet, is a "prestre fidelle" (line 54); the feminine gender of the adjective underscores his union with the "Belle." Not only does he praise the cosmic principle of change, he also "celebrates" (in both senses of the term) its incarnation in the human mind, the "cervelle" where Inconstancy finds an ultimate "sejour." This can only be understood as a paradox: in what is fleeting, habitation. The transience of strophe 5 takes on a new dimension. In the final line of the poem, the poet accedes to a deeper consciousness of time; by participating in the ceaseless inconstancy of thought and of the world, he knowingly lives out its "change immortel." As in states of religious ecstasy, the ephemeral and the eternal fuse.[55] The recurring rhymes on *el(le)* symbolize that fundamental unity: tolling like a bell, they measure a steady revolution around a central point, where change and permanence are one.

---

[54] Cf. R. J. Quinones' remarks about the spirit of "open comedy" in Renaissance literature: "The vision of open comedy does not look to the vanity of our dreams, but rather to their sufficiency and reality. Yet it does not cling to any notions of permanence. Those who belong in the world of open comedy accept things as naturally passing, but that does not detract from their pleasures, which they pursue and possess with gaiety and strength" (*The Renaissance Discovery of Time* [from the chapter on Montaigne], p. 213).

[55] In *The Late Renaissance and Mannerism* (p. 100), Linda Murray calls "the momentary movement caught and held" a typical device of Mannerist art; in a sense, the "Stances à l'Inconstance" represent a literary transposition of that device (see my Conclusion).

The devotional overtones in the "Stances à l'Inconstance" have prompted a number of critics to associate Durand with the *libertins*. Warnke bluntly avers, "I include Durand in the group on the basis of the implications of his poetry" (p. 34, note 41), by which he apparently means the "Stances" alone; as I mentioned earlier, he even goes so far as to claim that "the hymn opens with a blasphemous application of Eucharistic imagery" (p. 35). Tardieu speculates that "il serait... intéressant de savoir si E. Durand fut un esprit fort, un 'libertin'. Le fait qu'il ne nous ait laissé aucune poésie religieuse n'est, certes, pas un suffisant indice. Plus significatif, peut-être serait l'accent philosophique et presque matérialiste de ces stances où 'l'Inconstance', divinité abstraite, est pour ainsi dire mise à la place de Dieu..." (p. 193). For him the opening invocation possesses "l'allure d'une poésie sacrée, transposée dans une vision 'scientifique' de l'univers, héritée de Lucrèce" (loc. cit.).

On an ethical plane, S. A. Varga poses the problem as follows:

> L'inconstance est une notion morale. La façon grave dont elle est traitée ici, lui confère une auréole, une valeur qu'on ne saurait retrouver dans la plupart des charmants badinages que l'on consacre généralement à ce sujet. Est-ce dire qu'il faut y voir une manifestation de l'esprit libertin? Certains éléments, assez rares il est vrai, dans ses autres poèmes, nous engagent également à répondre par l'affirmative. En tout cas, on pourrait dire: oui, plutôt qu'autre chose, plutôt qu'un spécimen de poésie baroque ou précieuse. L'attitude est celle de Viau, des poètes à venir, plutôt que celle de d'Aubigné et des poètes du passé. (pp. 257-8)

In the last two sentences, chronology and terminology seem slightly muddled. Théophile was Durand's junior by a mere five years. His poems were already being circulated in manuscript by 1611, when the *Méditations* were published; like Durand, he staged an important ballet at Court in 1617.[56] He cannot be called a "poète à venir" in relation to Durand. The term "baroque" is usually applied to both Théophile and Durand, while "poésie précieuse" did not come to the fore until the 1620s. In reference to the date of Du-

[56] Cf. Jeanne Streicher, intro. to Theophile's *Oeuvres poétiques*, vol. I, pp. XIII, IX.

rand's death, the *Précieux* are the "poètes à venir." If Varga is alluding here to a phenomenon of style, his remarks are well taken; a few more observations along this line may help to clarify the question of Durand's *libertinage*.

Modern critics who have studied the "Stances à l'Inconstance" agree that in its rhapsodic power, the poem far surpasses other variations on the inconstancy theme. Sixteenth century versions of the *topos*, as well as those of Durand's immediate contemporaries, fall well behind his in intensity and complexity – two of the chief criteria in twentieth century esthetic judgements. La Roque and Motin alone, in a few of their verses, attain something of the hymnic tone of the "Stances." As for the other poets of the time, the reader only has to glance at Vauquelin des Yveteaux's or Lingendes's inconstancy poems to realize how vastly they differ from Durand's (see Rousset's *Anthologie*, vol. I, pp. 77-80, 87). Such "charmants badinages" as theirs – to borrow Varga's apt phrase – consist exclusively of the most nugatory motifs which occur in the "Stances à l'Inconstance": their subject is amorous inconstancy in its most jocose and limited sense. Durand's example did not exercise any perceptible influence on succeeding treatments of the theme, such as those of Frenicle (p. 149), Resneville (p. 244), Godard (Rousset, vol. I, pp. 94-7), or Scudéry (ibid., p. 105); all these poets continue the feather-headed vein of Vauquelin and Lingendes. The "Stances à l'Inconstance" mark the culmination of the inconstancy motif, after which it settles into facile preciosity and graceful wit.

All the same, the witty aspect is present in the "Stances à l'Inconstance" as well, and it would be misguided to interpret the poem exclusively as a subversive attack on accepted belief. After all, Inconstancy is addressed from the outset as the "Esprit des beaux esprits." I noted earlier that the very extravagance of the praise which Durand bestows on her can be understood as ironic exaggeration, and must be seen in the light of more straightforwardly comic versions like Motin's. The exceptional intricacy of the "Stances" may imply their ultimate joke: an ornate attempt to capture what is, by definition, impossible to grasp. In this context of wry anomaly, a brief reference to Lucretian atomism does not warrant suspicions of *libertin* materialism; atomistic notions were "in the air" at the time. Similarly, the pseudo-philosophical paradoxes dispersed throughout the poem belong to the stock-in-trade of current love poetry. In his sardonic "Pourtraict d'un amant sans pair, representé en [d]es Stances pleines d'une profonde doctrine,"[57] the anonymous author teasingly reproaches "Philosophes menteurs, qui de vains arguments/ ...abuse[nt] les Amans" (p. 130); summing up his own "profonde doctrine," he declares: "C'est autre chose Amour que la Philosophie."

The same could be said of Love and Religion. Though religious allusions often occur in the amorous verse of Durand's time, they were not necessarily considered "blasphemous" by the poets and their habitual readers, as Warnke claims of the "Eucharistic imagery" in the "Stances à l'Inconstance." At the very least, literary historians must differentiate between the laxity of the Court and the strictures of the Church. More prudently, S. A. Varga stresses the ambivalence which pervades the poem at all levels of style and meaning (see p. 258). Perhaps he also goes too far when he writes: "Il y a, incontestablement, surtout au début, une parodie de l'hymne religieux. Qu'est-ce, par example, que cette 'seconde essence', sinon, avant tout, un blasphéme, Dieu étant 'l'essence premiére'?" (p. 257, note 4) The fact that Durand identifies Inconstancy with the secondary sphere of reality already excludes any substantial "heresy." In any case, the quasi-religious tone of the invocation belongs to the conventions of its thematic genre. While Durand accentuates that tone considerably, one still cannot speak of an outright "parodie" or "blasphème," much less deduce from the "Stances" that their author was a *libertin*. Varga omits to list the other "éléments" in the *Méditations* which support his more cautious affirmation (cf. the longer passage quoted earlier); but whatever the "attitude de Viau" really was, it cannot automatically be attributed to Durand.

This is not to say that the "Stances à l'Inconstance" are only an exercise: the mock encomium often harbors a grain of truth. The hymnic solemnity of Durand's poem does convey a disturbing sense of shifted values, of sceptical displacement. The critics I have quoted are right to perceive in Durand's poem some reflection of that moral ambivalence which Père Garasse will soon denounce as characteristic of the age.[58] I only object when they equate rhetorical

[57] *Le Cabinet des Muses*, vol. I (1612), pp. 128-35.

[58] See Antoine Adam, op. cit., especially pp. 339-54.

poses with individual belief (or disbelief). Durand does not make his ethico-religious stance nearly as clear as Montaigne, for example, had done; there are no other sources of information about the poet's convictions, as exist in ample measure for the essayist. The ambiguous overtones of the "Stances à l'Inconstance" permit no distinct conclusions as far as Durand himself is concerned; and without that ambiguity, in fact, the poem would lose some of its appeal.

When the same questions are raised on a general level, and applied to Durand's era as a whole, the evidence displays a different consistency and carries a greater weight. At the height of the Renaissance a trio of idealisms – neo-Platonism, Petrarchism, and reverence for Antiquity – is joined with a rarefied Christianity; the result is an art which at times achieves a lucid equilibrium, and at others seems locked in a frigid remoteness. It is no accident that Durand dedicates his neo-Petrarchist cycle to Urania, the Muse of Astronomy, the embodiment of all that is fixed and eternal, suspended in a heaven beyond disintegration and change. That vision of an otherworldly balance, of an autonomous completeness, is progressively undermined as the Renaissance draws to a close. When Durand denies his emblematic "Uranie" in a random "Meslange," he makes the quintessential gesture of his age. The rise of the inconstancy motif betrays a cultural trend, a gradual implosion of spiritual values; it gathers force throughout the sixteenth century and comes to a head at the beginning of the seventeenth. Like a tracer element, the invocation *topos* signals the final crisis of the Renaissance. Replacing the orderly music of the spheres, Inconstancy is hailed (and/or jeered) as the only perceptible principle which "rules" (by not ruling) the universe: this is "chaos theory" long before the term was coined. As the finest example of the genre, the "Stances à l'Inconstance" make manifest the deep erosion – from within – of the traditional symbolic order, with its hierarchical distinction between essences and accidents, the timeless and the transient, the absolute and the concrete. After Durand's vivid ex-voto to ceaseless change, as Bonnefoy writes (p. IX), it is "bien clair désormais qu'il ne peut y avoir de poésie que par abandon de ce que les néo-platoniciens appelaient l'Idée. L'Intelligible, le transcendant qui faisaient Délie ou Olive n'est plus que cette 'flamme déserte', fascination jugée pernicieuse. Des siècles de hantise finissent là, dans l'affirmation d'un 'présent' qui est à la fois l'instant pleinement vécu et le don que l'on fait de soi dans une infinie, une extatique dépense."

Here again literary history can only speak of collective artistic strategies, not sincerely held beliefs. In this purely textual sense, the (ir)religious overtones of the "Stances à l'Inconstance" point to another crucial feature of the poetry of Durand's age: one which lies, not in the sphere of conviction, but in that of rhetoric. As I indicated earlier, since the *Roman de la Rose* Christian allusions have often cropped up in amatory works. But Durand and his contemporaries combine sacred and profane motifs in a distinctive manner; they seem intent on an arbitrary blurring of boundaries, rather than on an effect of ennobling adornment (as in Marot) or dramatic contrast (as in D'Aubigné). A similar conflation of terms characterizes the restless debate in their verse between constancy and inconstancy. This desultory game of mixed thematic signals is paralleled on the semantic plane: a pervasive "poetics of inconstancy," at work on every level of this labile and divided discourse, culminates in a mocking deflation of language itself.

Chapter IV

THE POETICS OF INCONSTANCY

The inconstancy praised by Durand and his contemporaries transcends the bounds of simple infidelity: it represents a universal principle of instability and change. The rising popularity of this *topos* toward the end of the sixteenth century reflects a shift, not only in literary poses, but also in literary practice. If the original tenets of Petrarchism are undermined by a new stance toward the beloved, the poetic technique of Durand and other Petrarchists of his time undergoes a parallel evolution. It is revealed, for example, in the treatment of religious motifs within an amorous context, where they function in an appreciably different manner than in previous love verse. No longer a source of dramatic heightening, such motifs are indiscriminately combined with the secular clichés of Petrarchism, so that the line between the devotional and the profane is blurred. The thematic inconstancy of Durand and his contemporaries complements their pretense of amorous inconstancy, since it leads to a deflation of meaning: whereas Laura or Délie had been exalted by religious imagery and diction, the later poets vitiate the very terms in which they celebrate the mistress.

Even without this more specific correlation, both phenomena illustrate the same underlying principle, whereby a poetry of pure convention "collapses inward" once it has reached a stage of maximum elaboration. As Petrarchists search for untrodden ground within a highly formulaic tradition, the thematic range expands until its opposing elements cancel each other out. Similarly, the inherited devices of their poetic discourse become increasingly mannered: in the end, they appear inflated to the point of parody, or deflated to the point of semantic emptiness. These tendencies proceed in concert as the Renaissance draws to a close.

1. Thematic Inconstancy

From the publication of Scève's *Délie* to that of Desportes's *Diverses amours*, lyric poetry in France is dominated by love verse. But during the latter part of his career (c. 1583-1603), Desportes reserves his talents for religious works alone, and many other poets trace a similar development.[1] After the Petrarchist compositions of his youth, the subsequent lyric verse of d'Aubigné is mainly devotional; even the licentious Papillon de Lasphrise, on retiring from the Religious Wars, wrote mostly sacred poems in his final years. While a great deal of amorous verse continued to be published in France, by the end of the sixteenth century – with the poetry of Chassignet, Sponde, and later La Ceppède – the balance of important work had shifted heavily toward Christian themes.[2]

By the time Durand was writing, devotional *topoi* belonged just as much to the stock-in-trade of the poet as mythological allusions and Petrarchist conceits. Practically all poets of the early seventeenth century exercise their skills in both amatory and religious verse; often the same volume will contain both types of poetry,[3] which was very rarely the case in the mid-sixteenth century. The collective anthologies which appear with such profusion under Henry IV almost always include verses both sacred and profane. As in the case of books by individual authors, the two genres are usual-

[1] Du Plessis, Le Digne's literary executor, attributes his shift in genre to the social upheavals of the era: "J'ay encor une partie de ce qu'il a faict à la Cour, durant ces derniers troubles, où il a formé plus de force, & gaigné plus de cognoissance. Ses Dernieres oeuvres aussi ont un air beaucoup plus relevés que ces premieres..." (non pag.).

[2] As I noted above, it is no accident that in modern anthologies the mid-century is represented mainly by love poems, while in the selections for the late sixteenth century, religious verse predominates. Cf. for example the anthologies of A. M. Boase (vol. I) and A.-M. Schmidt (*Poètes du* XVI*e siècle*).

[3] This tendency sets in after 1583, under the influence of Desportes, whose collected works of that year contain a new section devoted to religious poems. By the early seventeenth century, this arrangement has become the norm: cf. most of the relevant listings in my biblio. The devotional verse usually appears at the end of the book, and is presented as proof of the author's alleged conversion to a higher life, after the frivolity of his youth. More accurately, in his article "Sur les *Sonnets et poèmes sprituels* de Desportes," in the collective volume *Amour sacré, amour profane*, J. Rieu refers to the poet's "parole 'hybride', où le pétrarquisme se mêle aux emprunts bibliques..." (p. 38).

ly separated into different sections; but sometimes they are mixed indiscriminately throughout the volume.[4]

Predictably, this "ambidextrous" approach leads to a marked interpenetration of amorous and devotional themes. The Petrarchist and Marinist aspects of religious verse in the late Renaissance could easily form the subject of a full-length study, so ample is the material at hand. The reverse phenomenon – the influence of sacred poetry on love verse – clearly has more bearing on the works of Durand which have survived. If he had prospered long enough he would probably have followed the fashion, and added a devotional section to his collected poems. When considering his amatory verse and that of his contemporaries, one must always understand the hybridization of the two thematic genres as mutual and complementary. The rise of the anthologies after 1597, and their immense popularity in the early seventeenth century, not only testifies to the eclecticism of the age: the appearance of sacred and profane poems in the same volume points to the lack of distinction between the two. The conflation of genres is succinctly underlined by the amalgamated terms of the "Argument de ce Livre" (p. XI), which serves as a preface to the *Muses francoises ralliees* (1599):

> Triomple, Amour, espoir, absence, dueil, rigueur,
> Mespris, congé, recherche, esperance perduë,
> Changement, liberté, blasme, propos moqueur,
> Les meslanges, Tombeaux, louange au Ciel renduë,
> C'est toute la matiere en ce livre espanduë.

Jumbled together indiscriminately, "propos moqueur" and "louange au Ciel" take their place in a mosaic of themes, all of which are given equal weight by the editors.

The presence of a religious element in love verse is nothing novel in itself: the *Roman de la Rose* and Marot's "Temple de Cupido" have already been cited in these pages. As I recalled in the preceding chapter, Petrarchism has its roots in a profoundly Christian

---

[4] For examples of the latter arrangement in works by individual poets, see Du Souhait, *Marqueteries ou Oeuvres Diverses* (1601); Claude Hopil, *Meslange de poesie* (1603); Du Ryer, *Le Temps Perdu* (1610 – particularly the *Autres Meslanges*); and La Charnay, *Vers* (1632). For examples among the collective anthologies, see *Le Nouveau Parnasse* (1609), *Les Fleurs des plus excellents Poetes de ce Temps* (1611), and *Le Cabinet des Muses*, vol. II (1620).

tradition. To the saintly icon of Laura, neo-Platonism adds a further spiritualization; like the works of Scève and Labé, the early love poems of the Pléiade are informed by an idealizing ardor which the later "restoration" of Desportes will never equal. But with the appearance of the *Continuation*, soon after their introduction into France, the Christian-Platonic fundaments of the inherited conventions are distinctively transformed. In Italianate Petrarchism the Christian overtones are serene and beatific; in Jodelle, d'Aubigné, and the late Ronsard, they become strident and furious. The vehemence of the French variant might be attributed to the ongoing crisis of the Religious Wars; in any case, it does prefigure the dramatic chiaroscuro normally associated with the Baroque. While the *Sonnets de l'Honneste Amour* of Du Bellay or the love verse of Olivier de Magny are suffused with the Platonic purity of their Italian models, the devotional strain in the *Derniers vers* or the *Printemps* deepens the violence of a rhetoric of contrast. This tactic may be well observed in the following sonnet from Jodelle's *Amours*:[5]

> Chaque temple en ce jour donne argument fort ample
> De joye, refaisant son haut feste sonner,
> Et d'un chant gay son choeur et sa nef resonner,
> Où chaque image à nu découverte on contemple.
> En l'eglise je pren de l'eglise l'exemple,
> Je veux le dueil, la peur, la peine abandonner,
> Et en blancheur soudain telle noirceur tourner,
> Si je te puis sans robe adorer dans ton temple.
> Le grand jour de demain disposé d'estre beau
> Peut avec un Printemps me tirer du tombeau,
> Si de vaincre ma mort tu prens soudaine envie:
> Je diray, sans vouloir rien à Dieu comparer,
> Que s'il peut revivant nos vies reparer,
> Revivant par toymesme, à toy je rendray vie.

Here a whole nexus of religious motifs, centered on the Catholic rites of Easter, is paired with amorous equivalents. At the end of Lent, the dark cloths covering the holy images in the church are removed: the lover wishes to see the beloved "uncovered" in the "temple" of her bedchamber. Like Christ after the resurrection, the mistress has the power to save him from eternal death. Through the

[5] *Poètes du* XVI*e siècle*, ed. Schmidt, p. 730.

vivifying strength of their passion, the lovers can offer each other a mutual salvation on earth. The phrase "sans vouloir rien à Dieu comparer" boldly underlines the ambivalence of these analogies.

The religious undertones in Jodelle, d'Aubigné, and the late Ronsard always retain – if not the substance of conviction – at least the integrity of its terms. In the antithesis between sacred and profane, a vociferous faith throws into relief its opposite, a fiercely expressed eroticism. The love verse of Durand's time no longer possesses that tension of darkness and light; the sharp polarity subsides into suave equivalence or careless discrepancy. "Italianized" again by Desportes, but temporally barred from the freshness of the early Pléiade, late Petrarquism maintains itself through a strategy of convergence. In César de Nostredame's *Les Perles ou les Larmes de la Saincte Magdeleine* (1606), a languidly amorous tone permeates the whole:[6] conversely, the amatory verse of the period often appears interchangeable with the devotional genre. Poems such as Jodelle's, with its explicit Christian imagery, stand out as audacious exceptions in the sixteenth century. In the early seventeenth century, Durand and his contemporaries routinely blend Christian motifs with

[6] Cf. these lines from the title poem (p. 12), which depict Mary Magdalene at the tomb of Christ:

> Au lict royal, contre la sepulture,
> Ou ce Medor ce beau Dieu de nature
> Pasle & sanglant, las & mort fut posé
> Apres qu'il eust ses armes deposé,
> Donnant aux vents sa tresse nonchalante,
> Son Angelique esplorée & dolente
> Panchoit son corps de tristesse ennuyé
> Au droit genouil le bras droict appuyé,
> Dedans sa main que maint Opale arrose
> Portoit couché son visage de rose...

Prostitute turned saint, the Magdalene provides the early seventeenth century with an ideal focal point for thematic ambivalence. La Roque's "Larmes de la Magdaleine" (in the *Oeuvres* of 1609, pp. 785-803) is only slightly less languorous than Nostredame's version; one can understand the amusing error of La Roque's printer, who headed the last two pages of the poem "Les Amours de la Magdaleine." For a parallel in the visual arts, cf. Jacques Bellange, whose "Trois Maries" stand coquettishly before the sepulcher, coiffed with jewels and wearing lascivious gowns. Susan Haskins, in *Mary Magdalen: Myth and Metaphor*, asserts that in the art of the era "the saint became little more than a beautiful woman, an idealised feminine body rather than a repentant sinner, similar to the many paintings of courtesans of the period, her attributes – the jar or skull – often being the only means by which she might be distinguished" (p. 257).

secular themes. The individual beliefs of the later poets are not at issue; I would only suggest that the rhetoric of contrast has diminished. Religious conceits invade their amorous verse to an unprecedented degree, not by way of counterpoint, but by way of a sardonic indifference to the time-honored assignation of certain motifs to certain genres of verse.[7]

The distinction I am drawing is difficult to pin down "objectively," because it is largely a question of tone. As with the puncturing devices discussed earlier, only extensive familiarity with the poetry of the period allows the reader to discern its subtle shadings of wit; but even having acquired that familiarity, different readers may justifiably agree to disagree. No interpretation of the elusive nuances of mood and inflection in literature can ever be absolute or exclusive. As an example open to discussion, consider the following sonnet by Du Mas, published in 1609 (p. 110):

Qu'avois-je faits, devois-je miserable,
  Perir par fer, & puis grisler au feu,
  Respondez-moy qu'aviez-vous apperceu,
  Qui ne fust propre, & ne fust agreable?
Ce m'est encor une fin honnorable,
  Heureux tourment, mais non toutes-fois deu:
  Car sainct Laurens, & sainct Paul ont receu,
  Pareille peine, & martyre semblable.
L'un decolé pour l'orthodoxe foy,
  L'autre rosty soustenant nostre loy:
  Mais tous les deux, par des bourreaux infames.

---

[7] While one must steer clear of confusing literature with belief, the readiness with which these poets adopt opposing stances toward religion in the same book of verse does seem inconsequential, from an orthodox point of view. For example, several of the love poems in Guy de Tours's *Premieres Oeuvres...* (1598) denounce the mistress' intention to enter a convent in the most scabrous terms. Cf. fol. 145 ro, where he warns her: "Ne pense pas, qu'aymant un Boutecu/ Mieiux que ton Guy, le grand Dieu te pardonne." In another poem on the same page, he "prays" to Cupid: "...s'elle y va, fais si bien ton devoir,/ Qu'en bref le froc elle jette aux orties." In a milder form, the plea against joining a nunnery is a *topos* of erotic light-verse throughout the Renaissance; but it takes on a particularly virulent and disrespectful note after 1598 (cf. Bernier, fol. 83 vo, and Du Ryer, p. 20). On the other hand, further on in the same volume (fol. 226 vo) Guy attacks a "petit Atheiste" for daring to "blasfemer" "contre Jesu-Christ, ...son Eglise, ...[et] la Chrestienne foy." Whatever his true opinion of the Church and the Christian faith may be, his willingness to use conflicting *topoi* reveals an indifference toward the rhetorical consistency of themes, if not toward their content as well.

Moy par les mains de Diane & Vesta,
Mourant helas! cela me contenta,
Tel fust Orphee assassiné des fẽmmes.

Du Mas goes much further than any sixteenth century poet would have done in drawing an analogy between the "martyred" lover and the Christian martyrs. Though the cliché of "martyrdom" often appears in Petrarchist verse, it had traditionally remained a discreet, vague allusion. Du Mas does not hesitate to compare his agony with those of two specific saints; and what is more revealing, he places the martyrdom of Laurence and Paul on the same level with the dismemberment of Orpheus, making no distinction between Classical myth and Christian hagiography. The final phrase of the poem, where Diana and Vesta are equated with the wild women who killed Apollo's son, reduces even the mythological allusions to a pleasantry. The exquisite skill deployed elsewhere by Du Mas (in the sonnet discussed at the end of Chapter II, for example) would seem to confirm that these deflating effects are not the fruit of mere incompetence.

For the Christian, the fate of his soul in the fight between good and evil is no small matter: an eternity of bliss awaits him, should good triumph; the pains of hell, should evil win control. The following sonnet by Scalion (1599) diverts this grave debate to lighthearted ends (fol. 58 vo):

Pour vray ne suis je pas digne d'aimer un Ange,
Les uns regnent au Ciel, les autres en Enfer,
Ceux qui sont tentateurs, taschent à eschauffer
Nostre sang pour nous mettre en un malheur estrange:
L'Ange bon nous incite à chanter la louange
De Dieu qui delivra les bons de Lucifer,
Et l'infernal voulant de son ongle agriffer
Nostre ame, emplit nos yeux de vicieuse fange:
Sous espoir de passer nostre âge à follatrer,
Il nous fait en aimant la femme idolatrer,
Qui nous rend bien souvent triste et melancholique.
Ainsi l'amour mondain cault & pernicieux,
Transmue les effects des plus ingenieux,
Et l'humeur d'Angelique en la Diabolique.

To grasp the irony of this poem one must realize that the name of Scalion's mistress was Angélique; in a sense the entire sonnet is a *jeu de mots*. The conceit on which it is based is pointedly religious: Angelique is assuredly an angel, but perhaps a satanic one; under her "diabolical" influence, the lover experiences a hell on earth. Though the conceit derives from serious theology, it is treated like any other Petrarchist bagatelle; Christian belief, far from heightening the tone as in Jodelle's sonnet, is again reduced to the level of a joke.[8]

Both Du Mas and Scalion use the religious framework in a manner markedly different from that of Marot, whose "Temple de Cupido" derives from the allegorical tradition of the Middle Ages. In Marot's poem the "cathedral" in which the lovers "pray" corresponds point for point to a Christian church; like the garden in the *Roman de la Rose*, it occupies the lower level in a pious hierarchy, symbolic of and continuous with its upper reaches. In Du Mas and Scalion, the beloved is identified with evil rather than good: human love does not reflect God's love, as in the medieval and Petrarchan models. On the other hand these poets do not – like Jodelle or d'Aubigné in certain poems – forcefully associate the mistress with demonic powers, much less satanic ones. She is on the side of evil, but her wickedness boils down to feminine caprice. Equally devalued, both "good" and "evil" serve as false antitheses which converge in a playful *pointe*.

Whether Durand wrote devotional poetry himself is unknown, but his love verse contains the same religious accents as that of Du Mas, Scalion, and other poets of his time. A striking example is sonnet XXXI of the *Méditations*:

> Où te cacheras-tu, ma cruelle Uranie,
> Quand le Ciel courroucé la terre enflamera?
> Qui plaidera ta cause, & qui t'excusera
> Des maux que tu m'as faict endurer en ma vie?
> Tu me voudras nier ta longue tyrannie:
> Mais mon coeur plein de traicts alors t'accusera;
> Et monstrant ton portrait le Ciel te blasmera
> D'avoir contre toy-mesme addressé ta furie.

[8] Cf. sonnet XII of Trellon's *Amours de Felice*, which decries "Le jour de Sainct André, ce jour plein de disgrace," when the poet was rebuffed by his mistress; at the end of the sonnet, he quips: "Je ne t'adresse plus Sainct André mes prieres,/ Puis que tu es si fort contraire à mes Amours" (*Le Cavalier Parfait*, fol. 132 ro).

Pour moy, sans tes beautez mon mal sera caché;
Leur force inevitable excuse le peché:
Mais si le Tout-puissant qui les ames preside
A tout peché commis attache un chastiment,
Il faut que nous soyons punis egalement,
Moy comme un idolatre, & toy comme homicide.

The first quatrain launches the poet's condemnation by means of a vigorous rhythmic structure: two questions of equal length, both arranged as expanding triads, propel the movement forward. Throughout the poem, the impetus is reinforced by a dramatic vocabulary ("courroucé," "enflamera," "idolatre," "homicide"), in the context of which even the most conventional terms of Petrarchism ("cruelle," "maux," "endurer," "tyrannie") seem to retrieve their original meaning. Similarly, the scene which Durand sets – the Last Judgement – invests such words as "mal," "peché," "ames," and "chastiment" with the full force of their religious connotation. (Cf. the use of "peché" and "repentir" in the "Stances à l'Inconstance.") The poet even dares to evoke the "Tout-puissant" Himself – not in His more abstract aspects as the Creator or the Holy Spirit, but as Christ the avenging Judge of the human soul. With only a few alterations, this sonnet could easliy have appeared in a book of devotional verse.

That is the whole point. The poem unfolds within a Petrarchist framework: in the sonnet which precedes it, Durand develops a frivolously "Alexandrian" anecdote. Again the question arises: What function do the religious language and imagery serve? It would be hard to argue that they transfigure the beloved, as in Petrarch's holy vision of Laura after her death, or as in the ambiguous poems of Michelangelo, where the word *Signore* often seems to carry a double significance. It would be equally dubious to claim that they render the portrayal of passion and torment more acute, as in the *Printemps* or the *Derniers vers*. When Durand calls himself "idolatre" and Uranie "homicide," he is alluding to the Ten Commandments, the transgression of which entails a dreadful "chastiment"; the use of these terms to create a witty *pointe* deflates their substance. Rather than infusing the sonnet with dramatic power, the religious motifs collapse into playfulness: not only by virtue of the Petrarchist context, but also through their rhetorical function within the poem. By contrast, the final sonnet of the *Hécatombe à*

Diane steers clear of such a devaluation, even though it also alludes to the Last Judgement. D'Aubigné keeps within the bounds of a discreet analogy: from the outset, it is only a "tribunal d'amour" before which the mistress must appear. Christ Himself and the *dies irae* do not figure directly within an amatory conceit as they do in Durand's sonnet, where the suitability of tone and theme is mockingly ignored.

Particularly revealing of this "thematic inconstancy" is the infernal imagery in the *Méditations*. In the sixteenth century, d'Aubigné, Birague, Nuysement, and other poets had elaborated lengthy comparisons of the lover's torments with those of Hades.[9] The "Stances" on pp. 76-7 of the *Méditations* seem at first to be a simple continuation of this tradition.[10] At the beginning of the poem, the "Ombres" are summoned to leave their "manoirs gemissans" in order to bear witness to the poet's pains: Tantalus, Ixion, Sisyphus, and the other familiar figures are then invoked in turn, each bearing some analogy to the lover's sufferings. But the final *stance* sends the poem in a different thematic direction:

Quand les Dieux ont damné ces pauvres miserables,
Ils ont veu que deux maux estoient insupportables:
Chacun n'a que le sien, mais j'ay celuy de tous.
Comme plus que les Dieux je vous trouve puissante,
Retirez de ces maux mon âme languissante:
Pour damner et sauver il n'appartient qu'à vous.

The terms "damner" and "sauver" have a distinctly Christian resonance;[11] but they seem to bear as little weight as the Classical myth of Hades. Of these "Stances" Mathieu-Castellani has observed (p.

[9] The frequency of such infernal evocations is a characteristic of late Renaissance poetry which sets it off from the love verse of the Pléiade: cf. Mathieu-Castellani, pp. 376-83. Among Durand's immediate contemporaries, Le Masson develops the theme most fully in his "L'Enfer d'Amour" (op. cit., fols. 59 ro – 61 vo), which is – appropriately enough – dedicated to the Cardinal Du Perron.

[10] For a poem by Durand which does continue it, with few overtly Christian overtones, see the "Stances" on pp. 77-9.

[11] The Christian implications are made explicit in a poem by Du Mas (p. 232):

Si celuy qui peut tout d'une voix prophetisse,
Nous escrie qu'il veut refrenant son courroux,
Non la mort du pecheur mais qu'il se convertisse,
Dois-je moins esperer de clemence de vous?

428): "Lorsque Durand invoque les Ombres, il se défend mal d'un certain scepticisme... L'Enfer a perdu ses couleurs d'épouvante, et les dieux leur pouvoir: si on appelle les Ombres, on leur demande de témoigner de leur peu de réalité, et le texte s'achève par une pointe désabusée, qui met en cause tout un système de croyances, et l'aveu d'une incrédulité manifeste." While not accepting the view that such lines give conclusive proof of Durand's "incredulity," I can readily concur with her assessment of their tone.

In his *Amours de Narcize* (1609), S.-G. de La Roque traces a contrary movement: rather than summoning the shades like Durand, he descends among them to hell. But when he compares his torments to theirs, he reaches precisely the same conclusion (*Oeuvres*, p. 131):

> Et bien que de mes jours la fin soit à l'occase,
> Encor' de mon ardeur j'ay du resentiment,
> Courant au regne obscur de l'eternel tourment,
> Si l'amour et l'amant y peuvent trouver place:
> Et si comme en la vie, ore que je trespasse,
> Je porte en mon esprit vostre object seulement,
> Arrivant aux Enfers je diray justement,
> Qu'on n'y voit point de feu qui ma flamme surpasse.

In this and the other passages under review, Durand and his immediate contemporaries blur the distinction between Hades and the Christian hell to a much greater degree than Birague and other sixteenth century poets had done. Consider also the conflating (and deflating) word-play on the "feu" of damnation and the "flamme" of love. The interpenetration of the sacred and profane thematic registers becomes especially evident in such lines as the following – again by La Roque, but this time from the *Oeuvres Chrestiennes* at the end of the volume just quoted (p. 753):

> L'enfer est un palais d'estrange architecture
> Du fleuve Stigieux enclos de tout costez,
> Un theatre où Pluton fait voir ses cruautez,
> Ou l'on sent de la mort l'eternelle pointure.

Here the inferno of the Christian tradition is explicitly described in terms of pagan mythology, and demoted to a mere "theatre."

Another passage from Durand (p. 81), at the beginning of the "Stances de l'Absence," pushes the thematic fusion of the lines just cited even further:

En vain par les destins, redoutables enfers,
Vos cachots sont remplis de supplices divers
Pour punir les forfaits des criminelles ames:
Estans comme elles sont absentes de leur Dieu,
Ceste absence les doit tourmenter en ce lieu
Plus rigoureusement que vos fouëts ny vos flames.

Vos rouës, vos rochers et vos coulantes eaux
Que des filles en vain versent dans leurs vaisseaux,
Ne peuvent approcher de ceste violence:
L'absence est le bourreau qui gehesne vos esprits,
Et si nous voulons croire aux plus doctes escripts,
Tous les maux de l'enfer ne sont rien qu'une absence.

Despite the Classical trappings of lines 7-8 [12] Durand is evoking the most terrible punishment which the Christian religion foresees for the damned: no mere physical torture, like the eternal fire, but a spiritual agony of infinite proportions, *damnus* itself. [13] Possibly Durand had read some of the numerous descriptions of *damnus* in the Church Fathers or later theologians; in any case, he was clearly well versed in the Catholic doctrine of hell.

In the "Stances de l'Absence," Uranie is made equivalent to God; the lover's absence from his mistress causes the same torment as the sinner's separation from his Creator. [14] Such a grandiose anal-

[12] Cf. Ovid, *Metamorphoses* IV, line 463: "Assiduae repetunt, quas perdunt, Belides undas." The daughters of Danaus, son of Belus, killed their own husbands at their father's behest; in Tartarus, the Danaids were forced to refill forever a perforated water jar. For another example of this unusual motif, see Le Masson, fol. 55 ro.

[13] Cf. the horrifying definition in the *Dictionnaire de théologie catholique*, vol. IV, columns 9-10. Much too long to quote in full, it states in part: "La peine du dam est incomparablement la plus terrible de toutes les peines de l'enfer. Auprès d'elle, le tourment même du feu éternel, si atroce soit-il, n'est presque rien... Pour infliger au pêcheur le tourment le plus formidable qui puisse être, Dieu n'a qu'à se retirer complètement de lui."

[14] For a similar argumentation in the amorous context, see Bertaut (re-edn.), p. 348. Cf. also the lines by Jacques de Constans quoted in Janik, p. 104; and Janik's remark: "So ähnlich wird in mittelalterlichen Gottesbeweisen argumentiert." Even so, in the austere love verse of Constans – comparable to that of Sponde (see below) – the religious allusions carry an altogether different thematic charge.

ogy can only fall flat, simultaneously devaluing both the Petrarchist motifs and the religious ones.[15] The phrase "*si nous voulons croire* aux plus doctes escripts" (line 11) might indicate that this derisive effect is not involuntary. The name chosen by Durand for his beloved was conventionally associated with an inspiration truly divine. Urania is the Muse invoked by Du Bartas throughout his *Sepmaine* (1578), which recounts the story of the Creation. Later Milton apostrophizes her at length in Book VII of *Paradise Lost,* and addresses her in Book I as the "Heav'nly Muse." According to Merritt Hughes,[16] Du Bartas exercised such a pervasive influence on succeeding poets that for them Urania could only be a Christian Muse, not a pagan one. When Durand drags her through the mud in two of his "Elegies" (see below), accusing her of faithlessness and vile behavior, there is a peculiar resonance to his words.

As Terence Cave makes clear in his study of devotional poetry in France, the very title of the *Méditations* would ordinarily have been applied to a religious work. The flourishing devotional literature of the time produced many "meditations" on the life of Christ or the saints, the techniques of which have been analyzed by Louis Martz in *The Poetry of Meditation*. Another curious ambivalence in Durand's book is the vignette which appears prominently on the title page:[17] is this charming figure an Amor or an angel? As he is chastened by the fire which surrounds him, he turns his face from the torch of profane love to the lamp of sacred love – but he holds both torch and lamp aloft. It seems symptomatic of the thematic convergence of the age that the same vignette also adorns the works

---

[15] The analogy, and its devaluation, are even more pronounced in these lines by Le Masson (fol. 30 ro):

> Ainsi qu'aux bien heureus Dieu sert de Paradis,
> D'espoir aux penitents & d'Enfer aux maudits,
> Donnant aux uns plaisir & aux autres des flames.
> Ma belle est le brazier des infidelles coeurs,
> Purgatoire aux legers pour les rendre plus meurs,
> Et le vray Paradis des plus loyales ames.

[16] See pp. xlv-xlvi of his intro. to *Paradise Lost* for a dissertation on the figure of Urania; and compare A.-M. Schmidt, op cit. pp. 27-33, on her appropriation as "sacred Muse" in French poetry, following the example of Du Bartas. Rieu, in his article on Desportes, loc. cit., points out that one of the best-known anthologies of religious verse in the period (first published in 1591) was intitled *L'Uranie*.

[17] Reproduced as the frontispiece to the recent edn. cit.

of Claude Hopil, one of the greatest devotional poets of Durand's time. In Hopil's *Meslange* (p. 81), the vignette introduces the "Hymne chrestien, Des Elemens," which ends the collection on a strongly religious note; at the beginning (p. 3) of the *Oeuvres chrestiennes* (1603), it reappears opposite the "Elegies, ou Meditations Chrestiennes."

In Durand's title – as in the vignette and the name of his Muse – there may be a hint of parody: one can "meditate" on the profane as well as the sacred. More disturbingly from an orthodox point of view, all three instances may betray an utter indifference to such distinctions. Théophile was condemned in 1623 for having openly denied the immortality of the soul; Durand, like most of his contemporaries, does not take a firm position on doctrinal matters. The professions of orthodox faith which come at the end of most poetry collections in this period cannot be taken at face value, precisely because they do constitute a formula. The archetype in this respect is *Le Cavalier Parfait* (1597 – republished 1614) by Claude de Trellon, whom I have already discussed as exercising a major influence on the "poets of inconstancy." The full title of his book is *Le Cavalier Parfait, où sont comprinses les Amours de Sylvie, les Amours de Felice, les Meslanges, & l'Hermitage*: the implication being that the final conversion to higher things is all part of playing the perfect gentleman. More often than not, the "hermit" turns out to be a "Hermite Amoureus." [18] Though Desportes and Passerat had already exploited this humorous theme in the 1570s, [19] it becomes far more frequent in the early seventeenth century. The fact that the *topos* appears alongside "serious" vows of renunciation renders it – and them – more ambiguous than before. [20]

In the "Stances à l'Inconstance," the note of Lucretian materialism is subsumed in a mock encomium: the ambivalence remains intact. Similarly, the indiscriminate fusion of amorous and devotional motifs in the poetry of Durand and his contemporaries cannot be considered *in itself* a symptom of loss of faith. All the same it is

[18] See the long poem by that title in Le Masson, fols. 25 ro -28 ro.

[19] See the two sonnets in Desportes's *Diane*, pp. 207-8, and notes.

[20] As noted in the previous chapter, Trellon himself places his verse under the sign of deliberate deception; nor is it an accident that Pizzorusso has identified "la dissimulazione" as a dominant theme in Durand's work (see art. cit.). And cf. Puleio, op. cit., pp. 63-82, where she develops the theme of "la transgressione dissimulata."

striking that while they constantly employ religious themes in their love verse, they do not appeal to the stabilizing supernatural framework of the Petrarchan model. The "equivalence principle" of the sacred and profane in poetry – like the increasing autonomy of natural science – might be said to prepare later developments in the secularization of thought; in that sense, literary language could well be "ahead" of current belief-structures. Although Durand calls Inconstancy a "seconde essence," within the space of his poem no "premiere essence" intervenes: the changing material world seems to obviate the notion of a higher permanence, as though endless metamorphosis were eternity enough.

Appropriately, a principal example of the thematic instability of the late Renaissance may be found in the constancy-inconstancy debate itself. The praise of inconstancy can be understood as the secular twin of a religious obverse. Durand and other "poets of inconstancy" employ familiar devotional motifs in a gaily amorous context: they turn them on their head by embracing the ephemerality of the sublunar world rather than decrying it. Both the sacred and the profane registers of this thematic scale spring from a common source; they reflect an important current in the popular philosophy of the time, the *Renaissance du stoïcisme au XVIe siècle* which Léontine Zanta has documented.

The neo-Stoic moralists themselves exhibit a high degree of thematic inconstancy, especially when they try to reconcile pagan ideals of behavior with traditional Christianity. For example, they are hard put to resolve the contradiction between Stoic principles of indifference to suffering and the Christian emphasis on redemption *through* suffering (whether Christ's or man's). But whether writing in an antique or a Christian mode, Lipsius, Charron, Du Vair, and other neo-Stoics all agree in condemning the innate flightiness of human nature. Pierre Charron's chapter on "Inconstance" in *De la Sagesse* (1601)[21] reveals the decisive influence of Montaigne on his style and thought; it also demonstrates his firm refusal to adopt his model's positive attitude toward inconstancy. "L'irresolution d'une part," he writes, "puis l'inconstance & l'instabilité est le plus commun & apparent vice de la nature humaine" (p. 124).

---

[21] Book I, chapter XXXVIII; reprinted in *Toutes les Oeuvres* (1635), vol. I, pp. 124-5.

In praising inconstancy, Durand and his contemporaries are playing tricks with a moral *topos* as well as a religious one. From both perspectives, their stance remains ambiguous. Inconstancy is Durand's outstanding theme, but his "thematic inconstancy" prevents it from becoming dominant. Constancy figures just as prominently in the *Méditations*, even if it does not correspond entirely to the faithfulness of traditional Petrarchism – or to the fortitude of neo-Stoicism. A brief comparison with Sponde may clarify these distinctions.

As Gérard Genette[22] and Mathieu-Castellani (pp. 489-501) have pointed out, the love poetry of Sponde displays a remarkable unity of purpose; the same is true of his religious verse and prose. The *Amours*, the *Stances et Sonnets de la Mort*, and the balanced periods of the *Méditations* all revolve around an identical *Leitmotiv*: constancy in love, whether toward the beloved or toward God, in the face of an inconstant world. Like most of his contemporaries, Sponde was an avid reader of the ancient Stoics and the modern neo-Stoics; Alan Boase[23] has analyzed the influence which Seneca, Lipsius and others exercised on his thought and rhetoric. The "pagan" backdrop of Sponde's work is also revealed by his imagery, which abounds in the examples from Greek and Roman history employed by Stoics such as Plutarch to illustrate their philosophy. In the *Amours*, Caesar, Horace at the bridge, the city of Numantia, Fabius Cunctator (who helped defeat Hannibal), Alexander – and so on – set examples of fortitude in adversity which the poet aspires to imitate; in the constancy of his love, he will show a similar heroism:

On n'eust jamais cognu le Scevole Romain
Sans le beau desespoir des deux coups de sa main,
Cesar sans les Gaulois, Scipion sans Carthage.
Le sommeillant repos endormoit leur courage,
Et leur nom dans la mort s'alloit desja plonger,
S'il n'eust trouvé sa vie en cherchant le danger.
Mon Amour cherche ainsi, pour se montrer si brave,
Des perils de l'Amour le peril le plus grave,
A la fin on verra, pour marque de vertu,
Qu'il scait que c'est de batre et non d'estre batu.[24]

---

[22] See the essay on Sponde in his *Figures I.*
[23] In the intro. to his edn. of Sponde's *Méditations.*
[24] *Poètes du XVIe siècle*, ed. Schmidt, p. 917.

At the end of the sixteenth century, the comparisons made by Sponde would have seemed neither extraordinary nor incongruous,[25] even though such comparisons occupy a place of particular prominence in his verse. Like the neo-Stoic philosophers of the time, French poets were used to dramatizing their own emotions and actions by means of historical parallels from Anitiquity,[26] in addition to the mythological ones favored by the early Renaissance.

The poets of Durand's generation continue and augment this neo-Stoic legacy; a prime example is Sonnet IV of the *Méditations*:[27]

Brute voyant mourir la liberté Romaine,
 L'ayant suivy vivant, la suivit au tombeau:
 Caton voyant sa vie et sa mort incertaine,
 Fit entrée à la mort par son propre cousteau:
Annibal accourcit et sa vie, et la haine
 Des Romains par le suc de son petit anneau:
 Et Socrate, en prison par la rage inhumaine
 Des tyrans, de son coeur fit oeuvre de bourreau.
Si ma liberté meurt, si ma vie est douteuse,
 Si je suis poursuivy d'une rage amoureuse,
 Si mon coeur est aux fers, à la mort apresté:
Pourquoy languis-je plus en l'ardeur qui me tuë?
 Que ne mouray-je en Brute avec ma liberté,
 Ou du moins en Socrate après l'avoir perduë?

The supreme act of Stoic virtue is suicide; by choosing the moment of his death and dispassionately accomplishing it, the Stoic displays his mastery over the vagaries of fortune and the petty fears of common mortals. "Philosopher, c'est apprendre à mourir." By their moral premises (or poses), as well as by the models they cite, many of Durand's poems are unthinkable outside the context of neo-Stoicism;[28] to this extent, his work resembles that of Sponde.

---

[25] Genette wrongly assumes the contrary in his essay, p. 248.

[26] In addition to the examples cited below, cf. Desportes, *Hippolyte*, p. 106; and Le Masson, fols. 4 vo and 28 vo.

[27] The rhetorical form, the historical conceits, and even certain phrases of this poem (particularly the last two lines) derive from a sonnet by Desportes (*Cléonice*, pp. 19-20). According to Graham (p. 19, note 1), Desportes's own source was a sonnet by Bernadino Rota.

[28] The premises were so familiar that they could also be playfully subverted. Bertaut, also referring to Cato, makes slavery a source of Stoic virtue by cleverly "collapsing" an antithesis (re-edn., p. 328):

They differ in one essential point: for Sponde, reason is on the side of love – it underpins his constancy toward the beloved; for Durand, reason and passion are antonyms,[29] eternally at war. Even in his amatory verse, Sponde adopts the attitude of a devotional poet, for whom Stoicism provides a means of salvation: faced with universal instability, he clings to his faith against all odds. It is immaterial whether the object of that faith is called "God" or "Love"; in his amorous works, as Mathieu-Castellani observes, "la constance désigne moins la victoire d'amour que la victoire de l'esprit, sur la Chair et le Monde ligués contre lui" (p. 497). By contrast, Durand and most love poets of his generation conceive of their passion as a defeat, an irresistible doom which overwhelms them. Once Petrarchist love has become divorced from its Christian and Platonic background, it can no longer be pursued as a spiritual exercise – whether leading toward God, as in Petrarch, toward an apprehension of Love in its transcendent ideality, as in Scève or Du Bellay,[30] or toward heroic self-control, as in Sponde.

The devotional poet draws on Stoicism as a method which will maintain his loyalty to the Absolute, despite the changing winds of circumstance; the characteristic love poet at the end of the Renaissance envisages constancy from an entirely different angle. He still hopes to win the mistress' favors through a show of fidelity; in this sense, his approach is still that of traditional Petrarchism:

J'employe vainement des souspirs et des larmes,
Esperant meriter avec fidelité
Tout ce que vostre humeur donne à la nouveauté:
Au moins si vous avez à bien-heurer une ame,
De ces cheres faveurs que merite ma flame,
Qu'elle ait ainsi que moy par ses desirs constans
Surmonté les desdains, les jaloux, et le temps.

Pourquoy resisteroy-je, en rompant mon cordage,
Au destin qui m'ayant dans ses noeds arresté,
Veu qu'un si glorieux et si noble servage
Me soit ce qu'à Caton estoit sa liberté.

[29] As I shall try to explain, they do not oppose each other as fixed values, in the manner of medieval allegory or traditional Petrarchism (cf. the first sonnet of the *Amours de Cassandre*).

[30] As I suggested in the previous chapter, the dissolution of this continuity between worldly and spiritual love is already implicit in the amorous verse of Ronsard.

But this passage from Durand (pp. 117-18) also reveals the rupture with the past which has occurred: Uranie is not portrayed as a virtuous mistress. The poem just cited, "Elegie IV," is a long and passionate denunciation of her inconstancy; it begins: "Qui ne seroit jaloux vous voyant tous les jours/ Tenir la porte ouverte à nouvelles amours...?" (p. 115). The lover even goes so far as to give his mistress the following cynical advice (p. 116):

Rangez cent mille coeurs dessous vostre pouvoir,
Leur donnant s'il vous plaist de leurs maux allegence:
Il n'importe, pourveu qu'il soit sans apparence:
Non, je ne vous veux pas moins prompte à vous brusler,
Mais bien plus advisee à le dissimuler.

Loose and faithless, Uranie is not worthy of the poet's constancy. She may appreciate it in some way, but only as a quality which she herself does not possess. "Pourquoy si fort prisez-vous la constance,/ Les longs desirs, et la perseverance?" the lover asks in "Elegie II" (p. 110), adding bitterly: "C'est estimer ce que vous n'avez point..."

Traditional Petrarchism derived its value from the virtue of the beloved; all the better if the poet's passion was unrequited – he was chastened by the contemplation of an ideal. But if the object of the lover's adoration is frivolous and unworthy, his allegiance loses its higher meaning. The lack of conviction which colors the final phase of Renaissance love verse translates itself in the indiscriminate imagery and deflated language often noted in these pages. While devotional poets are by no means safe from this confusion of boundaries – witness Nostredame or the religious verse of La Roque – certain of them manage to rejoin "la lumière de la permanence."[31] Still, it is significant that they discover meaning only *beyond* this world: a world no longer envisioned as a harmonic whole, leading by degrees to God,[32] but as a realm of disjuncture and instability. The love poets of the age harbor a similar view of sublunary existence;

[31] Cf. the poems grouped under this heading in Rousset's *Anthologie*, vol. II, pp. 240-82.

[32] Cf. G. Castor, p. 176: "The sixteenth-century world picture was still based on a fusion of the Platonic cosmology (strongly tinged with Aristotelianism) with that of the Old Testament. The universe it portrayed was a beautifully ordered universe arranged in a fixed system of multiple hierarchies..."

but for them, after the erosion of the Christian-Platonic underpinnings of Petrarchism,[33] there is no redeeming absolute: no Constancy, no Love. Urania has truly been dethroned.

The lover's constancy claimed by Durand and his contemporaries stems from the Petrarchist tradition; but it is identified with passion alone, and so belongs to the earthly realm of degradation and – paradoxically – inconstancy. Unlike the constancy of the devotional poet, the constancy of the lover can no longer be deemed a Stoic virtue, much less a path to transcendence. Among the "poets of 1600" love is reduced to a moral and even psychological imperfection. In the "Stances de l'Amour" (pp. 103-05) Durand methodically strips love of its spiritual and mythological trappings;[34] he scoffs at those who would "fai[re] un Dieu d'une folie" (p. 103):

> Non, ce n'est point un Dieu, ce n'est qu'un nom d'excuse,
> Qu'emprunte folement un esprit qui s'abuse
> A rechercher de l'aise où vole son desir,
> Nom qui selon le temps sur ses lèvres se glisse,
> Que son adversité fait un Dieu d'injustice,
> Et sa prosperité fait un Dieu de plaisir.

Love does not possess a higher spiritual meaning; it is merely a function of the individual mind (ibid.):

---

[33] Cf. Felperin, who refers to "a neoplatonic poetic, certainly available to an Elizabethan poet and often invoked by Spenser, that asserts the eternality of spiritual form over its mutable material embodiments..." (p. 157). This is the traditional schema which the "poets of 1600" increasingly reject.

[34] Cf. the long passage at the beginning of his pastoral novel, the *Espines d'Amour* (pp. 10-15), where Durand debunks the allegory of Love by clinically describing love's "real" effects. For example:

> Les traicts esbranlez dans sa paulme infantive, semblent tesmoigner, que leur faincte est inutile, & seullement inventee pour faire naistre un abuz aux esprits rustiques: ou sont les coeurs qui quelquefois affligez de ceste passion, ont jamais ressenty la poincture de quelque traict? le propre d'un traict, est d'enfanter à son arivee un sacrifice de sang, & au contraire, ou l'amour dresse ses batteries... le sang faict sa course aux lieux plus esloignez des extrémitez; le visage... devient pasle, ...& toutes les autres parties du passioné abandonnent leur chaude fonction, pour espouser la froideur d'une glace, qui s'empare incontinent des membres inopinement affligez.

Foible divinité, qui ne recoit son estre
Que du bien ou du mal que le desir fait naistre,
Et qui sans nous en nous ne peut avoir de lieu...[35]

In the end, passion is a self-contradiction: both attraction and repulsion, possession and loss; "L'Amour n'est à la fin qu'une fuitte d'Amour,/ Et sa possession de la perte est suivie" (p. 105).

The "Stances de l'Amour" reflect the profound mutation which transforms amatory verse as the Renaissance draws to a close. The crumbling of inherited ideals affects not only the image of the beloved and of the lover, but the very language in which love is expressed. The similes used by Durand in this poem are no longer those of the old Petrarchism, with its ornate conceits and mythological allusions: instead they are simple, almost bare, based on images borrowed from everyday reality.[36] The "naturalism" of such comparisons corresponds to a more sober evocation of love itself; love is viewed, not in philosophical or quasi-religious terms, but as a psychological phenomenon. Passion has significance only for the individual consciousness: far from transfiguring the soul, it only degrades the moral faculties, gradually destroying the will and the capacity to act. Durand's analysis of love resembles that of the Stoic moralists,[37] who considered all passions to be a disease. The poet's constancy toward Uranie is a *mauvaise constance*, an evil which he must overcome. The rational alternative is inconstancy. As a distant throwback to Petrarchan values, a farewell gesture toward the Renaissance inheritance, he denies himself this solution in the *Méditations* proper – but not in the *Meslange*, with its hymnic "Stances à l'Inconstance."

Like the shifts between profane and religious motifs, the endless oscillation between constancy and inconstancy epitomizes the "thematic inconstancy" of Durand and his contemporaries. The collective anthologies of the period are full of poems in praise of incon-

---

[35] For similar demystifications of love, see Bertaut (re-edn.), pp. 374-5; and La Vallettrie, *Les Oeuvres Poetiques*, fol. 6 ro.

[36] Cf. lines 52-3: "Comme un ver qui, naissant d'un bois par pourriture,/ Ronge le mesme bois, et s'en sert de pasture"; lines 59-60: "Comme un joueur qu'un feu d'avarice devore,/ Qui perd tout ce qu'il a pour vouloir s'acquitter"; lines 71-2: "Comme le bastelier mene à bord sa nasselle,/ Encor qu'en l'y menant il y tourne le dos."

[37] See for example the discussion of love in Du Vair's *Philosophie morale des stoiques* (1599), ed. G. Michaut, pp. 137-8; and cf. Zanta, p. 305.

stancy, interspersed with equally convincing pleas for constancy.[38] In the *Méditations* proper, the same poems which celebrate inconstancy and announce the lover's liberation often lead back to constancy in the end. The fifth "Elegie" (118-21) for example, which begins with the firm resolution to abandon the mistress, falters toward the middle; finally, the poet recognizes that his love is "trop fort.../ Pour [lui] permettre d'estre un momment infidelle" (lines 75-6).[39] But his attachment has nothing to do with the beloved's virtue; on the contrary, it is her faithlessness which makes him want to shake her off: "Je fuis une inconstance et suis une beauté" (line 81). He can flee from Uranie's inconstancy only by himself becoming inconstant; but her beauty forces him to remain constant: his fidelity is to the embodiment of infidelity. His absurd fate is sealed by the trivial accident of her physical charms: "Fuyant l'esprit je suis par le corps arresté" (line 82).

Here the tenets of traditional Petrarchism have been turned on their head: the mistress represents no higher virtue or spiritual beauty, and the lover's constancy is a meaningless passion, which he seeks to overcome through inconstancy. Nothing could be further removed from the age-old debate between reason and love, which depends on fixed values in formal opposition. In the alternation between constancy and inconstancy, the terms are ceaselessly shifted back and forth until their semantic charge fades away. In a double reversal, the inconstancy theme is itself subverted in certain poems. Le Digne, throughout his "Stances. De l'Inconstance" (fols. 113 ro-114 ro), employs all the familiar motifs of change only in order to deny their validity:

> ... la Mer, ny les vents de soy ne sont muables,
> Les saisons et les fleurs en leur temps sont semblables,
> l'Inconstance n'est point en ces comparaisons.

---

[38] Cf. in particular *Les Muses francoises ralliees* of 1606, fols. 185 ro – 229 vo, and *Le Parnasse des plus excellens poetes de ce temps* (1618), pp. 149-89. In both cases the inconstancy and constancy poems are indiscriminately mixed.

[39] A typical rhetorical pattern in this period; cf. d'Urfé's "Irrésolues resolutions. Stances," in *Les Delices de la Poesie Francoise* (1620), vol. I, pp. 306-7. Such poems demonstrate how closely the breakdown of Petrarchan constancy in late Petrarchism is related to the "rhetorical inconstancy" of the last stage of the Renaissance (the subject of the section which follows).

I could marshall a number of similar examples, where Inconstancy is shown to be unfaithful to her own nature.[40] As in the case of sacred and profane motifs, the poles of constancy and inconstancy are switched so many times that they end up by losing their force of contrast; or as Expilly would have it, in words which hinge – fittingly enough – on an affirmative negation: "Non, c'est être constant changer de volonté/ En ce monde leger, qui sans cesse varie."[41]

Like most verse collections of the period, the *Méditations* exemplify the poetic practice of inconstancy throughout, at all levels of structure and meaning. If the opening salvo of the *vers liminaires* invokes the poet's abandonment to "legereté" (p. 35), the last poem of the *Méditations* proper is a "Voeu à l'Amour" in which he promises to "vivre pour jamais en la flame cruelle" (p. 132) of his love. If the first part of the book presents the complaints of the unrequited lover as a continuous soliloquy, the final section is a *Meslange* of heterogeneous styles, forms, and contents. Such incongruencies are typical of amatory verse at the end of the Renaissance. The poetic inconstancy of the era is reflected not only in shifting *topoi* and a lack of global design, but also in the very fabric of which these larger structures are composed. As I observed in Chapter II, the question of theme resolves itself into a problem of rhetoric. At the dawn of the seventeenth century, the fixed constellations of *Délie* and *L'Olive* give way to a different mode of poetic discourse. An upstart goddess defies the heavenly Muse, and Urania yields to the Inconstancy of words.

2. Rhetorical Inconstancy

I have touched on the subject of this section many times in the preceding pages: now it is time to draw a number of threads together, all of which reveal a similar trend. Chapter I pointed out that throughout the *Méditations*, Durand uses Petrarchist motifs in a subversive manner; a turn of phrase often reduces the given theme to a hollow *jeu de mots*. The subsequent chapter suggested that

---

[40] For other reversals of this type see Expilly's "Cartel. Pour les Chevaliers de la Constance, contre les Chevaliers de l'Inconstance" (1624 edn., pp. 160-1); Le Masson, fol. 30 ro; and Scalion, fol. 85 vo.

[41] Edn. cit., p. 75; the poems of Expilly were originally published in 1596.

such verbal tricks characterize the style of the entire period. Playfully, the "poets of 1600" treat the traditional *topoi* with such perverse refinement that the subject retreats from view. The rise of the counter-Petrarchan elements discussed in Chapter III – the baseness of the beloved, the praise of inconstancy, etc. – goes hand in hand with an alteration on the plane of language. In the final stage of the Renaissance, rhetoric no longer serves to intensify, or even to convey the amorous conceit; more often, it serves to undermine it. In destabilizing the *topos*, this discourse becomes unstable in itself. After building up the theme through brilliant devices, the poet topples his construction with a witty *pointe* or syntactic anomaly – also a feat of rhetoric, but a corrosive one. Like the thematic structure of late Petrarchism, its language collapses inward, deliberately vitiating its own most forceful effects.

The stylistic inconstancy of the age does not end here: the deflating techniques often observed in this book go further than mere irony. Developed to an extreme, they tend to reverse themselves once again, falling back into their original position. By an act of double rhetorical inversion, the *thématique* of Petrarchism reemerges at a level different from before. The inconstancy of discourse, like that of the inconstancy motif itself, implies an alternation between constancy and inconstancy. These phenomena can best be demonstrated by a close analysis of specific examples: four sonnets from the *Méditations*.

Chapter I concluded that the beloved, the supposed inspiration of Durand's verse, seems strangely absent from it; Chapter II described the dissolution of Petrarchist themes through rhetorical refractions as a "disappearing act." Both traits are not only symptomatic of the age, they also reinforce each other. The figure of the mistress recedes along with the *topoi* that surround her; at the close of the Renaissance, center stage is occupied by the verbal coruscations of the poem itself.

In 1597 a sonnet "Sur les yeux de Madame de Beaufort" (Gabrielle d'Estrées, mistress of Henri IV) appeared in the *Recueil de diverses poésies*; its author, Laugier de Porchères, must have been pleased with the enormous success which it achieved. For the next two decades his poem served as the prototype for countless variations by versifiers all over France. It could justifiably be said to represent the stylistic quintessence of the "poets of 1600" (as their younger colleague Colletet would certainly have agreed):[42]

Ce ne sont pas des yeux, ce sont plutost des Dieux,
    Ils ont dessus les Rois la puissance absoluë:
    Dieux, non, ce sont des Cieux, ils ont la couleur bleuë,
    Et le mouvement prompt comme celoy des Cieux.
Cieux, non, mais deux Soleils clairement radieux
    Dont les rayons brillans nous offusquent la veuë:
    Soleils, non, mais esclairs de puissance incogneuë,
    Des foudres de l'amour signes presagieux.
Car s'ils estoyent des Dieux feroyent ils tant de mal?
    Si des Cieux, ils auroyent leur mouvement esgal:
    Deux Soleils, ne se peut: le Soleil est unique.
Esclairs, non: car ceux-cy duront trop et trop clairs:
    Toutefois je les nomme, afin que je m'explique,
    Des yeux, des Dieux, des Cieux, des Soleils, des esclairs.[43]

The rhetorical scheme used by Porchères epitomizes a number of the tendencies which I have already identified as characteristic of the period: the inversion of conventional motifs; the progressive negation of what has gone before (here by means of a chain of repetitions, or *gradatio*); and above all, the twists and turns of a pseudo-logic. Porchères wittily underlines the incongruity of his speculations in the final lines, where he "explains himself" by lumping together the things listed, after having denied the appropriateness of each in turn. This amounts to the opposite of an explanation: the quintuple positive is a multiplied negative, an emphatic self-cancellation. The discourse enacts its own indeterminacy; it calls attention to itself as a void.

Writing of this sonnet in 1658, as a champion of Malherbe and member of the Académie Française, Colletet severely condemns "ce genre de Poësie de Sonnets & de Stances, qui presque ne consistoient alors qu'en certaines pointes affectées, qu'en redites pueriles,

---

[42] See the discussion of Porchères's sonnet in his *Art poétique*, part II, pp. 51-3. Colletet contrasts the style of Porchères's age with his own "siecle délicat & raffiné" (p. 53), in which the principles of the Malherbian school ("les veritables Poëtes") have triumphed.

[43] Text of 1604, reprinted in Raymond and Steele, anth. cit., p. 111; as denoted by the title of the poem in their collection, by this time Gabrielle d'Estrées had been elevated to the title of Marquise de Monceaux.

& qu'en petites cheutes & contrebatteries de mots, dont les intelligens & les veritables Poëtes se mocquoient avecque tant de raison" (p. 52). His remarks are a valuable endorsement of my own observations, since he isolates a number of features I have discussed as endemic to the "pre-Classical" age: elaborate word-play, pronounced *conduplicatio* ("redites"), and internal contradiction ("contrebatteries de mots"). The qualifiers "affectées" and "pueriles" point to the willful artificiality and trivialization I have indicated as typical of the verse of Durand and his contemporaries. In this context, one might reconsider the connotations of the term *chute*: in Colletet's usage, as opposed to a *pointe*, it seems to imply the intentional deflation of poetic effect I have repeatedly singled out. The adjective "petites," applied to "cheutes" and "contrebatteries de mots," suggests that the "fall" in question is a diminishing of verbal force, caused by countercurrents of opposing words. These are the stylistic traits which Malherbe, Colletet, and the other "veritables Poëtes" had supposedly expunged by the middle of the seventeenth century. When Colletet stresses their intellectual understanding (cf. "intelligens"), he marks the divide between the old school and the new as one of childish mystification (cf. "pueriles") versus mature clarity of expression. Here again he highlights a phenomenon I have pinpointed in these pages: the playful bafflement which runs like a teasing thread through late Renaissance verse.

Affirmation, negation: throughout Porchères's poem a definition is proffered, then removed. But a reversal of the denials is inherent in the guessing game; though the eyes are none of the things named, they still have something of all of them. The *redditio* of the second tercet underscores the paradox: "Esclairs, non: ...des eclairs." Durand's sonnet XIX, an obvious imitation of Porchères, rehearses this procedure even more succinctly:

Beaux yeux, qui recelez tant de traicts et de feux,
    Que rien ne sçauroit fuir de vostre obeyssance,
    Vous n'estes point des yeux, mais des soleils heureux,
    Soleils, non, mais des Dieux d'immortelle naissance.
Mais comment puis-je avoir de vous ceste creance?
    Des yeux ne pourroient pas estre si dangereux,
    Des soleils n'auroient pas une telle influence,
    Et des Dieux ne seroient jamais si rigoureux.

Les yeux sont pour le bien, vous estes pour les peines,
   Le Soleil entretient, vous consommez les veines,
   Les Dieux donnent la vie, et vous faites mourir.
Qu'estes-vous donc, mauvais? des beaux yeux en essence,
   En beauté des soleils, et des Dieux en puissance
   Descendus icy-bas pour nous faire souffrir.

Durand employs several tactics to achieve greater concentration. In the first place, he reduces the terms of the comparison from five ("yeux," "Dieux," "Cieux," "Soleils," "esclairs") to three ("yeux," "Soleils," "Dieux"). Second, he states his reasons for believing that the eyes are *not* eyes (lines 6, 9), whereas Porchères never fills this hole in the logical structure. Third, Durand justifies the clustering of all three terms in the final affirmation: though in reality ("en essence," line 12) these are eyes, they possess the beauty of suns and the power of gods. Like the heavenly orbs of astrology, they rule the lover's fate.

Here again, the tables are easily turned. Since Porchères never fully "proves" that the eyes are not what they seem, he does not call their fundamental nature into question. Durand, by twice challenging their identity as eyes, plunges their true status into still deeper obscurity than his model has done. J.-M. Vianey (p. 241-4) trenchantly observes that Desportes becomes vague and inflated precisely because he tries too hard to be clear. As the Renaissance draws to a close, this explanatory obfuscation becomes more and more pronounced; in the early seventeenth century, a chain of mock elucidations often leads to virtual opacity.

In all the poems derived from the sonnet "Sur les Yeux de Madame Beaufort,"[44] the mistress has disappeared both as person and as *topos*. Though such verses echo the old Petrarchist schema of the arrows of love that dart from the mistress' pupils, the theme has been fragmented to the point of total abstraction: these are the shards of a tradition in decay. The eyes are simply the starting point for a rapid succession of metaphors, a string of *pointes* which relay each other in swift verbal revolutions.[45] When the wheel of conceits

[44] For other examples, see Bertaut (re-edn.), p. 333; Baddel, fol. I vo; Deimier, p. 34; Du Souhait, fols. 4 vo-5 ro; and Rosset, fols. 56 vo-57 ro.

[45] Cf. Lafay, pp. 200-2, 372-3; one cannot agree with him that the "images" used by Porchères in this sonnet retain a "pouvoir émotif" (p. 202) – except in the impersonal sense defined below, at the end of the present chapter.

rolls to a halt in the final verse, nothing has been described. By contrast with the earlier *blason*, here there is no portraiture: no details about a physical trait, however stereotyped. In this respect Durand goes even further than his predecessor. In memorializing Mme de Beaufort, Porchères emphasizes the blueness of her irises; the "beaux yeux" addressed by Durand lack a specific color – just as the subject of his anti-portrayal bears no name, not even the fictitious one of "Uranie."

More markedly than the Petrarchism of the mid-Renaissance, that of Durand's generation debunks the beloved as a literary pretext. This is poetry which calls attention to itself chiefly as language – not as the expression of traditional themes, much less of personal sentiments. Porchères himself underlines that autonomous quality when he writes: "je les nomme," "je m'explique" (line 13). External reality and *topos* are submitted to the arbitrary will of the poet; it is he who draws the disparate elements together – "des yeux, des Dieux, des Cieux, des Soleils, des esclairs." But this shaping impulse is not based wholly on individual "authority," since the pieces are brought together in large part by the requisites of rhythm and rhyme. The organizing principle lies above all in the discursive form itself. It comes as no surprise that the rhetorical framework perfected by Porchères was used as a vehicle for other subjects than the mistress' eyes. But it is still more significant that two poems of the period, by Corbin and Deimier,[46] substitute the poet's verses for the original object of praise. Here poetry itself appears even more openly as the real centerpiece – though once again, an inconstant rhetoric swings round to the opposing side: like the *topos* of the mistress, that of the verses recedes behind the shifting surface of the words themselves.

---

[46] See the sonnet "Sur les Amours de Sieur de Deimier" by Jacques Corbin, in Deimier (ninth liminary poem, non pag.); and Deimier's own sonnet LII (pp. 52-3). It is interesting to note that Deimier uses the same rhetorical formula in another sonnet which praises the mistress' portrait, rather than herself: an artistic parallel to the substitution of rhetoric for reality. The poem approaches incoherence when Deimier writes that the portrait "n'est pas Cypris, il est plustost les Cieux,/ ...Les Cieux, non, mais les Dieux..." Similarly, in the sonnet on his verses he concludes with more than the usual number of convolutions:

> Pensees, non, mais feux elles fondent vos glaces,
> Non feux: mais c'est mon coeur qui devient par vos graces
> Feux, pensees & vents, & souspirs amoureux. (p. 53)

Chapter I indicated that the retreat of the beloved from a focal position in the *Méditations* corresponds to an increased emphasis on the lover; throughout the book, the lyric *je* dominates the scene. That its identity stands in some relation to the poet's own – not necessarily as "lover" – seems self-evident; but just as in the case of the mistress, the rhetorical inconstancy of its presentation often calls into question the integrity of the lyric *je* itself. Durand's sonnet III provides a particularly good example of this anomaly, especially since it takes its point of departure in the most conventional of Petrarchist themes and tropes: nothing out of order here, at first glance. The usual antitheses unfold in a predictable manner, their semantic equivalence reflected in the parallel structure, a series of infinitive phrases (or as I termed it in Chapter II, a "syntactic *conduplicatio*"):

Geler dedans les feux, et brusler dans la glace,
 Ne pouvoir à mes yeux accorder le sommeil,
 Vivre de desespoir attendant le cercueil,
 Effroyable porter la mort dessus ma face:
Verser, non pas des pleurs, mais du sang de mon oeil,
 Mesler la joye aux pleurs, et la craincte à l'audace,
 Gisant dedans mon lict n'arrester point en place,
 Ci tost que le jour vient detester le Soleil:
Errer en un moment entre mille desirs,
 Faire dès leur naissance avorter mes plaisirs,
 Sont les seuls entretiens de mon ame affligée,
Lors que je considere avec quelles douceurs
 Elle fut par tes yeux à t'aimer obligée,
 Pour n'avoir à la fin que des feux et des pleurs.

The first line is based on the archetype of all Petrarchist paradoxes, the fire-ice dichotomy. Either element should kill, but in the realm of passion they cancel each other out: the lover cannot die, yet he cannot live... and so on. Whether he suffers from the coldness of the mistress or the burning of desire is irrelevant: they merely form two sides of the same coin, which is perpetually reversed from one side to the other. Psychologically, the Petrarchist antitheses represent a paralysis of the will, a numbness which obliterates the distinction between contrary feelings. Poetically, the same pattern pertains; in Durand's sonnet the successive pairs of opposites neutralize themselves and each other.[47] Meaning no longer evolves, but rather turns in circles. In the Petrarchist paradigm of the emotions, oscillation between extremes produces the rigidity of indecision; similarly, the semantic movement of the poem subsides paradoxically into a mobile stasis. The vacuous rotation and arrest are "metamimetically" portrayed by the *redditio* which links lines 1 and 14 ("feux-glace": "feux-pleurs"), while the melting of ice to tears neatly sums up the dilution of the hackneyed motifs.

Line 2 introduces a further aspect of the psychology inherent in Petrarchist language: the disintegration of the self. It is symbolized by the division of the body into its component parts.[48] Here the poet speaks of his eyes as though they were separate from himself. In lines 3-5 Durand develops a more unusual thematic scheme: the violence of tone and imagery recalls that of d'Aubigné and the "pétrarquistes noirs." But in line 6 Durand typically deflates the effect; though he had just said in the previous verse that he does not weep tears, now he mixes joy with his tears. Presumably, line 5 was distinguishing between tears of water and tears of blood; still, a debilitating note of confusion accompanies the "contrebatterie de mots," to borrow Colletet's apt expression. In the last two verses of the quatrain a similar inconsistency occurs, this time on the plane of rhythm. Line 7 already breaks the previous pattern of an infinitive in each initial hemistich; in line 8 the disruption is accentuated by rhythmic means. The irregularity of the verse, which recalls the wrenched meters of Jodelle, imitates the lover's outburst against the dawn which he detests.

The first tercet returns to the previous syntactic and rhythmic pattern. Rhetorically, it continues and then rounds off the development of the quatrains; in its final line the suspense aroused by the incomplete syntax of the infinitive chain is resolved. Accordingly, the second tercet sounds like an afterthought. The sense of detach-

[47] While antitheses are a feature of all Petrarchist poetry, as the Renaissance draws to a close they become particularly accentuated and all-pervasive. Cf. Raymond, art. cit., p. 115: "Au XVIe siècle, le maniérisme rhétorique est une composante nécessaire du pétrarquisme, de son style antithétique, 'pointu', lequel se prolongera, en se codifiant en quelque sorte, dans la préciosité." As I noted in Chapter I, by the time Colletet published his *Poésies diverses* in 1656, "cette facon d'escrire par Antitheses" (p. 189) was no longer thought to be consonant with "Classical" taste.

[48] See the discussion of this theme in Chapter I in relation to sonnet VII, where the poet's eyes argue with his heart; and cf. the examples given in the footnote.

ment is increased by the somewhat analytical term *considérer* (line 12), and by the distracting pronoun "elle" (line 13), the antecedent of which does not immediately spring to mind. In passing from line 11 to line 12 the reader naturally assumes that "mon ame" (line 11) and "je" (line 12) refer to the same subjectivity. Oddly, line 13 throws this equivalence off balance: what "je" is considering is the "ame" itself: so "je" must occupy a different vantage-point from the "ame." Throughout the poem the speaker had seemed to be describing an inner state, the state of his soul. Suddenly the perspective goes awry; the self appears to stand back and observe the soul from without. It sees the soul seduced, betrayed, then abandoned to torment and sorrow.

Are those agonies still felt by the self, in its transposed form as the lyric *je*? The phrase "Lors que" (line 12) does not signify a duration in which the self suffers, but one in which the self "considers" the soul. The soul seems to obey its own time: before, it was lured by "douceurs" (line 12); now it is plunged into "feux" and "pleurs" (line 14). The temporal clause which should fuse "je" and "mon âme" into a single consciousness divides them instead. Who is suffering then? Who is speaking? If the speaker is separate from his suffering, then he has retreated into the background of his verse as well. It might be objected that these questions are not legitimately posed in the poem. In my attempt to follow the meanders of a divided discourse, I am only positing them myself. But it would be wrong to dismiss such an interpretation out of hand, as simply another case of modern obscurantism. Colletet in his elder Malherbian years, censuring a sonnet by one of Durand's contemporaries, Angot de l'Éperonnière, comes to a similar conclusion about the inner contradictions of late Petrarchist poetry. "Les deux premiers quatrains sont beaucoup plus obscurs & plus hérissez d'espines que les bois mesmes ausquels [le poète] s'adresse... Car à vray dire il est malaisé de juger si c'est lui qui soit absent de ce bocage ou si c'est sa maistresse qui en soit esloignée. Je scay bien que le second quatrain faict bien voir que c'est luy qui en est esloigné; mais aussy scay-je bien que le premier marque tout le contraire, en disant que sa vie y perd ses voeux & que son coeur y est dans une langueur perpétuelle. Ainsy, comme au jeu des gobelets, on peut dire qu'il y est & qu'il n'y est pas."[49]

[49] "Vie de Robert Angot," in Angot's *Nouveaux Satires*, ed. Blanchemain, pp. XII-XIII.

Chapter II maintained that dislocations of tone and perspective are characteristic of the final phase of Renaissance verse. These lead inevitably to the same kind of "disappearing act" that Durand stages in sonnet III, where "on peut dire qu'il y est & qu'il n'y est pas." As the poet uses the given motif straightforwardly, then subverts it through irony or murkiness, he also undermines the unified identity of the lyric *je*. Pure Petrarchism – or pure anti-Petrarchist parody – keeps the putative self intact; but the "poets of 1600," in their fondness for modulating styles, metaphors, the dramatic context, the speaker's attitude, etc., *within the course of the poem*, dissolve that fiction. At one level the Petrarchist "self" and the associated themes are everywhere present, just as before; but like the *topoi* surrounding it, the lyric subjectivity unevenly withdraws from the foreground. What remains at closest range is the opaquely shifting rhetoric of the poem, which calls attention to itself primarily as language.

If the conventions of the supposed love-experience, and even the pretense of the lyric *je*, no longer form the unifying substance of late Petrarchist verse, then one must seek it at the level of the words themselves. A commonplace of much twentieth century criticism regards the work – or on a larger scale, the *oeuvre* – as a system of signs; the relationships between these signs constitute the meaning of the whole, which does not depend on any outside sphere – biographical, historical, or other. The formulaic poetry of the Petrarchist tradition lends itself especially well to this type of analysis, since the thematic vocabulary it uses is limited, inbred, and autonomous. Petrarchism functions mainly by its own inner laws, rather than taking its cue from external influences (as would be the case, for example, in political satire).

There are exceptions to that rule. The *Canzoniere* contains a number of poems (e.g. CXXVIII) which allude to recent historical events, and the same is true of the *Délie* (e.g. XIX-XXI). Ronsard's *Amours* appeal with some frequency to exterior circumstances: personal, national, etc. But it is symptomatic that after Ronsard, such elements become increasingly scarcer in amatory verse, particularly in love poem cycles. Late Petrarchism accentuates the inbred autonomy of the tradition; the sophisticated self-irony of Durand and his contemporaries goes hand in hand with a further separation of the literary sphere from the outside world. To no work could the notion of a *monde clos* be better applied than to the *Méditations* proper; in this verse of unadulterated convention, discourse becomes "auto-referential." Meaning doubles back on itself in a perpetual retreat from the reader, a semantic *mise en abime.*[50]

As the preceding pages have suggested, such implosions occur when they are least expected – when one's attention has been dulled by a series of clichés. The rhetorical repetitions studied in Chapter II, like the thematic ones examined in Chapter I, put the reader off his guard: this too may be a strategy, a preparation for surprise. In his sonnet II, for example, Durand employs a familiar device – the comparison of the lover's fate with that of a mythological figure – to unexpected ends:

> Battus ayant promis de garder le silence
> Au larcin qu'avoit faict Mercure en un troupeau,
> Le trompa neantmoins par un profit nouveau,
> Dont Mercure outragé soudain prit la vengeance.
> Ainsi la Parque ayant achevé mon fuseau,
> Le destin me promit heureuse recompence,
> Si je pouvois dompter la douce violence
> Du Dieu qui porte aveugle un funeste flambeau.
> Mais luy m'ayant promis un plus riche salaire,
> J'ay trompé mon destin, qui depuis par colere
> M'a faict comme Battus en pierre transformer.
> Et comme il fut depuis une pierre de touche,
> On peut voir par mes vers que c'est de bien aimer,
> Et le silence peut s'apprendre de ma bouche.

Here it is not only *topos* and lyric subjectivity which dissolve, but the fabric of the discourse itself. At the beginning of the poem, the word "silence" appears perfectly straightforward; by the time it is repeated in the final line, it has become an enigmatic commentary on the *Méditations* as a whole.

The legend evoked by Durand in sonnet II is an unusual one, at least in the Petrarchist context. More likely than not, he drew on

[50] Cf. the energetically "contemporary" exegesis of Shakespeare's sonnets by Felperin (pp. 147-99), who asserts that we should never underestimate the self-awareness of late Renaissance authors. As he affirms (p. 200): "The recent paradigm-shift toward theory, which has enabled such texts to be read as never before, and writerly modernity to be radically backdated, may itself be only the latest phase of that larger change in the status of writing which enabled such self-critical and self-destabilizing texts to be produced in the first place, the academic institutionalization of a textual self-consciousness long since in train."

the original source: *Metamorphoses* II, lines 676-707, where Ovid recounts a monitory tale. Mercury stole some cattle from Apollo's herd, and hid them in a forest. Battus, an aged shepherd, was the only witness of the theft; in return for the bribe Mercury gave him, a fine heifer, the old man promised to keep quiet. Later the god returned in disguise to test the shepherd's trustworthiness. He offered Battus an even better reward than before – a heifer and a bull – if he would tell him where the cattle were. Battus accepted the offer, breaking his earlier promise. In revenge, Mercury turned him to stone.

Though the myth is uncommon, Durand employs it in a highly conventional fashion – or so it seems at first. According to the typical Petrarchist scheme discussed in Chapter I, the tragic fate of the mythological figure is compared point for point with that of the hapless lover. As noted earlier, Vianey reproaches Desportes with "une poursuite excessive de la clarté" (p. 241). Similarly, in Durand's sonnet, the simile appears *too* clear: "Battus (line 1)... Ainsi (line 5)... comme Battus (line 11)... comme il fut (line 12)" – a mechanical structure, without mystery. On closer inspection, the parallel betrays some perplexing incongruities. The easy equivalence of Battus-lover and Mercury-destiny already breaks down in the second pair: Mercury returned incognito to tempt the shepherd; here the lover seems to be led astray by Amor, not Mercury. Though Amor represents an aspect of the lover's "destin" (line 6), "destin" and the "Dieu" of love (line 8) are presented as two distinct entities; the former is personified by "Mercure," but it is emphatically "luy [Amor]" who promises the poet "un plus riche salaire" (line 9). Or is the reader to understand after all that the lover's "destin" only *appears* to be Love? In any case, the embodiment of "destin" as distinct from the "Parque" (line 5) strikes a discordant note in itself. As opposed to the Fate,[51] who merely spins the thread of human life, "destin" figures here as an independent god, subject to "colere" (line 10) and fits of vengefulness just like Mercury. Owing to these facets alone, the simile emerges as more complex and sub-

[51] According to Cartari (p. 455), the youngest of the Fates holds the distaff; the middle in age, the spindle ("fuseau"); and the eldest cuts the thread. The "fuseau achevé" (line 5) would be the fate or destiny which had already been determined – and which, by definition, could no longer be "trompé" (line 10): another case of inconsistency.

tle than one had initially imagined – but the crowning anomaly comes in the final tercet.

The word "silence" in the last verse of the sonnet echoes the "silence" evoked in line 1: Battus' silence is equated with that of the poet. Just as Battus was turned to speechless stone, so the poet has been struck by vengeful destiny with the "immobile ecstasy" of unrequited love – yet the poem itself, and the book of poems, are in conflict with the parallel. If the poet is silent in that he dares not talk of his love face to face with the mistress, as stated in the epistle "D. à son Uranie" (p. 34), he does speak out in his poems. Attention is deflected from this thematic contradiction by a fanciful verbal trick. Without any basis in traditional mythology, Durand styles the petrified shepherd a "pierre de touche" (line 12), and extends the simile beyond the bounds of logic by comparing him to the touchstone of amorous devotion formed by his verses. The symmetry of the comparison is maintained, but at the expense of semantic consistency. Battus is a "pierre de touche" only by virtue of the pun which allows some analogy with the verses, not because of any genuine correspondence between the myth of Battus and the lover's fate. By a curious effect of ricochet, the conceit suddenly bounces from the level of allegory to that of words. Not only does this quirk point up the disharmony between the myth and the amorous theme, it also deflates both sides of the extended simile by reducing the whole poem to a *jeu de mots*.

So far sonnet II appears to be just another exercise in punctured meaning – more extreme than those previously discussed, though not radically different. Through inconsistency and verbal playfulness, both the *topos* and the lyric subjectivity give way, flattening out into a blank wall of discourse. Here the game becomes more complicated, in that the *topos* in question concerns poetry itself: the poem expresses (or does not express) the fact of expression (or non-expression). Eliminating the lyric *je*, the words achieve an autonomous "reflexivity"; they talk about themselves. The theme of the poet's ability to "parler par son taire" – to paraphrase Durand's "Elegie VI" (p. 122) – appears in the French Petrarchist canon as early as Scève; for example, *dizain* VIII of the *Délie* begins as follows: "Je me taisois si pitoyablement/ Que ma Deesse ouyt plaindre mon taire." But in Durand's sonnet the poem becomes a substitute for direct speech: it is a "speaking silence"; like an emblem, it is seen but not heard – "On peut voir par mes vers..." (line 13). Whereas Scève uses the theme in its traditional sense – the lover's passion is so strong that it "speaks out" without needing to be said in words – Durand converts it into a commentary on writing.

What does the poem actually say about itself? Like the central simile on which the sonnet is based, the final *pointe* seems ambiguous, even contradictory. Battus forms a "pierre de touche" (line 12) only because the verses do; the "silence" of line 14 cannot be compared to that of line 1, since the whole poem would make no sense – the violation of a promised silence being precisely the starting point for the simile. If the poet says "le silence peut s'apprendre de ma bouche" (line 14), then he represents the opposite of Battus. The silence which can be learned from these poems is one of meaning: in fact, they say nothing at all. At the end of this sonnet, the inner structures of poetic language have been collapsed; even the sound of the words lapses back into silence – though the silence after speech is not the same as the silence before.[52]

In the three sonnets by Durand analyzed above, the foundations of Petrarchism appear thoroughly demolished: the mistress and the *topoi* surrounding her, the lyric *je*, and even the cohesion of poetic technique ultimately evade the reader. Still, here again the terms undergo a further inversion: through the self-contradiction and emptiness which remain, the *thématique* and poetic substance of Petrarchism re-emerge at another level.[53] In sonnet XIX the retreat of the beloved (or her *topos*) behind a series of metaphors demonstrates the obsessive, idealizing character of Petrarchist love, which "loses sight" of its object. The Petrarchist confusion of desire evoked in sonnet III – "Errer en un moment entre mille desirs" (line 19) – is embodied by a confusion of identity, a confusion of

[52] Cf. Felperin (p. 129): "No conceivable... system of rhetoric can bring interpretive sense or consensus out of a text that is simultaneously 'there' and not 'there,' that says and unsays itself in one and the same breath."

[53] Cf. Lafay's observation that the love poetry of Porchères "n'est pas aussi gratuite qu'elle peut en donner d'abord l'impression: elle a un retentissement humain profond. La frivolité, la subtilité, les complications quintessenciées et jusqu'aux images et aux thèmes légués par le pétrarquisme, y compris dans ce qu'ils ont à la fois d'outré, d'artificiel, voire de commun, sont significatifs et suggestifs d'un aspect essentiel, au sens plein du mot, de la sensibilité amoureuse" (p. 373). As the author underlines, he is speaking of essences here, not of specific emotions: the "beloved" of Petrarchism, especially in its final phase, is poetry itself – a brilliant display of language, an aspiration which fulfills itself only by never being fulfilled.

temporality, a confusion of syntax and meaning in the poem itself. Similarly, the symbolic disjunction of sonnet II mirrors its principal theme: the Petrarchist's incapacity to express his passion simply or directly, "struck dumb" as he is by the violence of unrequited love.

The existence of a personal love need not be invoked; on the contrary, the poet's yearning for fulfilment may be understood as concentrating on the impersonal. His desire is directed toward the "poetic moment" itself, in which the self is exteriorized into words. That moment – continually approached, never fully attained – represents a fusion of subject and object (or the self and the "other") into one. The first sonnet of the *Méditations* succinctly illustrates this principle, which provides the key to the cycle as a whole:

> Languissant nuict et jour en un égal martyre,
> Voicy ce que mon coeur a tousjours medité,
> Tantost en adorant les loix de ton empire,
> Et tantost par douleur contre elles despité.
> Non, c'est plustost Amour qui lamente et souspire
> De voir contre mon bien ton courage irrité,
> Et qui semble vouloir par ma plume te dire
> Qu'en me blessant tu blesse aussi sa deïté.
> Je suis son ame mesme, ou plustost son essence,
> Tous mes tourmens aussi luy tiennent lieu d'offense,
> Il souffre en mes douleurs, et languit en mes fers.
> Voy donc ses mesmes cris, et ses mesmes alarmes,
> Et permets pour le moins qu'il t'asseure en ces vers
> Combien ils m'ont cousté de souspirs et de larmes.

Already in line 1, the opposites "nuict et jour" collapse toward a central identity, "un égal martyre." On a rhetorical level, such antitheses as those of lines 3-4 reflect the same mutual cancellation as they express on a moral plane: an ineffectual paralysis, brought about by inner contradiction. Line 2 introduces another aspect of the dilemma. Like antitheses, or the many figures of repetition discussed in Chapter II, the various forms of metonymy are more than just automatic, unconsidered devices. Here the substitution of "coeur" for the lyric *je* corresponds to the mental process of poetry, as a force which acts on the mind in its turn, divorcing the poet from himself as completely as does the passion imposed on him from without according to the Petrarchist schema. The word "Voicy" (line 2) presents the poems, which have been continuously "meditated" ("tousjours medité"). As lines 3-4 reveal, one movement of the heart countermands the other; the continuity lies not in the lover's fidelity, but in the poet's contemplation. Through poetry, the focus on desire achieves a singleness of purpose which desire alone does not possess. By the same token, in this concentrated effort toward clarity, the experience itself (whether the amorous or the poetic impulse) is set aside, becomes detached from the feeling subject.

The inner process which either poetry or desire can initiate evolves on three planes simultaneously. The first corresponds to the first person: the forces of the self are directed toward a unique object – "inspiration" or "objet amoureux" – by which it enters fully into the role of subject. But the self is also submitted to the power of the other, the second person invoked in the phrase "ton empire" (line 3). This dominion robs the self of its independence – the poet's heart is stolen, according to one of the most common Petrarchist images. On a third level, corresponding to the third person, subject and object are fused in a higher awareness. Such a schema, though vastly over-simplified, forms the basis of Petrarchism: both of its thematic psychology and of its poetic discipline.

The rest of Durand's sonnet tersely enacts the three-fold evolution outlined above. The second quatrain begins by denying that it is "mon coeur," i.e. the subjectivity, which expresses itself in the love poem cycle; instead it is "Amour," the embodiment of desire, who dictates the poet's meditations. By this playful shift to the third person, Durand inscribes a complex event. In pursuing the amorous (or the poetic) impulse to its extreme conclusion, the self experiences a strange reversal: it attains that part of consciousness which is impersonal, which lies at the threshold of the inhuman. Far more than the beloved, Amor represents the radically other. The beloved can be singled out, can be identified; Love cannot. All the same, Amor is intrinsic to the lover's suffering. In transferring his torments to the god, the poet stands outside himself: the subjectivity becomes objectified.[54]

[54] In the *Phaedrus*, Socrates imagines that every soul follows its patron god in a procession across the sky, before being born into the mortal sphere of decay and death. "Ce qui fait qu'un homme est aimé d'un autre, c'est que ce dernier croit retrouver en lui l'image de son dieu, et les efforts qu'il fait pour façonner et pour parfaire cette image suscitent en lui un effort parallèle pour imiter la vie divine, pour en retrouver en lui-même l'image" (Léon Robin, *La Théorie platonicienne de l'amour*, p. 146).

In the tercets, the fusion of the lover and the god, the poet and the god, is complete. From the moment passion takes hold of the mind, a double life begins: a new self rises up within the old, vaster and more distant. In this poem which introduces the *Méditations* as a whole, the god seems to represent the farthest removed of the poet's selves, which in its endless retreat appears at times to reunite with him. As in all Petrarchist poetry, this enlargement can take place only because of the second person which mediates between the first and third, whether that medium is understood as the beloved or the poetic moment itself. The second tercet summons the beloved to hear the cries of a tormented love; but significantly, they are seen rather than heard: "*Voy* donc ses mesmes cris..." (line 12). In the end, they are verses on a page.

The last two lines of the sonnet bind all the threads together, with laconic ambivalence. There are three agents at play: the beloved ("permets"), the god ("qu'il t'asseure"), and the verses ("ils m'ont cousté"). The first of these is also an object ("qu'il *t'*asseure") – because the beloved, while acting upon the lover, is also the intended object of Amor's plaints. The lover himself, as an agent, is absent; he survives only as a passive instrument ("ils *m'*ont cousté"). A force larger than himself appears to suffer in his place – this is a measure of inner distance. At the farthest reach of the poet's consciousness, his passion and his creation detach themselves; as autonomous agents, they exist at a remove from himself. In the final line it is not love that makes the poet suffer, but the verses themselves. The last two lines *also* represent the lover speaking to the beloved of his torments, his "souspirs" and his "larmes." The progressive fusion of the poet with the god, and of the god with the poems, cannot be arrested at the end: it works in both directions. If the poet seems to disappear into his passion and his creation, he returns as the sentient mortal in the final words. The "souspirs" and "larmes" are *his*.

Then again, notice the past tense: the price has been paid by the lover; but the poet speaks in the present. The poetic moment refunds his amorous despair, reinscribes it here and now. The message to the beloved always demands a "double reading," an "overturning gesture" which leads back to the poem itself – not that a second movement or a third or any number is enough; not that any discourse ever annuls the terms which it assumes, much less the ones that lie outside it. "Lover, beloved, poet, god" – or even the fabric of the words themselves: no element can dominate the rest, no dead polarity can block the next progression or return to "ghostlier demarcations, keener sounds." The poem frames but never occupies "a field of nonpresence as other than lack of presence."[55] By reliving the worn tropes and *topoi* of a moribund tradition, Durand and his contemporaries affirm the power of poetry to revive its most ossified conventions, and start anew.

One of those contemporaries triumphantly asserts that the present is only strengthened by what has been. "In me thou seest the twilight of such day,/ As after sunset fadeth in the west..." But he ends the sonnet: "This thou perceiv'st, which makes thy love more strong..."[56] In his Petrarchist sequence Shakespeare takes the stance of an older man writing to a youth: like the lover's, his passion gathers force from "the remembrance of things past." His verse is a poetry of sameness, a repetition which recalls the repetitions from before. In sonnet 76 he asks himself:

> Why is my verse so barren of new pride,
> So far from variation or quick change?
> Why with the time do I not glance aside
> To new-found methods, and to compounds strange?
> Why write I still all one, ever the same...?

In the couplet he answers: "For as the sun is daily new and old,/ So is my love still telling what is told." For late Renaissance verse as a whole, memory is the medium of renewal; the tomb of precedent is the house of resurrection. Sonnet 31 addresses the lover as other lovers – itself as other poems. The poetic moment is now; but it re-

[55] Cf. J. T. Nealon, *Double Reading...*, pp. 29-30: "For Derrida, contra many of his followers and critics, deconstruction is not merely a move toward neutralization... Rather, this deadlock, this undecidability, this unreadability is only the first gesture in a double reading. It is the 'overturning' gesture which shows the untenability of the 'classical opposition,' the fact that the (present) privileged term in the opposition can structure itself only with reference to the (absent) non-privileged term, leaving nonpresence as a structuring principle of presence and calling into question the privilege of the master term over the subservient term. This overturning gesture is indeed first-level deconstruction, but it leaves the crucial operation of Derrida's thought unperformed: the wholesale displacement of the systematics of binary opposition and the reinscription of the opposition within a larger field – a 'textual' field that can account for nonpresence as other than a lack of presence."

[56] Sonnet 73; the phrase which follows is from 30.

members other moments: it projects them toward the future, toward the readers that we are. It counts us as other visitants – lost and saved and lost again – among the endless selves it reinvokes:

Thou art the grave where buried love doth live,
Hung with the trophies of my lovers gone,
Who all their parts of me to thee did give:
That due of many now is thine alone:
    Their images I loved I view in thee,
    And thou, all they, hast all the all of me.

Conclusion

THE END OF RENAISSANCE VERSE

In the love verse of Durand and his contemporaries, a wayward rhetoric reverts to ultimate fidelity, only to rebound toward disjunction once again: and so the somersaults proceed, in a ceaseless chain. No matter how obliquely, the thematic subversions, puncturing devices, and playful inconsistencies of this poetry still portray, on a stylistic plane, the inner conflicts of a Petrarchist psychology. But this "metamimetic"[1] allegiance to the traditional *thématique* is also labile; as I noted in Chapter II, all forms of literary repetition circle toward, and *away from*, a central identity. Late Petrarchism differs from its previous stages: in its final expression it no longer manifests the Petrarchan continuity between the human and the divine, the profane and the Christian. The stabilizing intellectual structures which underpin *Délie*, *L'Olive*, and the amatory works of Sponde, do not hold firm in the early seventeenth century. Just as the *topos* of inconstancy implies an alternation between constancy and inconstancy, so the rhetorical inconstancy of the age impels a frequent return to the tropes in their conventional usage – but mainly in order to twist, deform, and disrupt them anew.

At the end of the Renaissance stylistic constancy and inconstancy exist simultaneously, like a Petrarchist antithesis writ large. This combined exaggeration and undermining of inherited devices has

---

[1] As I noted in the Introduction, in his discussion of Shakespeare's sonnets (p. 193), Felperin notes that the "dark lady" may be equated with poetry, in "the 'metamimetic' project of representing nothing other than linguistic difference itself." Similarly, in late Petrarchism inconstancy may be taken to signify the indeterminacy of all language, poetic or otherwise (see the final paragraphs below).

often been compared to Mannerism in the visual arts: a perverse prolongation of earlier traits, already tending toward the Baroque.[2] But as the persistent debate about its esthetic identity demonstrates, the "pre-Classical" period is harder to pin down than most. It is symptomatic of the poetics of inconstancy I have described that it resists all labels. Again and again, literary historians have found themselves obliged to invent fresh name tags: no doubt the current ones will be discarded in their turn. In trying to grasp the essence of this era, critics face a dilemma: its eclecticism deepens the rift between analysis and evidence; its mutability confounds all definition. If one substitutes "theory" for "philosophy," the remarks of Terence Cave[3] apply *a fortiori* to the "poets of 1600":

> Ever since the Greeks invented philosophy, attempting to separate a language of truth from the tropical languages of myth and rhetoric, rational discourse has continued to impose constraints on its supposedly non-serious twin. But literature, in its turn, continually reasserts its liberty by rewriting itself. Like Proteus, it always seeks to evade the moment when allegorization or equivalent procedures force it to reveal "the truth."

Criticism, with its categories and distinctions, is one of those "equivalent procedures" which poetry eludes, and never more deftly than at the conclusion of the Renaissance. As long as the poetics of inconstancy is recognized as only one among many possible "holds" on the epoch – rather than as a fixed historical concept competing with other esthetic terms – Proteus is still free to assume his myriad disguises. As I insisted at the outset, the multifarious masks that literature adopts – especially in the era under discussion – impose a thorough initiation into the individual authors, without preconceived notions about how they must "fit" into a stylistic formula. No matter how far criticism pushes toward generalization, no matter how many echoes it perceives in this immense *conduplicatio* of meaning and form, at any given moment its primary focus must rest on the particular poet, the specific work, the actual poem, as

---

[2] Cf. Mirollo, p. 162: "...literary mannerism does not seem to share with visual mannerism and baroque, or with literary baroque for that matter, a clear stylistic profile of its own. It is not so much an autonomous style as a mode or modulation of the Renaissance literary style..."

[3] *The Cornucopian Text: Problems of Writing in the French Renaissance*, p. 333.

though nothing else were there. If criticism theorizes, it can never be from without: it must always be from within.

Throughout this book I have examined the love poetry of the late Renaissance in the light of its most powerful theme, universal inconstancy. My study has flowed from a single (and singular) case: not only is Durand the greatest exponent of that *topos* in France; through a curious concordance, he seems almost to embody it. Though the parallel is only a coincidence, previous Durand criticism has made so much of the topic that I could not neglect it in this monograph without leaving a serious gap. As even the most sceptical reader would concede, rarely has an author been more consistent in his inconsistency than the poet of the "Stances à l'Inconstance." Like the "Stances," Durand's entire biography appears dominated by change, instability, and inner contradiction. Though himself a commoner, Durand was closely related to the aristocratic Fourcys. His novel, *Les Espines d'Amour*, is dedicated openly to his cousin; by contrast, the *Méditations* are addressed to an "Uranie" whose identity remains unknown. The novel, published in both Paris and Rouen, seems to have been distributed through the normal channels; the book of verse was apparently printed in the utmost secrecy. The public roles played by Durand as "contrôleur des guerres" and "maître de ballet" (in themselves an odd combination), make this privacy seem all the more anomalous. As for Durand's character, the charming figure depicted by Colletet differs sharply from the rapacious schemer denounced by Boitel. The participation in the plot against Luynes could be ascribed either to greedy opportunism or to selfless loyalty toward Marie de Médicis. Finally, the discovery of the incriminating documents, found by accident as they floated down the river, seems like a parable of inconstant Fortune. This is how Durand's contemporaries viewed his meteoric rise to favor and sudden disgrace, which epitomize the instability of the Queen's ephemeral reign.

Admittedly, there is an irony in the fact that Durand's writings were burned along with him at the execution: in this drastic image of transience, Amelia Bruzzi perceives "una tragica coerenza fra vita e opera." With the advantage of hindsight, some readers may choose to consider these poems a reminder of mortality, of defeat and loss. Instead, I would stress the capacity of poetry to restore part of that loss, through a few fine moments of crystallization.

Here again, the "vanishing act" is not complete. As the Renaissance fades, Petrarchism disintegrates only to re-emerge on a different plane. Despite the cruel immolation of Durand, the authorities could not destroy all imprint of his brief and exemplary existence. Several decades after his death, Colletet lamented: "Certes la France perdit en la personne de Durand l'une de ses lumières futures et l'un de ses plus grands ornemens" (Lachèvre edn., p. XI). The *Méditations* date from 1611; no one will ever know how many later verses went up in flames in 1618, along with the ill-advised libel. Jean Tardieu has observed that in the "Stances" Durand unwittingly traced "son portrait mythique et sa propre épitaphe" (p. 195); of course, no mythmaker would expect a poet of impermanence to leave behind, in Horace's proud phrase, a "monumentum aere perennius."

In fact there is no need to appeal to a correlation between Durand's biography and the major theme of his time: on internal evidence alone, his oeuvre displays a high degree of esthetic *inconstantia*. In the first place, the sheer multiplicity of literary genres within such a limited corpus is striking. Not only does it include a novel, ballets, a book of verse, and a political tract, but the variety within the single work is also immense. In the *Espines d'Amour*, Durand intersperses the prose narration with long poems and epistolary passages. The "déscriptions de ballet" reveal his talent as a court chronicler, scenarist, producer, dance-master, and lyricist for operatic songs. The *Méditations* are divided into three disparate parts, and contain almost every conceivable type of verse: a Petrarchist cycle, narrative poems, *folâtries*, satire, occasional verse, an encomium to Louis XIII, *vers de ballet*, etc. Translation and paraphrase appear alongside the original pieces. The variety of stanzaic forms is also impressive: odes, *stances*, elegies, *discours*, madrigals, *chansons*, sonnets, and an epyllion. In the eclecticism of his genres and versification, Durand typifies the epoch in which he wrote.

In his lyric poetry, the most acute contrast arises through comparing the *Méditations* proper – the Petrarchist cycle at the beginning of the volume – with the *Meslange* at the end of the book. The cycle is a self-contained body of verse, dominated by a familiar set of traditional themes; the miscellany presents a hotchpotch of different styles and contents, from the official ode to the *gaulois* joke. The *Méditations* proper exalt the lover's constancy to a single mistress – despite her un-Petrarchan worthlessness; the *Meslange* derives its chief distinction from the "Stances à l'Inconstance." There is nothing unusual about such a discrepancy: that is the whole point. By the end of the Renaissance (as opposed to the era of *Délie*, *L'Olive*, and the early Ronsard) it was customary for authors to add a *mélange* to their works. The universality of this practice reveals a change in attitude. No longer concerned to round out his poetry collection as a perfect monument to Petrarchan love, the poet allows it to trail off in a literary equivalent of *non finito*. If the *Méditations* proper close back on themselves in a vast movement of *redditio*, the *Meslange* represents an open-ended inconclusiveness. Even in its simplest formal outlines, such a volume of verse reflects the poetic contradictions of the age.

The internal conflicts go deeper than the obvious disjunction between different sections of a work. The poetics of inconstancy extends to all levels of composition. By concentrating on the *Méditations* proper throughout my book, I have tried to demonstrate that instability pervades even the supposedly predictable conventions of the Petrarchist cycle itself. On the one hand, all the thematic and rhetorical formulae of the tradition remain recognizable; on the other hand, they are subtly transformed. Like the repeated words in the various types of *conduplicatio*, reiterated themes and tropes change their meaning with each new repetition. The union of stability with movement is certainly a feature of all poetry; but in late Petrarchism the pace of metamorphosis seems to accelerate, straining the inherited conceits and figures to the point of overload and final collapse. As Adorno writes in his *Aesthetic Theory*: [4] "While technique is the epitome of the language of art, it also liquidates that language. This is art's inescapable dilemma."

The dissolution of poetry through the brilliance of its own technique proceeds apace as the Renaissance draws to a close. Even in the standard love verse cycles, familiar motifs are often deformed and undermined, either by consistent omission or by sardonic verbal tricks. The development of a classic *topos* such as the invocation to Sleep suggests that the distortion of Petrarchist themes becomes particularly radical and diverse in the early seventeenth century. In the variations by Grisel, Deimier, Le Digne, Du Mas, Bouchet, and Durand, the *topos* is ingeniously refracted through inversion, blurring, negation, shifting perspectives, tangential side-motifs, and un-

---

[4] Cited by Nealon, p. 183.

expected metaphors. Their poems oscillate across a wide spectrum of opposing styles, even within the space of a single sonnet. On a strictly rhetorical plane, a similar lability makes itself felt: Durand and his contemporaries use *conduplicatio* in all its traditional forms, but they also show a penchant for carrying such devices to extremes.[5] In the works of Du Mas and Le Blanc, as in the innumerable *vers rapportés* of the period, the familiar impact of repetition is thrown off balance, alternately vitiated or intensified through sheer accumulation. Like the chains of metaphors which they support, these extended figures waver at the borderline between complex meaning and semantic emptiness.

Still more obviously than in transformations of the thematic and rhetorical heritage, the esthetic *inconstantia* of the age is embodied in the inconstancy motif itself. It would be specious to overemphasize the link between this *topos* and the social upheavals of the late Renaissance; but its rise does correspond to a change in poetic practice. At one level, the shift in technique appears as a natural outgrowth of the theme: the notion of inconstancy calls up certain images – waves, lightning, wind – which are then stylistically portrayed. As suggested in Chapter III, the themes of movement and discontinuity which dominate the invocations to Inconstancy may be traced deep into their structure and metrical articulation. Even this consistency between motif and rhetoric is disrupted in its turn: for example, the hymnic tone adopted in most invocations clashes oddly with the things evoked – bubbles, straw, fluff, etc. Again the reader enters a metamimetic no man's land, where style and content serve only to enact disparity itself.

On a broader level, the fact that the inconstancy *topos* can emerge and flourish within a Petrarchist tradition which it flagrantly contradicts seems to signal the end of an era. Not only have the formulae of Renaissance love verse become mannered, the willful effort to renew them through novel turns and twists leads to a chronic instability, both in composition and in meaning. The arbitrary treatment of sacred and profane motifs, and the vagaries of the constancy-inconstancy debate itself, form but two examples

---

[5] A tendency which been identified with literary Mannerism. Cf. Raymond, art. cit., p. 115: "Un instinct ludique préside aux exploits de ce style, qui est accidenté, mouvementé, agité, excessif. Le maniérisme, dit Shearman, 'est le style des excès'. Et souvent des excès contraires."

of the thematic inconclusiveness of the "poets of 1600." Similarly, their verbal feints and dodges seem to manifest a characteristic type of rhetorical dislocation. Far from being the result of individual caprice or awkwardness, these phenomena are so widespread that they appear to spring from a collective method, an unconscious or unstated stylistic program. This is clearly the point of view expressed by Colletet when he repudiates the poetic techniques of the previous generation as belonging to a recognizable "school." While inconstancy has often been discussed as a theme of the late Renaissance, one must also acknowledge how fully *inconstantia* pervades its practice of writing.

The esthetic inconstancy of the age reveals itself almost quantifiably in the sphere of literary models: here the unifying pattern is disunity alone. Though Mathieu-Castellani reaffirms the predominance of the "double tradition 'magistrale'" of Ronsard and Desportes from 1570 to 1600, she also emphasizes the rise of several new poetic trends at the end of the period – especially the "réalisme amoureux" of Trellon and his imitators.[6] These innovations do not replace the Petrarchist and pastoral traditions: they simply grow up alongside them, and no attempt is made to reconcile the conflicting elements. Appropriately, no one poet in the early seventeenth century achieves a marked pre-eminence over his rivals, as Ronsard, then Desportes, had done in the previous century. The huge popularity of the anthologies from 1597 onwards testifies in itself to the eclectic tastes of the era: poems of every conceivable sort, both old and new, are included, sometimes without mentioning the authors' names. As the title of one of the first and most successful of the collections makes known, these are truly *Muses ralliées de diverses pars*. The literary pluralism of Durand and his contemporaries shows forth in the individual work as well. In the *Méditations*, for example, five cases of direct influence can be identified – but with one exception, each involves a different poet: Desportes (the "Adventure de Sylvandre" and sonnet IV), Motin (the "Stances à l'Inconstance"), Laugier de Porchères (sonnet XIX), and Durant de la Bergerie (sonnet XX).

---

[6] On the vogue of Trellon's verse in the early seventeenth century see also Lafay, pp. 330-1.

It is striking that despite Durand's collaboration with Malherbe on court entertainments,[7] no echoes of the latter are perceptible in his verse. Once again, this is characteristic of the age. As Henry Lafay has pointed out, even at the height of his official prestige in the 1620s, Malherbe was no more influential over younger writers than other senior poets like Motin. Boileau's tribute to Malherbe, and his subsequent enshrinement as the founder of French Classicism, have distorted the importance of his "doctrine" in his own lifetime.[8] Deimier's *Académie de l'Art Poétique*, published in 1610, does gesture toward the supposedly Malherbian precepts of reason and clarity. But Deimier does not niggle over points of diction and grammar,[9] like Malherbe in his commentary on Desportes; and in practice, the thematic convolutions of Deimier's own verse are hard to follow.[10] By the mid-seventeenth century, a new concern for rigor may be perceived in Colletet's critical remarks, quoted in Chapters III and IV. With Malherbian precision, he picks out the "faults" which were rampant in his youth: the verses of Porchères, Angot, and others, as well as his own early poetry, are condemned as incoherent, obscure, grammatically unsound, and "pointus" – i.e., excessively complex in their tropes and conceits. As noted above, it is significant that he contrasts the defects of "ce type de poésie" with the stylistic purity now upheld by the Académie Francaise;[11] by implica-

---

[7] See the "déscriptions de ballet" listed in the bibilography, which include verses by Malherbe and Bordier as well as Durand.

[8] In his poem "Le Malheur des Poetes" (*Les Divertissemens*, pp. 56-65), published in 1631, Colletet depicts Malherbe as having ended his days in poverty and neglect. Accordingly, when Boileau later hails him as a precursor, it is to some degree a case of "rediscovery."

[9] He devotes a chapter (pp. 71-99) to demonstrating that every hemistich should have an independent sense, that auxiliary verbs should not be separated from the past participle by the caesura, etc., but on the whole Deimier's expositions display a "critical inconstancy" which seems consonant with the period. Cf. Houston, pp. 231-32: "At the end of the sixteenth century, where we may situate a mannerist current of style, if we wish to make the distinction, and the beginnings of a baroque mode, still another kind of poetry was coming into being. This is the French neoclassical style, which we must not see as a simple antithesis to baroque poetry, but as a parallel and in some ways related style."

[10] See Chapter IV, note 46.

[11] Cf. the dubious improvements in metrics and diction which he suggests in discussing one of Durand's poems (Lachèvre edn., p. XIII). At the end of his commentary, which is reminiscent of Malherbe's on Desportes, Colletet concludes: "Mais ce sont des grâces et des beautés qui ne sont guère connues que des poètes de l'Académie françoise ou de ceux qui ont le goût assez bon et assez délicat pour en estre."

tion, he categorizes the "poets of 1600" as partaking of a shared and identifiable literary trend, just as I have done in this book.

To define "pre-Classical" poetry as esthetically inconstant is not merely to evade defining it. The verbal legerdemain and bafflement it flaunts correspond to a crisis in Renaissance poetics. The breakdown of the Petrarchan model in Ronsard already foreshadows the anomalies later observed at the turn of the century. The decline of Ronsard's reputation can be attributed in part to the fact that love verse as a whole is slow to assimilate his innovations. For a time, Desportes assures the continuance of neoclassical Petrarchism; but his final collections follow Ronsard in openly invoking amorous inconstancy. The *Diverses amours* reject both the formal coherence of the *Canzoniere* and its stance of hopeless devotion to a single mistress: as in Ronsard, the spiritual discipline of Petarchism is undermined along with its poetic unity. Arguably, this disillusionment is already inherent in the earlier amatory cycles to Diane, Hippolyte, and Cléonice. Not only do they tacitly acknowledge a Ronsardian plurality of loves: written on commission, they read like an exercise. "Le poète... se laisse dévorer par le langage, seul point de contact entre lui et le monde." In her discussion of Desportes (pp. 209-311), Mathieu-Castellani describes his work as a "poésie sans sujet," a long evocation of indifference, evanescence, discord, and inertia; in her conclusion, she calls him a "poète de l'incohérence."

It may not simply be *post hoc, ergo propter hoc* to suggest that the exhaustion of Petrarchism in Desportes naturally elicits the new *thématique* of "Amour sans passion" in Trellon and his successors, and the matching hollowness of their deliberately vitiated techniques. Revealingly, the abandonment of Petrarchist fidelity goes hand in hand with a mounting distrust of poetry itself: the power of the latter to seduce and delude is recognized as being equal to that of idealistic love. In Saint-Amant's "Inconstance," amorous betrayal and dissimulation are directly linked with the shams of art (ed. Gourmont, p. 131):

On devrait bien trouver estrange
Que ma muse n'ait mis au jour
Quelque oeuvre digne de louange
Sur le sujet de mon amour:

Je m'en estonnerois moy-mesme;
Mais, dans mon inconstance extresme,
Qui va comme un flus et reflus,
Je n'ay pas si-tost dit que j'ayme,
Que je sens que je n'ayme plus.
　　Il est vray que je scay bien feindre,
Et qu'il n'est esprit si rusé,
Lors que ma bouche se veut plaindre,
Que ne s'en trouvast abusé...

The harsh "réalisme amoureux" of the "poets of 1600" is prefigured in the final love poems of Ronsard;[12] but despite the doubts which imbue some of his later verse, he ultimately reaffirms the enduring validity of art: "J'ay vescu j'ay rendu mon nom assez insigne,/ Ma plume vole au ciel pour estre quelque signe..." (*Derniers vers*, sonnet VI) As Castor asserts,[13] Ronsard "exalted poetry above all else, making it sufficient unto itself, and not simply a stage through which the soul passed on its way to a final reunion with the godhead. Such a remodeling of the neo-platonic theory of divine inspiration exalted not only poetry, but also the poet himself." As opposed to this testament of faith in literature, which seems typical of the Renaissance as a whole, consider the following lines from an ode by d'Audiguier, published in 1614 (fol. 40 vo):

　　Toy discours vain & sans effet,
Tu ne seras pas sans suplice
D'avoir esté comme complice
Du tort qu'une ingrate ma'a fait.

A precedent for this passage may be found in the *Contre'Amours* of Jodelle, where he denounces his "traistres vers"; but in the mid-sixteenth century, Jodelle's sonnet appears as an original and isolated instance. By the early seventeenth century, such motifs form a *topos*. They are not restricted to the context of a farewell to love, in the manner of anti-Petrarchism; in a jarring departure from the tradition, Trellon and his epigoni decry the illusions of poetry *in the midst* of the love verse cycle.

[12] Cf. e.g. the ruthless sonnet "Vous estes dejà vieille, et je le suis aussi" (ed. Cohen, vol. II, p. 639).

[13] *Pleiade Poetics*, p. 197.

For clarity's sake I have confined this study mainly to French verse, but the phenomena I have described are actually pan-European in scope. As I noted in Chapter III, the inclusion of the goddess Inconstancy in Cesare Ripa's *Iconologia* of 1603 strongly suggests that the invocation *topos* was widespread throughout the continent by that date. A detailed perusal of the lesser-known authors of each national literature would yield ample material for further scholarship on this subject, and probably corroborate many of my conclusions here. In Italy, for example, among Marino and his followers, "le réalisme amoureux" also makes itself heard, and their self-parodic style, with its flippant twists and turns, stands at the threshold between Mannerism and *préciosité*. Their indiscriminate mixture of sacred and profane motifs, amusingly described by Benedetto Croce, [14] parallels the "thematic inconstancy" I have identified in France.

In the Spanish verse of the period the distinction between *conceptismo* and the *culteranismo* which eventually subsumes it – epitomized by Quevedo and Góngora, respectively – is illuminating: using ordinary words and displaying an ostensible simplicity, *conceptismo* arrives at the same opacity as *culteranismo* through "el sentido oscuro y difícil del pensamiento, como consecuencia de la asociación anormal de las ideas, de los frecuentes equívocos y retruécanos, y de los contrastes y antítesis..." [15] In other words, the habitual Renaissance *concettismo* is contorted to such a point around 1600 that it disrupts rather than advances the poetic discourse, just as in the French verse I have examined in this book; but in France as in Spain, it maintains an appearance of limpidity. Excessive *conceptismo* partakes of the Mannerism which Hatzfeld identifies with exaggerated tropes, transposing that rhetorical inspissation to the semantic level. *Culteranismo*, with its stately rhythms and recondite vocabulary, clothes a fundamentally simpler train of thought; it ushers in the more "exterior" complications of the Baroque, which wins the upper hand in both countries by the second third of the century. [16] In this schema, French Clas-

[14] *Storia dell'Età Barocca in Italia*, pp. 272-3. First published in 1929, Croce's extensive discussion of Marino and his followers (pp. 241-353) is a typical example of twentieth century critics' rejection of late Petrarchism as insubstantial: he goes so far as to call it "pseudo-poetry."

[15] E. Gutiérrez, *Literatura Española*, p. 359.

[16] On these distinctions cf. ibid., p. 358, especially the following comment: "La

sicism is a more restrained version of the Baroque, as Houston has indicated.[17]

The *Quijote* also affords some intriguing comparisons: given the common roots of Petrarchism and the chivalrous novel in the medieval concept of courtly love,[18] the central figure in Cervantes' novel can be taken as an ambiguous parody of the faithful, unrequited lover who haunts both genres. Cross-generically, Dulcinea would then correspond to the degraded image of the beloved which dominates the final stage of Petrarchist verse. The sudden changes of tone, style, and perspective, the simultaneous accentuation and undermining of well-worn themes and tropes, and the constantly paraded self-referentiality of its fictions *as* fictions, are suggestive facets in Cervantes' work[19] which have their analogues in the love poetry of the period. In the author's last romance, the *Persiles* of 1617, the amalgamation of conflicting elements is taken even further, and their extreme hybridization finds its emblem in the androgyne.[20]

As a form of *redditio*, I will close this chain of literary links as I began it in the Introduction, with Shakespeare's sonnets as my main touchstone outside France.[21] More than any other single work, they

---

oscuridad y dificultad del culteranismo radican en lo exterior del lenguaje, es decir, en la sintaxis y el vocabulario. La oscuridad y dificultad del conceptismo radican, en cambio, en los pensamientos. El conceptismo es, así, al pensamiento, lo que el culteranismo es al lenguaje." This does not mean that the two trends can be strictly divided, either stylistically or chronologically. In his comprehensive essay "Temas y problemas del Barrocco español," B. Wardropper remarks that "culteranismo" grows out of the "conceptismo" of the late Renaissance, but never wholly supplants it: "...tanto el culteranismo como el conceptismo llevan a sus últimos extremos unas técnicas que las generaciones anteriores habían utilizado con moderación" (p. 16). A similar development occurs in France and other countries, as the "Mannerism" of the late sixteenth century evolves into the "Baroque" esthetic of the first decades of the seventeenth, with the two styles coexisting through a lengthy transitional period.

[17] See note 9 above.

[18] This common ancestry is made explicit in Shakespeare's sonnet 106, where the ideals of Petrarchism are presented as synonymous with those of medieval tales of "ladies dead and lovely knights."

[19] On all these points see Gutiérrez, op. cit., pp. 216-31.

[20] See the article by D. de Armas Wilson in *Literary Theory/Renaissance Texts*, pp. 150-81.

[21] "Versions of two Q sonnets appeared in 1599... Otherwise the only certainty about the date of the 154 sonnets in Q is the publication date, 1609" (Booth, p. 545). Though most scholars date them between 1594 and 1599 (see Quennell, pp. 121-2), this is pure conjecture. The publisher's preface to the 1640 edition, which describes the sequence as being in its "infancy" at the time of Shakespeare's death (ibid., p. 134), would seem to imply that many of the sonnets were written in the first decade of the seventeenth century. In some of them, the poet takes the stance of an older man (see the final paragraph of Chapter IV above).

exemplify the poetic inconstancy of Petrarchism in its culminating phase – and the subsequent reactions to its shelved esthetic values. As I indicated at the outset, the labile rhetoric of these poems has puzzled readers for centuries. Mark Van Doren was not the first critic – or the last – to complain of their stylistic volatility: "[they] die as poetry at the couplet; or cease somewhat less suddenly at the close of a quatrain"; "the sequence is radically uneven, and so is the average sonnet within the series."[22] This is not a book about Shakespeare, and so I cannot undertake a lengthy review of alleged "weak" lines or "inferior" poems[23] (Auden's terms) in order to refute such claims, and show the vital function of each verse within the given sonnet and each poem within the sequence as a whole. The reader can derive his or her own extrapolations from my exegeses of French authors. Besides, Stephen Booth has proved my contention a thousandfold in his immense commentary of 1977, which accords equal weight to every line and every sonnet, amply demonstrating the richness of the verbal play even where the text seems most "tedious" or "frivolous." Since then his all-embracing enterprise – which brings out for example the importance and subtlety of the much maligned "Alexandrian" sonnets at the end of the sequence[24] – has helped inspire the "solemn" critics to give the "trivial" poems their due.[25]

---

[22] Quoted in ibid., p. 135; Quennell goes on to make the same kind of judgements himself in the next few pages. Such objections were not made by Shakespeare's contemporaries, who admired his sonnets for their "superlative wit and eloquence" (p. 134).

[23] One of the problems is that critics such as Auden, Van Doren, Quennell, Barber, and Wheeler (see my Introduction, pp. 31-2) rarely stipulate exactly what lines and poems they find so defective, aside from the last two sonnets in the series. As to entire poems, presumably they do not mean the ones that are regularly included in anthologies such as Auden's own (see my biblio.) Their general critical reactions are plainly manifest, however, and those are what interest me here. Blanket condemnations like theirs find a blanket refutation in Booth's all-inclusive commentary.

[24] See his commentary in edn. cit., pp. 533-38, and the further information on p. 545.

[25] Cf. Helen Vendler's comments (p. 237) on sonnet 128: "The sonnet finds in synecdoche a solution to the aesthetic problem of how one represents sexual jealousy in other than tragic or satiric terms. By understanding that a problem is being solved, we can understand the aesthetic gaiety of the comic solution, and we end by conceiving of this sonnet not as a frigid triviality (as the more solemn commentators would have it) but rather as a triumphant *jeu d'esprit* on the dangerous subject of sexual infidelity." Her exegesis, "Shakespeare's Sonnets: The Uses of Synecdoche" (in *The Sonnets*, ed. Burto, 237-44) follows Booth's lead in exploring the irony through which Shakespeare both inflates and deflates a light-hearted amorous con-

My thesis here is a general one, which concerns basic critical attitudes toward the last phase of Renaissance poetics. I would suggest that the unevenness deplored by Van Doren and others is part of an overall strategy of alternating inflation and deflation, such as I have outlined repeatedly in my book, and that the revaluation of *all* Shakespeare's sonnets which Booth has carried out can have broad repercussions in assessing the literary technique of late Petrarchism as a whole. Many French poems which are currently neglected because they are not "powerful" – i. e. consistent in the intensity of their effects – can bear the same kind of scrutiny as he has devoted to Shakespeare's "unanthologizable" sonnets. As Felperin asserts (p. 195), in his poems "Shakespeare confesses the mimetic invalidity of his art in order to assert its metamimetic validity." Drawing a close analogy with the French examples I have discussed, I would submit that the strained metaphors, lethargic interludes, and ironic "puncturing devices" deployed by poets throughout Europe in this period are not the result of incompetence. While re-enacting metamimetically the vagaries of Petrarchist love, they discredit it both as ideal and primary representation. At the same time, they continually reinscribe its conceits in wider arcs, expanding their scope, flexibility, and ultimate significance.

On the thematic level, the rancorous triangle (or larger polygon) evoked by Shakespeare's sonnets, which address a beloved of either gender (or "both"), is light years removed from the Petrarchan scheme. As in the French verse of the time, accusations of the inconstancy and unworthiness of the lovers crop up everywhere;[26] the fall (or Fall) of the Christian-Platonic ideals of the early Renaissance is aptly summed up by sonnet 142, which begins, "Love is my sin..." Here and throughout this open-ended sequence,[27] the casual slippage between amorous and devotional registers parallels the French tendencies discussed in Chapter IV. Alien even to the usual

---

ceit. Her analysis is symptomatic of the new attention being paid to the more neglected sonnets, and she will soon be publishing a full-length study of Shakespeare's lyric verse.

[26] For example sonnets 61, 91-94, 150-51. In 142 the lover tells his "dark" mistress: "[Your lips have] sealed false bonds of love as oft as mine, /Robbed others' beds' revénues of their rents." (The accent is Booth's emendation of Q.)

[27] In R. L. Coles' apt phrase (art cit., p. 29), it is a "sequence (or sequences, or series, or cycle, or cycles: the exact relation of the poems to one another is difficult to establish)..."

late Petrarchist eclecticism are many of the other motifs introduced, such as the imperative to procreate or the frankly stated plainness of the mistress' face. The congeries is studded with a wealth of earthy strokes: ordinary images and terms that undermine the arch hyperboles and lofty modes of speech, that jostle impishly with the metrical sonorities. I have alluded several times to the increased "realism" of metaphor and tone among the "poets of 1600" in France, but they cannot rival the runaway poultry of Shakespeare's sonnet 143 or the bumptious swagger of number 20. On the other hand, the obscene humor of the latter poem finds its pendant in Durand's sonnet XLII: both signal a jeering rejection of the chaste Petrarchan paradigm. The mention of genitalia *within* the amatory cycle is an iconoclastic gambit, and one which presages the final dissolution of the Petrarchist genre as a whole.[28] But like all the other fleeting moods in these "sugared sonnets," that caprice is brief. The shifts in perspective are rapid, and the "Shakespearean" verse-form accentuates their abruptness. The four divisions of the Italian sonnet encourage modulations from part to part in a more orderly, progressive form. The English version abets a sudden, final turnabout. Following on the three quatrains, the couplet packs the reductive charge of a parting shot: "But love, hate on, for now I know thy mind, /Those that can see thou lov'st, and I am blind" (149). At other times it serves as the opposite – a noncommittal shrug: "Thus have I had thee as a dream doth flatter: /In sleep a king, but waking no such matter" (87). The stanzaic form which Surrey pioneered and Shakespeare groomed to perfection is a fitting vehicle for the discordant poetics of the age.[29]

The late Renaissance valued wit as much as emotion: the two could be savored even more when combined. Many modern readers have trouble appreciating the sarcastic *pointe* or *chute*, which they experience as a falling-off of poetic concentration; *concettismo*

[28] See the discussion in Kerrigan and Braden, pp. 175-8, where they argue that the transition from late Petrarchism to the new English love poetry of the seventeenth century can be understood both metaphorically and literally as the crossing of a sexual threshold. Compare my remarks in Chapter I on the satiated, post-Petrarchist lovers evoked by Tristan l'Hermite and Théophile de Viau.

[29] The sonnet-cycle vogue in England was brief but prolific. For other practitioners of the "Shakespearean sonnet" besides the Earl of Surrey and Shakespeare himself, see Sir Philip Sidney (*Astrophel and Stella*, 1591), Samuel Daniel (*Delia*, 1592), and Michael Drayton (*Ideas Mirrour*, 1594).

as a whole may seem petty and jejeune.[30] Romantic criteria such as earnestness and exaltation are hard to exorcise, especially if they hide behind more contemporary tags like "coherence" or "impact." At the end of the sixteenth century, grandeur and jest go hand and hand. Shakespeare's sonnets are best understood as miniature versions of his final comedies, where spirits consort with louts. But when it comes to one major *topos* in particular, the aging poet harks back to a younger Renaissance, descanting almost obsessively on the triumph of poetry over time, the glorious permanence of art. Here the puckish tweaks are few, the eloquence largely unbroken.[31] Faith in love has died, but faith in verse perserveres still more staunchly than before: "Not marble, nor the gilded monuments/ Of princes, shall outlive this powerful rhyme" (55). As in the poems of Durand, the "master-mistress" retreats from center stage while the poet advances to the foreground; but Shakespeare is even more self-referential. The polymorphous beloved is never specified, even by a fictive sobriquet like "Stella" (or "Astrophel"). Where Petrarch rang the changes on Laura's name ("l'aura," "lauro," "l'auro," "l'oro"), Shakespeare weaves a complex *annominatio* around his own: "So thou, being rich in 'Will,' add to thy 'Will' / One will of mine, to make thy large 'Will' more."[32]

The resounding self-affirmation of such lines recalls Ronsard's proud rhyme of "signe" with "insigne," quoted above, a *derivatio* which writes his name in the sky. His quill soars heavenward: and through a play on words, though he is a dying swan, his work is a changeless star. In the magnificats of Shakespeare and Ronsard the late Renaissance rejoins the Humanist fervor of Petrarch, with a portentous shift of focus from the *exempla* of Antiquity to the wonders of their own craftsmanship. But for the generation which comes to

---

[30] In her art. cit., p. 238, referring to the central *concetto* of sonnet 128, Vendler comments that "readers can become impatient with such a conceit (a figurative expression); they feel they are being asked to concur in language inappropriate to a grown man."

[31] Even this proud theme is occasionally belied, as in sonnet 32, such is the penchant for self-negation. Overwhelmingly, however, the *topos* re-emerges – intact, vital, and assertive.

[32] Sonnet 135; for similar puns see 136 and 143. As noted above in Chapter II, the *Canzoniere* unfolds a series of puns on "Laura"; no matter how "unreal" she may be, the image of the beloved always occupies center stage. Ronsard and Desportes still give names, at least, to their successive loves; in Shakespeare's sequence their nameless simultaneity marks a further displacement of their presence in the poems, and a corresponding rise in the poet's own predominance.

the fore at the beginning of the seventeenth century, even this final remnant of the old ideals has vanished. True to late Petrarchist practice, and in "metamimesis" of its historical evolution, I will end this section on a *pointe* – or "quibble," as the Elizabethans might have said. Rejecting the outmoded credo of his elders, a later "Démon des Foux" scoffs at those who hope for immortality through art:

Ces rimeurs qui par des paroles
Pensent survivre à l'Univers
Et vifs sont rongez par les vers,
Ne vont-ils pas à mes escolles?

In these lines from one of Durand's last surviving poems, published in 1617,[33] the pun on "vers" cleverly implies that verse destroys an author's existence rather than prolonging it beyond his death. "Sky-signs" are only "worm-words" as the Renaissance draws to a close.

That the poetics of inconstancy is transnational and cross-lingual is only natural, in a Europe where new fashions have always circulated quickly; in addition, I would suggest that the tendency possesses definite parallels outside the literary sphere. In their problematic stance toward the tradition and their emphasis on their own deceptiveness, the "poets of 1600" reflect the *Crise de la renaissance* which André Chastel has discerned in the visual arts: the esthetic *inconstantia* of a diffuse and uneven transition from Mannerism to Baroque.[34] The *Méditations* were published in a decade which is often thought to mark the turning point between these two

[33] "Ballet pour M. le General des Galeres, Representant le Demon des Foux", from *Discours au vray du ballet dansé par le roi...*; reprinted in our edn. of the complete poetry, p. 224-5. In his "Elegie VI," Durand writes: "Voicy des vers mourans et des plaintes de Cigne,/ Qui sont de mon trespas et la borne et le signe" (p. 121). Though he splits Ronsard's pun into a rhyme, making it more explicit, here the emphasis is entirely on mortality: the swan does not fly heavenward, and the verses die with their author.

[34] Cf. Houston's book on rhetoric, p. 201: "...as our distinction is narrowly linguistic, it offers, instead of the dramatic confrontation of a somber mannerist and an exuberant baroque world view, a much more modest scheme which emphasizes elements of continuity and development between mannerism and baroque... One principle that obtains throughout all attempts at periodization of styles is the simultaneous existence of more than one stylistic current at any time..." But the very persistence of the debate about the esthetic identity of the early seventeenth century underlines the fact that in this particular period there is more overlapping than in others: again, this implies a pervasive poetics of inconstancy.

artistic phases, and ample evidence could be marshalled to link Durand's poetry with either of the two.[35] The feminine portraiture which Richard Sayce has described as peculiar to Mannerism is well represented in the *Méditations*, as are the exaggerated rhetorical figures which Helmut Hatzfeld and Marcel Raymond associate with Mannerist verse. The blurred edges, eclecticism, mixed registers, and parodic deflation of late Renaissance poetry are mirrored by Mannerist paintings, from Jacques Bellange to Bartholomeus Strobel.[36] Yet the motion and vigor of Durand's finest work, in particular the "Stances à l'Inconstance," seem closer to the forthright energy of the Baroque, the style with which his name has most often been connected in the past.

Tintoretto also spans the period of Mannerism and the Baroque; *mutatis mutandis*, the most accomplished poem in the *Méditations* can be illuminated through a comparison with one of his works. As I noted earlier, "the momentary movement caught and held" has been called a typical device of Mannerist art. No device would be more ambiguous. Does it regenerate the movement, recreate its sprung tension within the picture space? Or does it freeze the movement into immobility? At best, it does both. Tintoretto's "Dis-

[35] As Raymond asserts (art. cit., p. 113): "Si le maniérisme a pris le départ le premier (vers 1520, dans les arts figuratifs), il peut arriver que le maniérisme et le baroque composent ensemble, s'interpénètrent, s'entrelacent, chez un même poète, dans un même poème." While the work of Durand as a whole reflects a Mannerist eclecticism and disunity, the "Stances" seem to embody the esthetic of the Baroque; cf. Puleio's book. Raymond's definition of the difference between the two styles remains the clearest and most authoritative: "L'unité de l'oeuvre, chez les maniéristes, paraît morcelée, décentrée, atectonique. Le spectateur, le lecteur, est conduit d'une partie à l'autre, d'une surprise à une autre surprise... L'unité de l'oeuvre baroque est complexe à la fois et globale, que cette unité soit d'essence structurale ou énergétique. De plus, elle se fonde sur une alliance renouvelée de l'homme et de la nature, de la nature et de la surnature, du corps et de l'âme, qui s'incarne, ce qui entraîne l'élargissement... du clavier de l'expression" (art. cit., p. 134).

[36] On Bellange see Ch. IV, note 6. The genius of the Polish artist Strobel (1591-1644) has yet to receive its due; perhaps because of his "provincial" status, he prolongs the Mannerist style long past its prime. His monumental "The Beheading of St. John the Baptist and the Feast of Herod" at the Prado illustrates many of the poetic traits described in this study. On a thematic plane tragedy and caricature, the sacred and the profane, are indiscriminately mixed: contemporary portraits, such as those of Henri IV and Charles I, perversely contradict the Biblical setting, and the saint's head is presented at the garishly overladen table like just another dish. On the level of technique, hyper-realistic details combine with distortion, asymmetry, fragmentation, diffuseness and abstraction in a stunning visual display of the esthetics of inconstancy. (For a color plate of the work with notes, see *Museo del Prado...*, p. 377.)

covery of the Body of Saint Mark" dramatically illustrates this esthetic process. Within a dim funeral vault, the saint is shown presiding over two events at once: the lowering of his body from its tomb, and the rejoicing of the faithful over the already laid-out corpse. What immediately strikes the viewer of this scene is that the two events do not represent different episodes, but rather two successive *moments* of the same occurrence – as though consecutive frames from the film of a single gesture had been projected simultaneously. Before the "Discovery of the Body of Saint Mark," one is induced to a sense of timelessness by the very inconsistency of time within the *camera oscura* of the painting. In the "Stances à l'Inconstance," the transience of the universe culminates in a "change immortel," which is ephemeral and yet eternal.

Like Tintoretto's canvas, the "Stances" bespeak an art of internal contradiction – or if one will, of Mannerist disquiet. The "tableau fantastique" which the poets offers up to Inconstancy portrays a love emptied of sense and abandoned, a "flame deserte." The beloved is dismissed as a "folastre objet," and "l'amour et le jeu," "les femmes et les vents" are cynically equated. On the other hand, the picture is also a "divin tableau," one which evokes "les peintures du Ciel à nos yeux incogneuës." Despite the flippancy of certain lines, the "Stances" are pervaded by a note of "humeur melancolique"; though they end with a dynamic affirmation, they also dwell poignantly on the fragility of man, his vertigo before the fleeting transformations of the world and of the self. Unlike Sponde or Chassignet – or in another way, Tintoretto – Durand does not invoke an ultimate permanence in the beyond. In this sense, his tragic consciousness may be at least as great as that of the devotional poets, despite the easy distinction which has been made between "inconstance blanche" and "inconstance noire." [37] In fact there is a gamut of shades between the two: the "Stances" occupy a "gray" area between mockery and praise, despair and blissful assent. To draw another analogy with the Baroque, Bernini's zestful geniality does not make him any less profound than Borromini, his austere and visionary rival: both combine flights of fancy with a somber, histrionic éclat.

Tempting as such comparisons may be, I agree with Steadman (p. 162) that "one should, for the most part, regard these formal

[37] Cf. Rousset, intro. to anth., vol. I, pp. 6-9.

analogies between mannerist or baroque art and the literature of the late or post-Renaissance as suggestions only – as conceits and ingenious correspondences." Nothing could be more consonant with the era under discussion than the deployment of critical *concetti*; but why must they always relate to the visual sphere?[38] Most poets of the late Renaissance participated in music academies and the creation of songs, and their works are redolent with allusions to the sister art.[39] Durand collaborated with many musicians in the staging of his operatic ballets; he even provided the *vers liminaires* for two scores published in 1617, by the Court composers Antoine Boesset and Pierre Guédron.[40] In the midst of these cross-fertilizations, harmony between "words and music" on a larger scale seems inevitable. To cite one example, the esthetics of inconstancy I have outlined clearly informs Monteverdi's variegated sequence, the magnificent *Marian Vespers* of 1610. Like the poems of the age, as adumbrated in Chapter IV, they flicker unpredictably between the sacred and profane, splicing ascetic plainchant with jig-like instrumental tunes, enraptured melismata with wry echo-madrigals, the holy with the mundane.[41] As compared with the unswerving evenness and sublimity of Palestrina's style, this abrupt shift at the end of the Renaissance, and the parallel with literature, becomes all the more suggestive.

Monteverdi's relevance does not stop there: his long life (1567-1643) makes him a key figure in the transition from Mannerism to Baroque. As Denis Arnold writes in reference to the early seventeenth century, "although it is usually assumed that the term 'baroque' implies extravagance of feeling, this is certainly not true of most of the composers who flourished in what music historians have liked to call 'the early Baroque period'... Only those who had learned their art in the later decades of the previous century – Gesualdo and Marco da Gagliano in vocal music, Frescobaldi in instru-

---

[38] In the intro. to his anth., pp. 15-16, Raymond mentions music but declines to make any parallels with literature; as usual in such comparisons, the focus is exclusively on the visual arts.

[39] Cf. the examples among French authors given in ibid., and compare Shakespeare, sonnets 8 and 128.

[40] These poems are reprinted in our edn., pp. 227-9.

[41] Somewhat quizzically, the musicologist Wolfgang Osthoff states (p. 11, intro. to CD libretto): "With his *Vespers* of 1610, Monteverdi made what might be described as a secular contribution to sacred music."

mental music – retained the grand excesses typical of [the] inbred Northern Italian courts. They are, in fact, mannerist rather than Baroque composers, and Monteverdi is the greatest of them."[42] Similarly, framed by the Antique Classicism of the Pléiade and the French Classicism of the seventeenth century, the *maniera* of late Petrarchism appears as an idiosyncratic development which obeys its own stylistic laws. As opposed to Monteverdi, Lully is stately and measured; he represents the muted variant of Baroque style which informs the "grand siècle," and which has obvious literary ramifications. In this context the Artusi-"Monteverdi" controversy of 1600 to 1607[43] affords another set of paradigms: like a musical Malherbe, Artusi takes the composer to task for introducing too many dissonances, tonal feints, sudden modulations, modal mixtures, and inconsistencies into his work. In his defense the "Monteverdi" figure builds on a comparison already advanced in 1591 by Galilei, to the effect that a poet composes his sonnet so that "each quatrain and tercet, indeed each particular verse, is of a different mode from the rest. Whoever does differently... is accused of indolence and of lacking inventiveness" (p. 146). He cannot justify the liberties he has taken except to say that a dissonance will always be a dissonance, "but by circumstance (*per accidente*) it can well be otherwise, for there is no dissonant interval which is in itself one that by circumstance cannot be made good with reference to the accompaniments among which it is placed... And since you desire a proof, you will draw it very easily from this: you allow an excellent poet the metaphor purposefully used; similarly the [dissonance] is taken in place of the [consonance]" (p. 148). No document could be clearer in defining the discordant, multi-modal esthetic which informs the verse as well as the music of the late Renaissance.

If literary critics have largely confined their analogies to painting, it is partly because the concepts of Mannerism and Baroque derive from art history, and partly because the precept *ut pictura poesis* is a time-honored one. In the case of the "Stances à l'Inconstance," the correlation is made explicit by the imagery itself. But the mobile

[42] "Monteverdi and his Teachers," in *The New Monteverdi Companion*, p. 106.

[43] This complex esthetic disagreement is pieced together by Claude Palisca in ibid., pp. 127-158. Simply put, Artusi created a dialogue in which he debates musical points with a "Monteverdian" interlocutor. Later, Monteverdi's brother wrote a refutation on the composer's behalf.

"tableau" evoked by Durand, with its dramatic changes of lighting and perspective, resembles a coup de théâtre more than a picture in a frame. Again, such scenic effects could naturally be linked with his activities as the organizer of lavish spectacles at Court. These entertainments were truly *Gesamtkunstwerke*, global works of art combining poetry, narration, dance, painting, sculpture, and music both vocal and instrumental. Their increasing complexity and extravagance at the beginning of the seventeenth century heralds the transition toward a new esthetic which delights, above all, in celebrating the breach between *être et paraître*, in flipping back and forth between "be" and "seem." The thematic and stylistic reversals I have identified in the love poems of the period might be said to illustrate the same principle on another plane. It has often been pointed out that theater is *the* characteristic genre of the Baroque. Much has been said about images drawn from the stage, and the "theatricality" which gradually spreads to other forms of literature. But perhaps the critical corpus has not sufficiently stressed the way in which scenic procedures strike inward, reshaping the rhetorical ploys of lyric as well as dramatic verse. The poetics of inconstancy which permeates these deeper structures announces the rise of a different sensibility as the Renaissance meanders to a close: accompanied, in esthetic terms, by the creation of another language.

The artistic synthesis embodied in the Court festivities lends support to modern attempts at formulating a general esthetic for the period, whether designated as Mannerist, Baroque, or both. That some far-reaching change was in the air seems evident from my survey of late Petrarchism: though less a "decadence" than a culmination, in any case it calls for a renewal. By the end of the sixteenth century – without giving a negative sense to any of these terms – the tradition has become so formulaic, ornate, mannered, and fully-exploited that it collapses under its own weight, generating *topoi* which run counter to its basic tenets and verbal shadowplays which thwart its inherited tropes. This is the final scene which the "Stances à l'Inconstance" metamimetically enact, as the poet strips off one by one the outworn masks of amorous verse. The "sermens parjurez" of the "Belle" make any degree of fidelity to her a "peché": if her words are lies, then his will be fake as well. Belying a tired oxymoron, he disfigures all the figures: "Entre mille glaçons je sçay feindre une flame." Doubly false, the beloved is torn apart like a straw-filled effigy; her heart is an altar of mendacity, her "cervelle" a shrine of deceit. Thunderclaps and lightning-strokes – "les flammes des esclairs plutost mortes que veuës" – dramatize this bonfire of the vanities. The lover liberates himself, not just from the mistress, but from Petrarchism itself.

As in any transition, one cannot speak of a clean break: even in their negation, the consecrated terms are still employed. Like Mannerism, the Baroque is a modulation of the same melodic line in a different key; but it *is* a modulation, and one which continues to gather force. The labels assigned count for less than a general awareness that by the early seventeenth century a love verse cycle as cohesive as *Délie* or *L'Olive* has become unthinkable – and above all, that a poem written in 1630 no longer *reads* like one from eighty years back. The gradual progression toward another poetics is implicit in the first awakenings of the Renaissance. "Beginning with Petrarch, the belief in a reusuable, and therefore potentially analogous, past inspired the exacting study of antiquity, but the historically self-conscious philology developed for such study both presupposed and disclosed the radical distance between past and present."[44] Similarly, the deliberate adoption of the Petrarchan scheme as a model for amatory verse in the early French (or English or Spanish) Renaissance, especially since that model is so ostentatiously imported from another tongue and culture, opens the possibility of altering the frame of reference once again. The pressure to deny the prototype accumulates as the "radical distance between past and present" becomes more and more pronounced. The "Stances à l'Inconstance" – this is the source of their exuberance – mark an interval when poetry frees itself from a vast and overloaded *conduplicatio*, without having settled yet into the succeeding mode of repetition: though this, in turn, will build on what has gone before.

What transpires in that interval can only be the pleasure in language itself, though the poet makes clear it will never let the human mind seize any permanent truth: "Nostre esprit n'est que vent, et comme un vent volage." *Avant la lettre* and apparently without regret, he subscribes to the contemporary concept that "language holds out the promise of an end, while simultaneously

[44] Deborah Shuger, *Habits of Thought in the English Renaissance*, p. 261.

sweeping the ends of determinate meaning away..." [45] In late Petrarchism, all confidence in the capacity of words to portray love directly has been abandoned; [46] but as I have tried to suggest, where mimesis falters metamimesis takes its place. Felperin (p. 189) describes Shakespeare's sonnet 107 as "rooting out its own masonry, risking its monumentalizing immediacy, and counteracting its own enactment." The "Stances" stage a similar reversal, starting from the opposite direction: their methodical destruction of the old poetics founds a new language of desire, a "temple" in the here and now. As Bonnefoy writes in his essay on Durand (pp. VII-VIII):

> Dans ces mots, en effet, où l'être se dérobe, où la pensée tourbillonne sans points d'appui dans les choses, le désir est d'autant plus libre de s'attacher, ne serait-ce qu'une minute, à une apparence qui le séduit, ce qui permet à ses forces surabondantes de se dépenser, et c'est une joie. Quand les formulations de la vérité trahissent, ne laissant en leur place que la nostalgie ou le nihilisme, les mots du désir ont la qualité, au moins, de la soif qui cesse, ils abreuvent. Et n'est-ce pas là, dans la mutabilité infinie, dans l'universelle absence, comme un instant de présence, furtive mais d'autant plus émouvante?

The last stage of the Renaissance represents more than a historical style: it expresses, in its own specific idiom, the essential aspirations of poetry. Perhaps in an art of sheer virtuosity, of pure variation on given themes, these aspirations stand out more clearly than elsewhere. In the *Méditations* as in all amorous verse, the "beloved" can best be understood as the poetic moment itself – the moment when the creator (or the reader) becomes absorbed in a larger language than his own, so that the distinction between world and self is abolished. That "objet de plus haute vertu" remains an object of desire: it can only be approached, never fully realized. But true to

---

[45] Nealon, p. 183. At a more comprehensive level, the word "contemporary" can be taken here in a double sense, including Montaigne on the one hand and ourselves on the other.

[46] Cf. ibid., pp. 101-02: "Perhaps literature, what we call the literary, has always, from before the beginning, been that which poses the greatest danger to representation: it might be called the 'post' that has always haunted the 'modern,' the (im)possibility of representation which has haunted representation."

the form of Petrarchist paradox, the approach is already a realization; the poem signifies both the unbearable absence and the captured presence of the "beloved." In the words of René Char: "La poésie est l'amour réalisé du désir demeuré désir." The "Stances à l'Inconstance" elevate this paradox to a universal principle: the world and the self exist only insofar as they move toward dissolution; their being unfolds in a process of disappearance, a constant inconstancy. The poet is a "prestre fidelle" in the eternal liturgy of speech: a temporary vessel, supplanted before he begins. His words can only celebrate themselves – turning inward and spiraling away, wheeling in a "change immortel."

SELECT BIBLIOGRAPHY

I. Primary Sources

A. Works by Etienne Durand

Description du ballet de Madame, soeur aisnee du Roy [attrib. to Durand], Lyon (F. Yvrad), 1615.

Discours au vray du ballet dansé par le roi le dimanche 29e jour de janvier 1617, avec les dessins, tant des machines et apparences différentes, que de tous les habits des masques, Paris (P. Ballard), 1617. (Reprinted in Paul Lacroix, *Ballets et mascarades...*, Geneva, 1868-70 [Gay] and 1968 [Slatkine].)

Les espines d'Amour, ou sont traitées les infortunées Amours de Philadon & Caulisée. Par Estienne Durand. A Madamoiselle de Fourcy, l'aisnée, Paris (Gilles Robinot), 1604. – Another edn., Rouen (Pierre l'Oyselet), 1608.

Méditations de E.D., [Paris, 1611?].

Méditations de E.D., réimprimées sur l'unique exemplaire connu, s.l.n.d. (vers 1611), précédées de la vie du poëte par Guillaume Colletet et d'une notice par Frédéric Lachèvre, Paris (H. Leclerc), 1906.

Poésies complètes, ed. Hoyt Rogers and Roy Rosenstein, preface by Yves Bonnefoy, Geneva (Droz-T. L. F.), 1990.

B. French Love Verse, c. 1570-c. 1630

Angot de l'Éperonnière, Robert, *Les Nouveaux Satires et exersices gaillards de ce temps*, Rouen (Michel l'Allemant), 1637. – Ed. P. Blanchemain, Paris (Lemerre), 1877.

———, *Le Prelude poetique de Robert Angot, sieur de l'Esperonniere*, Paris (Gilles Robinot), 1603.

Aubigné, Agrippa d', *Le Printemps, Stances et Odes*, ed. F. Desonay, Lille-Genève, 1952.

Audiguier de la Menor, Vital d', *Les Oeuvres Poetiques Du Sieur Daudiguier*, Paris (Toussainct du Bray), 1614.

Baddel, B., *Poëmes d'amours. De. B: Baddel, Bassinois. Ou se voyent les diversités amoureuses*, Amsterdam (Paul Ravesteyn), 1616.

Beau-Jeu de Jeaulges, Christofle de, *Les Amours de Christofle de Beaujeu, Baron dudit Beau-jeu, et seigneur de Jeaulges*, Paris (Didier Millot), 1589.

Bernier de la Brousse, Joachim, *Les Oeuvres Poëtiques du sieur Bernier de la Brousse*, Poitiers (Julian Thoreau), 1618.

Béroalde de Verville, François (Fr. Brouart), *Les Souspirs amoureux de F.B. de Verville: Avec un discours Satyrique de ceux qui escrivent d'Amour, par N. le Digne*, Paris (Timothee Jouan), 1583.

Bertaut, Jean, *Les Oeuvres poétiques de M. Bertaut... Dernière édition*, Paris (Toussaint du Bray), 1620. – Ed. A. Chenevière, Paris (Plon), 1891.

Berthrand, François, *Les Premieres Idees d'Amour, de Francois Berthrand, d'Orleans*, Orléans (Fabian Hotot), 1599.

Birague, Flaminio de, *Les Premieres Oeuvres Poetiques de Flaminio de Birague, Gentilhomme ordinaire de la Chambre du Roy*, Paris (Thomas Perier), 1585.

Blanchon, Joachim, *Les Premières Oeuvres Poétiques de Joachim Blanchon*, Paris (Thomas Perier), 1583.

Bouchet d'Ambillou, René, *Sidere, Pastorelle. De l'Invention du sieur d'Ambillou. Plus les Amours de Sidere, de Pasithee, et autres Poësies du mesme Autheur*, Paris (Robert Estienne), 1609.

Boyssières, Jean de, *Les Premieres Oeuvres Amoureuses de Jean de Boyssieres, Montferrandin*, Paris (Claude de Montreuil), 1578.

Bretin, Filbert, *Poesies Amoureuses Reduites en forme d'un Discours de la nature d'Amour. Par Filbert Bretin Bourgongnon Aussonois. Plus les meslanges du mesme Auteur*, Lyon (Benoist Rigaud), 1576.

Certon, Salomon, *Vers Leipogrammes et Autres Oeuvres en Poesie, De S.C.S.D.R.*, Sedan (Jean Jannon), 1620.

Colletet, Guillaume, *Les Divertissemens de Colletet*, Paris (Robert Estienne), 1631.

Cornu, Pierre de, *Les Oeuvres Poetiques de Pierre de Cornu, Dauphinois...*, Lyon (Jean Huguetan), 1583. – Ed. Blanchemain, Turin (J. Gay et fils), 1870.

Courtin de Cissé, Jacques de, *Les Oeuvres Poetiques de Jacques de Cissé, Gentilhomme Percheron*, Paris (Gilles Beys), 1581.

Deimier, Pierre de, *Les Premieres Oeuvres du Sieur de Deimier, dediées à la Gloire*, Lyon (Claude Morillon), 1600.

Déplanches, Jean, *Les Oeuvres Poetiques de Jean Deplanches, sieur du Chastelier, & de la Bastonnerie*, ed. J. Bernier de la Brousse, Poitiers (Julian Thoreau), 1612.

Desportes, Philippe, *Les Amours de Diane*, ed. V. E. Graham, Geneva-Paris, 1959, 2 vols.

———, *Les Amours d'Hippolyte*, ed. V. E. Graham, Geneva-Paris, 1960.

———, *Cléonice, dernières amours*, ed. V. E. Graham, Geneva-Paris, 1962.

———, *Diverses amours et autres oeuvres*, ed. V. E. Graham, Geneva-Paris, 1963.

———, *Elégies*, ed. V. E. Graham, Geneva-Paris, 1961.

———, *Les Imitations de l'Arioste par Philippe Desportes, suivies de poésies inédites ou non recueillies du même auteur*, ed. J. Lavaud, Paris, 1936.

———, *La Rencontre des Muses de France & d'Italie, A la Reyne*, Lyon (Jacques Roussin), 1604.

Du Mas, S., *Lydie, Fable Champestre, Imitée en Partie de l'Aminthe du Torquato Tasso. Dédiée à la Reyne Marguerite. Par le S. Du Mas*, Paris (Jean Millot), 1609. (*Oeuvres meslees du Sieur S. du Mas*, pp. 95-306.)

Du Perron, Jacques Davy, *Les Diverses Oeuvres de l'illustrissime Cardinal du Perron*, Paris (Antoine Estiene), 1622, 2 parts in 1 vol.

Du Pin-Pager, Romain, *Les oeuvres poétiques du sieur Dupin-Pager*, Paris (J. Quesnel), 1630.

Durant de la Bergerie, Gilles, *Imitations du latin de Jean Bonnefons. Avec autres Gayetez amoureuses, de l'invention de l'autheur, Dernière edition reveue et corrigée*, Paris, 1610.

Du Ryer, Isaac, *Le Temps Perdu d'Issac Du Ryer. Reveu et augmenté par l'autheur* [3rd edn.], Paris (Toussainccts du Bray), 1610.

Du Souhait, Guillaume, *Marquetries ou Oeuvres Diverses...*, Paris (Jean Houzé), 1601.

Expilly de la Poëpe, Claude, *Les Poèmes du sieur d'Expilly à Madame la marquise de Monceaux. Le Second livre des poèmes...*, Paris (A. Langellier), 1596. Another edn., Grenoble (P. Verdier), 1624.

Frenicle, Nicholas, *Les Premieres oeuvres poetiques du sieur Frenicle*, Paris (Toussainct du Bray), 1625.

Godard, Jean, *Les Oeuvres de Jean Godard...*, Lyon (Pierre Landry), 1594.

Grisel, Jehan, *Les Premières Oeuvres Poétiques de Jehan Grisel Rovennois*, Rouen (R. Du Petit-Val), 1599.

Habert, Isaac, *Les Trois Livres des Météores, avecques autres oeuvres poëtiques*, Paris (J. Richer), 1585.

Hopil, Claude, *Meslange de poesie*, Paris (Francois Julliot), 1603. (Accompanied by Hopil's *Oeuvres chrestiennes*; contains a number of love poems.)

Jamyn, Amadis, *Oeuvres poétiques...*, ed. Ch. Brunet, Paris (Léon Willem), 1878-9, 2 vol.

La Borderie, J. de, *Les Préludes de Perroquet, Fluteur Tolosain*, Bordeaux (Gilbert Vernoy), 1620. (Contains parodies of Petrarchist verse alongside conventional love poems.)

La Charnay, *Vers du Sieur de La Charnay...*, Paris (T. Du Bray-A. Soubron), 1632. (A few love poems, mixed with other thematic genres.)

La Roque, Siméon-Guillaume de, *Les Oeuvres du Sieur de la Roque de Clairmont en Beavoisis. Reveues et augmentées de plusieurs poésies...*, Paris (Veuve Claude de Monstr'oeil), 1609.

La Vallettrie, *Les Oeuvres Poetiques du Sieur de la Valletrye...*, Paris (Estienne Vallet), 1602.

Le Blanc, Jean, *La Neotemachie Poetique du Blanc*, Paris (Francois Julliot), 1610. (Contains a few love poems.)

Le Digne de l'Espine-Fontenay, Nicolas, *Les Fleurettes du Premier Meslange de N. le Digne, Sieur de l'Espine-Fontenay. Rassemblees par A. de la Forest Escuyer, Sieur du Plessis*, (Jeremie Perier), 1601.

Le Masson, Nicolas, *Les Premieres Oeuvres... Dediez à la Reyne*, Paris (O. de Varennes), 1608.

Lespine (or L'Espine), Charles de, *Le Mariage d'Orphée, sa Descente aux Enfers, sa Mort par les Bacchantes. Tragedie: Et autres oeuvres Poëtiques du sieur Lespine...*, Paris (Henry Sara), 1623. (Contains a number of love poems.)

Loys, Jean, *Les Oeuvres Poetiques de Jean Loys Douysien, licentié es droits*, Douay (Pierre Auroy), 1613. (Some love poems.)

Nervèze, Antoine de, *Les Essais Poetiques...*, Poictiers (Francois Lucas) – Rouen (Théodore Reinsart), 1605.

Papillon de Lasphrise, Marc de, *Les Premieres Oeuvres Poetiques du Capitaine Lasphrise, Reveuës et augmentées par l'Auteur*, Paris (Jean Gesselin), 1599. – First edn., 1597. – *Les gaillardes poésies du capitaine Lasphrise, publiées d'après les éditions de 1597 et 1599*, ed. P. Blanchemain, Turin, 1870.

Passerat, Jean, *Recueil des Oeuvres Poetiques de Jean Passerat, Lecteur et Interprete du Roy. Augmentée de plus de la moitié, outre les precedentes impressions...*, Paris (Claude Morel), 1606.

(Bueil de) Racan, Honorat de, *Oeuvres complètes...*, ed. M. Tenant de Latour, intro. by A. de Latour, Paris (P. Jannet), 1857, 2 vols.

Resneville, Noël de, *Les Traverses du sieur de Resneville et ses Oeuvres Poetiques*, Paris (Toussainct du Bray), 1624.

Romieu, Jacques de, *Les Meslanges Vivarois...*, Lyon (B. Rigaud), 1584.

Rosset, François de, *Les XII Beautez de Phyllis. Et autres oeuvres Poëtiques...*, Paris (Abel l'Angelier), 1604.

Saint-Amant (Marc-Antoine de Gérard), *Les plus belles pages...*, ed. R. de Gourmont, Paris, 1907.

Scalion de Virbluneau, *Les Loyales et Pudicques Amours...*, Paris (Jamet Mettayer), 1599.

Soffrey de Calignon, *Vie et poésies de Soffrey de Calignon, chancelier du roi de Navarre, publiées sur les manuscrits originaux* par le Comte Douglas, Grenoble (Edouard Allier), 1874.

Sponde, Jean de, *Poésies*, ed. A. Boase and F. Ruchon, Geneva, 1949.

Trellon (or Trelon), Claude de, *Le Cavalier Parfait... Divise en quatre livres. Où sont comprinses les Amours de Sylvie, les Amours de Felice, les Meslanges, & l'Hermitage*, Lyon (Thibaud Ancelin), 1597.

———, *Les Oeuvres Poetiques... nouvellement reveues et corrigées*, Lyon (C. Michel), 1595.

Viau, Théophile de, *Oeuvres poétiques*, ed. Jeanne Streicher, Geneva-Paris, 1958, 2 vols.

C. Other Works

1. Works by individual authors

Bazin, M. A. (Anaïs de Raucou), *La Cour de Marie de Médicis, mémoires d'un cadet de Gascogne, 1615-1618*, Paris (A. Mesnier), 1830.

Belleau, Rémy, *Oeuvres poétiques*, ed. C. Marty-Laveaux, Paris (A. Lemerre), 1878, 2 vols.

Berni, Francesco, *Rime*, ed. G. Bàrberi Squarotti, Turin, 1969.

Boitel, Pierre, sieur de Gaubertin, *Le Théâtre du malheur sur qui la fortune présente les divers accidents tragiques des hommes illustres*, Paris (Toussaints du Bray), 1621.

Cartari, Vincenzo, *Les Images des dieux des anciens... traduites en francais, et augmentees par Antoine Du Verdier*, Tournon (Claude Michel et Thomas Soubron), 1606-7. Another edn., Lyon, 1610.

Charron, Pierre, *De la Sagesse*, in vol. I of *Toutes les Oeuvres... Derniere edition...*, Paris (Villery), 1635, 2 vols. (Slatkine Reprints, 1970).

Colletet, Guillaume, *L'art poétique du Sr Colletet*, Paris (Antoine de Sommaville), 1658.

———, *Poésies diverses de M. Colletet...*, Paris (L. Chamhoudry), 1656.

———, *Vies des poètes françois*, ed. Philonneste (Gustave Brunet), Geneva (J. Gay et Fils), 1867.

Cotgrave, Randle, *A Dictionarie of the French and English Tongues*, London (Islip), 1632. (1st edn. 1611.)

Deageant, *Memoires de Monsieur Deageant, envoyez a Monsieur le Cardinal de Richelieu...*, Grenoble (Charvy), 1668.

Deimier, Pierre de, *L'Académie de l'art poétique...*, Paris (J. de Bordeaux), 1610.

Du Bellay, Joachim, *Oeuvres poétiques*, ed. Henri Chamard, Paris, 1908-23, 5 vols.

Du Vair, Guillaume, *De la Sainte philosophie* [et] *Philosophie morale des stoiques*, ed. G. Michaut, Paris, 1945. (The *Philosophie morale* was first published c. 1599.)

Garel, Élie, *Les Oracles Francois, ou Explication Allegorique du Balet de Madame...*, Paris (Pierre Chevalier), 1615.

Jodelle, Étienne, *Oeuvres complètes*, ed. Enea Balmas, Paris, 1965, 2 vols.

La Ceppède, Jean de, *Les Théorèmes sur le sacré mystère de notre rédemption* [facsimile of the Toulouse edn. of 1613-22], intro. by J. Rousset, Geneva, 1966.

La Fontan, *Les jours et les nuicts du Sieur de La Fontan...*, Paris (Charles Sevestre), 1606.

Lemaire de Belges, Jean, *Oeuvres*, ed. J. Stecher, Louvain, 1882-91, 4 vols.

Lorris, Guillaume de, and Meun, Jean de, *Le Roman de la Rose*, ed. Lecoy, Paris, 1968-70, 3 vols.

Marot, Clément, *L'Adolescence Clémentine*, ed. V. L. Saulnier, Paris, 1958.

Milton, John, *Paradise Lost*, ed. Merritt Y. Hughes, New York, 1962.

Montaigne, Michel de, *Essais*, ed. Albert Thibaudet, Paris, 1937.

Nostredame, César de, *Les Perles, ou les Larmes de la Saincte Magdeleine*, Toulouse (la vefve de J. Colomiez), 1606.

Petrarca, Francesco, *Canzoniere*, ed. Piero Cudini, Milan, 1974.

———, *Dal Canzoniere/ Le Chansonnier*, ed. Gérard Genot, Paris, 1969.

Richelet, Pierre, *Dictionnaire Francois, Contenant les Mots et les Choses...*, Geneva (Widerhold), 1679-80. (Slatkine Reprints, 1970).

Ripa, Cesare, *Iconologia overo Descrittione di diverse Imagini cavate dall' antichità, & di propria inventione...*, Roma (Lepido Faciù), 1603.

Ronsard, Pierre de, *Les Amours*, ed. Henri and Catherine Weber, Paris, 1963.

———, *Oeuvres complètes*, ed. Paul Laumonier, Paris, 1914-67, 18 vols.

Scève, Maurice, *The "Délie" of Maurice Scève*, ed. I. D. McFarlane, Cambridge, 1966.

Shakespeare, William, *Shakespeare's Sonnets*, ed. with an analytic commentary by Stephen Booth, New Haven and London, 1977.

———, *The Sonnets*, ed. W. Burto, New York, 1964.

———, *The Sonnets and Narrative Poems*, ed. W. Burto, New York, 1988.

Spenser, Edmund, *The Mutabilitie Cantos*, ed. S. P. Zitner, London, 1968.

Sponde, Jean de, *Méditations, avec un essai de poemes chrétiens*, ed. A. M. Boase, Paris, 1954.

Tyard, Pontus de, *Oeuvres Poétiques*, ed. C. Marty-Laveaux, Paris (Lemerre), 1875.

2. *Anthologies*

Le Cabinet des Muses: Ou nouveau recueil des plus beaux vers de ce temps, Rouen (David du Petit-val), 1619-20. (Previous edn. in 2 vols., 1612.)

Le Cabinet satyrique ou recueil parfaict des vers piquans et gaillards de ce temps, Paris (Anthoine Estoc), 1618.

Les Delices de la Poesie Francoise. Ou, Dernier Recueil des plus beaux Vers de ce temps, Paris (Toussainct du Bray), 1620, 2 vols.

I Fiori delle Rime de' Poeti Illustri Nuovamente raccolti & ordinati. Da M. Girolamo Ruscelli..., Venice (Marchib Sessa), 1579.

Les Fleurs des plus excellents Poetes de ce Temps, Paris (Bonfons), 1601.

Le Nouveau Parnasse des plus excellents poètes de ce temps, Paris (Guillemot), 1609; re-edn., 1618.

Les Muses francoises ralliées de diverses pars, Paris (Guillemot), 1599.

Les Muses françoises, r'alliees de diverses pars. Par le Sieur Despinelle, Lyon (Thibaud Ancelin), 1606.

Les Satyres bastardes et autres oeuvres folastres du Cadet Angoulevent Quatrain, Paris (Ant. Estoc), 1615.

II. Secondary Sources and Modern Anthologies

A. *Reference Works*

Arbour, Roméo, *L'ère baroque en France: Répertoire chronologique des éditions de textes littéraires 1585-1615*, Geneva, 1977, 2 vols.

Creore, Alvin Emerson, *A Word-Index to the Poetic Works of Ronsard*, Leeds, 1972.

Dictionnaire de théologie catholique, ed. A. Vacant, E. Mangenot, E. Amann, Paris, 1924.

Godefroy, Frédéric, *Dictionnaire de l'ancienne langue française*, Paris, 1880-1902 (Kraus Reprint, Vaduz and New York, 1961).

The Johns Hopkins Guide to Literary Theory and Criticism, ed. M. Groden and M. Kreiswirth, Baltimore and London, 1994.

Lachèvre, Frédéric, *Bibliographie des Recueils collectifs de poésies, publiés de 1597 à 1700*, Paris, 1901-5, 4 vols.

———, *Les Recueils collectifs de poésies libres et satyriques publiés depuis 1600 jusqu'à la mort de Théophile (1626)*, Paris, 1914. – *Supplément. Additions et corrections*, Paris, 1922.

Lausberg, Heinrich, *Handbuch der literarischen Rhetorik: eine Grundlegung der Literaturwissenschaft*, München, 1960, 2 vols.

Nyrop, Kr., *Grammaire historique de la langue française*, Copenhagen, 1899-1910, 5 vols.

Princeton Encyclopedia of Poetry and Poetics, ed. A. Preminger, F. J. Warnke, O. B. Hardison, Princeton, N.J., 1974. (Enlarged edn.)

Sonnino, Lee A., *A Handbook to Sixteenth-Century Rhetoric*, London, 1968.

B. *Works by Individual Authors*

1. *Studies of E. Durand (for a more complete listing see the bibilography in* Poésies complètes, *ed. Rogers and Rosenstein)*

Bonnefoy, Yves, "Préface," in Durand, *Poésies complètes*, ed. Rogers and Rosenstein, pp. II-XIV. Reprinted under the title "Etienne Durand" in Bonnefoy, *Dessin, couleur et lumière*, Paris, 1995, pp. 7-22.

Bruzzi, Amelia, "Metafore e poesia nelle *Méditations* di Étienne Durand," in *Studi sul barocco francese*, Bologna, 1962, pp. 71-96.

Colletet, Guillaume, "Vie d'Etienne Durand," in Durand, *Méditations*, ed. Lachèvre, pp. X-XVII.

Normann, Luca, "Durand, Poeta Barocco," *Culture française* 10, 1963, pp. 42-59.

Pizzorusso, Arnaldo, "Sulla poesia di Etienne Durand," *Letteratura*, nos. 19-20 (Jan.-April 1956), pp. 34-47.

Puleio, Maria Teresa, *Estienne Durand tra manierismo e barocco*, Catania, 1983.

———, "Il 'Giocondo' dell'Ariosto e la 'Vagabonde inconstance' di Estienne Durand," *Le Ragione critiche*, Jan.-June 1980, pp. 51-72.

———, "Il ritratto di Alcina et il 'Portrait d'Uranie': imitazione e trasformazione di un tema ariostesco," *Le Ragioni critiche*, July-Dec. 1982, pp. 145-54.

———, "Il 'sonnet VI' delle 'Méditations': una variazione sul tema del 'songe amoureux,'" *Le Ragioni critiche*, July-Dec. 1981, pp. 197-203.

———, "Le 'Stances de l'Amour' di Estienne Durand, ovvero la profanazione del rito," in *Scritti in memoria di Pasquale Morabito*, Messina, 1983, pp. 396-408.

Rathmann, Bernd, "Remarques sur les 'Stances à l'Inconstance' d'Etienne Durand," *Papers on French Seventeenth Century Literature* 8:14,1 (1981), pp. 33-42.

Rogers, Hoyt, and Rosenstein, Roy, "Late Renaissance Petrarchism: The Rhetorical Inconstancy of Etienne Durand," *Papers on French Seventeenth Century Literature* 14:27 (1987), pp. 687-701.

———, "De l'inconstance thématique à une poétique de l'inconstance," *Neophilologus* 72 (1988), pp. 180-90.

Rogers, Hoyt, "Etienne Durand et l'esthétique de l'inconstance," in Durand, *Poésies complètes*, pp. 13-22.

Rosenstein, Roy, "Emblématique et poétique du feu: les sonnets d'Etienne Durand," in Yvonne Bellanger, ed., *Le Sonnet à la Renaissance*, Paris, 1988.

———, "Etienne Durand et les flammes de l'amour," in Durand, *Poésies complètes*, pp. 1-12.

Tardieu, Jean, "Etienne Durand, poète supplici," in *Le Préclassicisme français* (q. v.), pp.189-95.

Tricotel, Edouard, "Note sur un poète peu connu, E. Durand," *Bulletin du Bibliophile*, October 1859, pp. 656-62. – Reprinted in Tricotel's *Variétés bibliographiques*, Paris, 1883.

Varga, S. A., "Un poète oublié du XVIIe siècle: Etienne Durand et les Stances à l'Inconstance," *Neophilologus*, XXXIX (1956), no. 4, pp. 249-58.

2. *Other works*

Adam, Antoine, *Théophile de Viau et la libre pensée française en 1620*, Paris, 1935.

Barber, C. L., and Wheeler, R. P., *The Whole Journey: Shakespeare's Power of Development*, Berkeley and Los Angeles, 1986.

Bardon, Françoise, *Diane de Poitiers et le mythe de Diane*, Paris, 1963.

Baumal, F., *Molière, auteur précieux*, Paris, n.d.

Belowski, Eleonore, *Lukrez in der französischen Literatur der Renaissance*, Berlin, 1934.

Bosco, Umberto, *Francesco Petrarca*, Bari, 1961. (Revised edn.)

Braunrot, Bruno, *L'Imagination poétique chez Du Bartas*, Chapel Hill, N.C., 1973.

Burgess, Robert M., *Platonism in Desportes*, Chapel Hill, N.C., 1954.

Butler, P., *Classicisme et baroque dans l'oeuvre de Racine*, Paris, 1959.

Castor, Grahame, "Petrarchism and the Quest for Beauty in the *Amours* of Cassandre and the *Sonets pour Helene*," in *Ronsard the Poet* (q.v.), pp. 79-120.

———, *Pleiade Poetics: A Study in Sixteenth-Century Thought and Terminology*, Cambridge, 1964.

Cave, Terence C., *The Cornucopian Text: Problems of Writing in the French Renaissance*, Oxford, 1979.

———, *Devotional Poetry in France c. 1570-1613*, Cambridge, 1969.

———, "Enargeia: Erasmus and the Rhetoric of Presence in the Sixteenth Century," in *L'Esprit créateur*, XVI (1976), no. 4, pp. 5-19.

———, "The Love-Sonnets of Jean de Sponde: A Reconsideration," in *Forum for Modern Language Studies*, III (1967), no. 1, pp. 49-60.

Charmot, F., *La Pédagogie des Jesuites: ses principes, son actualité*, Paris, 1943.

Chastel, André, *La Crise de la renaissance, 1520-1600*, Geneva, 1968.

Chilton, P. A., *The Poetry of Jean de La Ceppède*, Oxford, 1977.

Cioranescu, Al., *L'Arioste en France, des origines à la fin du XVIIIe siècle*, Paris, 1939, 2 vols.

Clément, Michèle, *Une poétique de crise: poètes baroques et mystiques (1570-1660)*, Paris, 1996.

Clements, Robert John, *Critical Theory and Practice of the Pleiade*, Cambridge, Mass., 1942.
Croce, Benedetto, *Storia dell'Età Barocca in Italia*, Bari, 1967 (5th edn.).
Delley, Gilbert, *L'Assomption de la nature dans la lyrique française de l'âge baroque*, Bern, 1969.
Desonay, Fernand, *Ronsard, poète de l'amour*, Brussels, 1952-9, 3 vols.
Duval, Edwin, *Poesis and Poetic Tradition in the Early Works of Saint-Amant*, York SC, 1981.
Eias, Norbert, *The Court Society*, Oxford, 1983.
Ellrodt, Robert, *L'Inspiration personnelle et l'esprit du temps chez les poètes métaphysiques anglais*, Paris, 1960, 2 parts.
———, "Shakespeare the Non-Dramatic Poet," in *The Cambridge Companion to Shakespeare Studies*, Cambridge, 1986, pp. 35-49.
Felperin, Howard, *Beyond Deconstruction: the Uses and Abuses of Literary Theory*, Oxford, 1985.
Floeck, Wilfried, *Die Literarästhetik des französischen Barock: Entstehung, Entwicklung, Auflösung*, Berlin, 1979.
Friedrich, Hugo, *Epochen der italienischen Lyrik*, Frankfurt, 1964.
Fromilhague, René, *Malherbe: Technique et création poétique*, Paris, 1954.
Frye, Northrup, *The Anatomy of Criticism*, New York, 1968.
Gadoffre, Gilbert, *Ronsard par lui-même*, Paris, 1964.
Genette, Gérard, *Figures: essais*, vol. I, Paris, 1966.
Gordon, Alex L., *Ronsard et la rhétorique*, Geneva, 1970.
Graf, Arturo, "Petrarchismo ed antipetrarchismo," in *Attraverso il Cinquecento*, Turin, 1956, pp. 1-86.
Grammont, Maurice, *Le Vers français: ses moyens d'expression, son harmonie*, Paris, 1937.
Griffin, Robert, *Coronation of the Poet: Joachim Du Bellay's Debt to the Trivium*, Berkeley-Los Angeles, 1969.
Gutiérrez, Estrella, *Literatura española*, Buenos Aires, 1965.
Haskins, Susan, *Mary Magdalen: Myth and Metaphor*, New York, 1993.
Hatzfeld, Helmut A., "Mannerism Is Not Baroque," in *French Manneristic Poetry between Ronsard and Malherbe* (q. v.), pp. 225-33.
Hauser, Arnold, *Der Manierismus: Die Krise der Renaissance und der Ursprung der modernen Kunst*, Munich, 1964.
Houston, John Porter, *The Rhetoric of Poetry in the Renaissance and Seventeenth Century*, Baton Rouge, 1983.
Janik, Dieter, *Geschichte der Ode und der Stances von Ronsard bis Boileau*, Bad Homburg-Berlin-Zürich, 1968.
Kerrigan, W., and Braden, G., *The Idea of the Renaissance*, Baltimore and London, 1989.
Lafay, Henri, *La Poésie française du premier* XVIIe *siècle (1598-1630): Esquisse pour un tableau*, Paris, 1975.
Lanham, R. A., *The Motives of Eloquence: Literary Rhetoric in the Renaissance*, New Haven, Conn.-London, 1976.
Lavaud, Jacques, *Un poète de cour au temps des derniers Valois: Philippe Desportes* (1546-1606), Paris, 1936.
Lebègue, Raymond, *La poésie française de 1560 à 1630*, Paris, 1951, 2 parts.
———, *Ronsard, l'homme et l'oeuvre*, Paris, 1950.
Ley, Klaus, *Neuplatonische Poetik und nationale Wirklichkeit: Die überwindung des Petrarkismus im Werk Du Bellays*, Heidelberg, 1975.
Mariéjol, J. H., *Henri IV et Louis XIII (1598-1643)* (*Histoire de France*, ed. E. Lavisse, vol. VI-ii), Paris, 1911.

Martz, Louis, *The Poetry of Meditation*, New Haven, Conn., 1954.
Mathieu-Castellani, Gisèle, "La Poésie amoureuse française à la fin du XVIe siècle d'après les recueils collectifs (1597-1600)," *Revue d'Histoire Littéraire de la France*, LXXVI, no. 2, pp. 3-19.
———, *Les Thèmes amoureux dans la poésie française (1570-1600)*, Paris, 1975.
Minta, Stephen, *Love Poetry in Sixteenth-Century France: A Study in Themes and Traditions*, Manchester, 1977.
Mirollo, James V., *Mannerism and Renaissance Poetry: Concept, Mode, Inner Design*, New Haven, Conn., 1984.
Morel, Jacques, *La Renaissance [vol. III] 1570-1624* (*Littérature française*, ed. Claude Pichois, vol. V), Paris, 1973.
Mourgues, Odette de, *Metaphysical, Baroque & Précieux Poetry*, Oxford, 1953.
———, "Ronsard's later poetry", in *Ronsard the Poet* (q. v.), pp. 287-318.
Murray, Linda, *The Late Renaissance and Mannerism*, London, 1967.
McFarlane, I. D., "Aspects of Ronsard's poetic vision," in *Ronsard the Poet* (q. v.), pp. 13-78.
———, *Renaissance France 1470-1589* (*A Literary History of France*, ed. P. E. Charvet), London-New York, 1974.
McGowan, Margaret M., *L'Art du ballet de cour en France, 1581-1643*, Paris, 1963.
Nealon, Jeffrey T., *Double Reading: Postmodernism After Deconstruction*, Ithaca, NY, 1993.
Nelson, Lowry, *Baroque Lyric Poetry*, New Haven, Conn., 1961.
Ortali, R., *Un Poète de la mort: Jean-Baptiste Chassignet*, Geneva, 1968.
Osthoff, Wolfgang, "Claudio Monteverdi's *Marian Vespers* of 1610," intro. to libretto, *CD Das Alte Werk*, Vienna, 1966-67.
Panofsky, Erwin, *Studies in Iconology: Humanistic Themes in the Art of the Renaissance*, New York, 1972. (1st edn. 1939.)
Patch, H. R., *The Goddess Fortuna in Medieval Literature*, Cambridge, Mass., 1927.
Perkins, J.-G., *Siméon [de] La Roque: poète de l'absence, 1550-1615*, Paris, 1967.
Praz, Mario, *The Flaming Heart*, New York, 1958.
Quennell, Peter, *Shakespeare*, Cleveland and New York, 1963.
Quinones, Ricardo J., *The Renaissance Discovery of Time*, Cambridge, Mass., 1972.
Raymond, Marcel, "Aux frontières du maniérisme et du baroque," in *Être et dire: études*, Neuchâtel, 1970, pp. 113-35.
———, *L'Influence de Ronsard sur la poésie française (1550-1585)*, Geneva, 1965.
Reynier, Gustave, *Le Roman sentimental avant l'Astrée*, Paris, 1908.
Richards, I. A., *The Philosophy of Rhetoric*, New York, 1936.
Ricoeur, Paul, *La métaphore vive*, Paris, 1975.
Robin, Léon, *La Théorie platonicienne de l'amour*, Paris, 1964.
Rousset, Jean, *L'Intérieur et l'extérieur: Poésie et théâtre au XVIIe siècle*, Paris, 1968.
———, *La Littérature de l'âge baroque en France: Circé et le paon*, Paris, 1953.
Sayce, R. A., "Ronsard and Mannerism: The *Elégie à Janet*," in *French Manneristic Poetry between Ronsard and Malherbe* (q. v.), pp. 234-47.
Schmidt, Albert-Marie, *La Poésie scientifique en France au seizième siècle*, Paris, 1938.
Segre, Cesare, *Avviamento all'analisi del testo letterario*, Torino, 1985.
Shearman, John, *Mannerism*, London, 1967.
Shuger, Deborah K., *Habits of Thought in the English Renaissance: Religion, Politics, and the Dominant Culture*, Berkeley, 1990.
Spitzer, Leo, "The Poetic Treatment of a Platonic-Christian Theme," *Comparative Literature*, no. 3, pp. 193-217.
Steadman, John M., *Redefining a Period Style: "Renaissance," "Mannerism," and "Baroque" in Literature*, Pittsburgh, 1990.

Stone, Donald, *France in the Sixteenth Century: A Medieval Society Transformed*, Englewood Cliffs, N. J., 1969.
Tapié, Victor L., *La France de Louis XIII et de Richelieu*, Paris, 1952.
Todorov, Tzvetan, "Poétique," in *Qu'est-ce que le structuralisme?*, Paris, 1968.
Tillyard, E. M. W., *The Elizabethan World Picture*, London, 1963. (1st edn., 1943.)
Tortel, Jean, "Le Lyrisme au XVIIe siècle," in *Histoire des Littératures*, vol. III, pp. 335-403.
Varga, A. Kibedi, *Rhétorique et littérature: Etudes de structures classiques*, Paris, 1970.
Vianey, Joseph-Marie, *Le Pétrarquisme en France au XVIe siècle*, Montpellier, 1909.
Vickers, Brian, *Appropriating Shakespeare: Contemporary Critical Quarrels*, New Haven and London, 1993.
Wardropper, Bruce, "Temas y problemas del Barrocco español," in Wardropper, ed., *Siglos de Oro: Barrocco* [F. Rico, ed., *Historia y crítica de la literatura española*, vol. III], Barcelona, 1983, pp. 5-48.
Weber, Henri, *La création poétique au XVIe siècle en France: De Maurice Scève à Agrippa d'Aubigné*, Paris, 1965, 2 vols.
———, "Transformation des thèmes pétrarquistes dans le printemps d'Agrippa d'Aubigné," in *Mélanges d'histoire littéraire de la Renaissance offerts à Henri Chamard*, Paris, 1951.
Zanta, Léontine, *La Renaissance du stoicisme au XVIe siècle*, Paris, 1914.

C. *Collective Works*

Amour sacré, amour mondain: poésie 1574-1610, Cahiers V. L. Saulnier no. 12, ed. André Gendre, Paris, 1995.
French Manneristic Poetry between Ronsard and Malherbe, special number of *L'Esprit créateur*, VI, no. 4 (Winter 1966).
Literary Theory/Renaissance Texts, ed. P. Parker and D. Quint, Baltimore and London, 1986.
Museo del Prado, Catálago de Pinturas, Ministerio de Educación y Cultura, Madrid, 1996.
The New Monteverdi Companion, ed. D. Arnold and N. Fortune, Boston and London, 1985.
Le Préclassicisme français, ed. J. Tortel, Paris, 1952.
Ronsard the Poet, ed. Terence Cave, London, 1973.
Shakespeare Criticism: A Selection 1623-1840, ed. D. N. Smith, London, 1964.
William Shakespeare's Sonnets, Modern Critical Interpretations, ed. Harold Bloom, New York and Philadelphia, 1987.

D. *Modern Anthologies*

Auden, W. H., and Pearson, N. H. (eds.), *Poets of the English Language*, New York, 1973, 5 vols.
Boase, Alan M. (ed.), *The Poetry of France*, London, 1952-69, 4 vols.
Hösle, Johannes (ed.), *Texte zum Antipetrarkismus*, Tübingen, 1970.
Kemp, Friedhelm, and Koppenfels, Werner von (eds.), *Französische Dichtung*, München, 1990, 4 vols.
Menéndez y Pelayo, Marcelino (ed.), *Las Cien Mejores Poesías de la Lengua Castellana*, Ciudad México, 1984.

Mourgues, Odette de (ed.), *An Anthology of French 17th-Century Lyric Poetry*, Oxford, 1966.

Raymond, Marcel, and Steele, A. J. (eds.), *La Poésie française et le maniérisme, 1546-1610(?)*, Geneva-Paris, 1971.

Rousset, Jean (ed.), *Anthologie de la poésie baroque française*, Paris, 1961, 2 vols.

Rubin, David Lee (ed.), *La Poésie française du premier 17e siècle: textes et contextes*, Tübingen, 1986.

Schmidt, Albert-Marie (ed.), *L'Amour noir: Poèmes baroques*, Monaco, 1959.

———, *Poètes du XVIe siècle*, Paris, 1953.

Steele, A. J. (ed.), *Three Centuries of French Verse, 1511-1819*, Edinburgh, 1956.

Warnke, Frank J. (ed.), *European Metaphysical Poetry*, New Haven, Conn.-London, 1961.

NORTH CAROLINA STUDIES IN THE ROMANCE LANGUAGES AND LITERATURES

I.S.B.N. Prefix 0-8078-

Recent Titles

"EL ÁNGEL DEL HOGAR". GALDÓS AND THE IDEOLOGY OF DOMESTICITY IN SPAIN, by Bridget A. Aldaraca. 1991. (No. 239). *-9243-2.*

IN THE PRESENCE OF MYSTERY: MODERNIST FICTION AND THE OCCULT, by Howard M. Fraser. 1992. (No. 240). *-9244-0.*

THE NOBLE MERCHANT: PROBLEMS OF GENRE AND LINEAGE IN "HERVIS DE MES", by Catherine M. Jones. 1993. (No. 241). *-9245-9.*

JORGE LUIS BORGES AND HIS PREDECESSORS OR NOTES TOWARDS A MATERIALIST HISTORY OF LINGUISTIC IDEALISM, by Malcolm K. Read. 1993. (No. 242). *-9246-7.*

DISCOVERING THE COMIC IN "DON QUIXOTE", by Laura J. Gorfkle. 1993. (No. 243). *-9247-5.*

THE ARCHITECTURE OF IMAGERY IN ALBERTO MORAVIA'S FICTION, by Janice M. Kozma. 1993. (No. 244). *-9248-3.*

THE "LIBRO DE ALEXANDRE". MEDIEVAL EPIC AND SILVER LATIN, by Charles F. Fraker. 1993. (No. 245). *-9249-1.*

THE ROMANTIC IMAGINATION IN THE WORKS OF GUSTAVO ADOLFO BÉCQUER, by B. Brant Bynum. 1993. (No. 246). *-9250-5.*

MYSTIFICATION ET CRÉATIVITÉ DANS L'OEUVRE ROMANESQUE DE MARGUERITE YOURCENAR, par Beatrice Ness. 1994. (No. 247). *-9251-3.*

TEXT AS TOPOS IN RELIGIOUS LITERATURE OF THE SPANISH GOLDEN AGE, by M. Louise Salstad. 1995. (No. 248). *-9252-1.*

CALISTO'S DREAM AND THE CELESTINESQUE TRADITION: A REREADING OF *CELESTINA*, by Ricardo Castells. 1995. (No. 249). *-9253-X.*

THE ALLEGORICAL IMPULSE IN THE WORKS OF JULIEN GRACQ: HISTORY AS RHETORICAL ENACTMENT IN *LE RIVAGE DES SYRTES* AND *UN BALCON EN FORÊT*, by Carol J. Murphy. 1995. (No. 250). *-9254-8.*

VOID AND VOICE: QUESTIONING NARRATIVE CONVENTIONS IN ANDRÉ GIDE'S MAJOR FIRST-PERSON NARRATIVES, by Charles O'Keefe. 1996. (No. 251). *-9255-6.*

EL CÍRCULO Y LA FLECHA: PRINCIPIO Y FIN, TRIUNFO Y FRACASO DEL *PERSILES*, por Julio Baena. 1996. (No. 252). *-9256-4.*

EL TIEMPO Y LOS MÁRGENES. EUROPA COMO UTOPÍA Y COMO AMENAZA EN LA LITERATURA ESPAÑOLA, por Jesús Torrecilla. 1996. (No. 253). *-9257-2.*

THE AESTHETICS OF ARTIFICE: VILLIERS'S *L'EVE FUTURE*, by Marie Lathers. 1996. (No. 254). *-9254-8.*

DISLOCATIONS OF DESIRE: GENDER, IDENTITY, AND STRATEGY IN *LA REGENTA*, by Alison Sinclair. 1998. (No. 255). *-9259-9.*

THE POETICS OF INCONSTANCY, ETIENNE DURAND AND THE END OF RENAISSANCE VERSE, by Hoyt Rogers. 1998. (No. 256). *-9260-2.*

When ordering please cite the *ISBN Prefix* plus the last four digits for each title.

Send orders to: University of North Carolina Press
P.O. Box 2288
CB# 6215
Chapel Hill, NC 27515-2288
U.S.A.